D0072938

Human Stereopsis

Human Stereopsis
A PSYCHOPHYSICAL ANALYSIS

W. LAWRENCE GULICK
Hamilton College

ROBERT B. LAWSON
University of Vermont

New York
OXFORD UNIVERSITY PRESS
1976

To
Winifred
and
Jacqueline

Preface

Perhaps it was the quiet beauty of the northern hills that led us to wonder about the perception of distance. But, if so, it was our curiosity and our mutual interest in visual perception that took us into the laboratories at Dartmouth and the University of Vermont and ultimately led to our joining together to write a book about our labors. If nothing else, it has been an exhilarating experience. We have been both student and teacher to one another, and there is no honest way to attribute particular portions of the book to a single author. While the research was conducted in our respective laboratories, each of which had a slightly different flavor, periodically one or the other of us, usually with our students, would cross the Green Mountains to pay a visit. The rule was simple: Whether the guest traveled east or west was settled according to which one of us most needed the refreshment that comes with a brief respite.

R. B. L. wrote the initial drafts of Chapters 1, 2, 7, and 10 while W. L. G. wrote the remainder; but the final version of each was achieved by joint consensus after discussion and revision. Accordingly, the responsibility for what is good—and bad—rests upon us both.

We are indebted to Thorne Shipley who read the whole of the penultimate draft of the manuscript and made many important suggestions, and to Frank Romano who executed the art work with such skill. Finally, our special thanks are to Michele Rosinski who not only typed the manuscript, but showed us the way to stylistic consistency.

Clinton, New York   W. L. Gulick
Burlington, Vermont   R. B. Lawson
September 1974

Acknowledgments

Students who made major contributions

DARTMOUTH LABORATORY

J. Christopher Bill
Kenneth Fuld
John P. Galla
Sharon McH. Lawrence
Michael S. Pancoe
Jay H. Shaffer
William M. Youngs

VERMONT LABORATORY

Sally Andrews
Thomas D. Gibbs
Ronald T. Greene
Marvin M. Levy
David C. Mount
Marilyn Park
Cynthia G. Whitmore

The research reported in this book was supported, in part, by the following grants:

NSF (GB-2497), W. L. G.
NSF (GB-30579), R. B. L.
PHS (2T01-MH11983), W. L. G.
PHS (R01-00849), R. B. L.
University of Delaware Research Foundation, W. L. G.

Contents

Human Stereopsis

1
Introduction

The capacity of man to experience a three-dimensional visual world is of little wonder except to those who inquire of its basis. And the wonder grows as our ignorance is revealed, for we have yet to gain much satisfaction as to how the presentation of two-dimensional displays to the separate eyes is combined into stereoscopic depth perception. At the turn of this century we thought we understood the basis of stereopsis, but the view that disparate contours give rise to a three-dimensional world has, in the last decade, given way to open questions about what had only recently seemed so sure. Curiosity alone impelled us to inquiry, and this book contains the more important of our observations and ideas about stereopsis.

Needless to say, any student of visual perception is quick to recognize the utility of multiple and different persuasions among experimenters in their studies of depth perception. Indeed, history informs us that investigations of stereopsis form a rich tapestry, for we find in the record important contributions from physicists, physiologists, psychologists, philosophers, and artists. With interest piqued in so wide an arena, it is little wonder that much has been written about the topic.

While we have acknowledged the major contributors to our current state of knowledge about stereoscopy through an historical accounting in the chapter immediately following, our own inquiries have been limited to psychophysical studies of the perceptual effects brought about by manipulations of several stimulus parameters. Where appropriate, we

3

have related the results of our experiments to those obtained by others, particularly when by so doing an important principle could either be sustained or be found, in some measure, wanting.

We began the research reported in this book about ten years ago, and except for an occasional study, the data included here have not been published heretofore. As might be expected, stereopsis served as a point of departure for a number of empirical studies, some of which go beyond the strict limits of depth perception, but all of which have stereopsis as a common thread.

We do not consider this to be a textbook, for its scope is probably too narrow and the detail of its treatment too great. Rather, it is a forum to describe and relate a decade of research which has centered upon a psychophysical analysis of depth perception. No formal theory is advanced, but we have not hesitated to advance a number of theorems, each of which grew out of, and is sustained by, the results of our experiments. While reference occasionally is made to the work of others, this book is *not* an apporpriate source to represent the broad state of affairs on stereopsis. Instead, it represents what the authors think about a selected handful of phenomena.

METHODS

Throughout the work reported here we have limited ourselves to the methods of psychophysics. It is assumed that the reader is familiar with the established methods of psychophysics and scaling, but we have included enough detail in descriptions of our methods to allow readers to grasp quickly the essential features of the tasks set for our observers. We have relied heavily upon the method of magnitude estimation, and in every instance our observers were trained in the method employed. It was our practice to obtain repeated measures from a small number of observers, and unless otherwise stated, each experiment may be assumed to have involved different observers who, although practiced in the method, were naive as to our experimental purpose.

Visual Criteria. In general we only employed observers who met a rather strict set of visual criteria, as follows: uncorrected visual acuity in each eye between 20/17 and 20/25, lateral and vertical phoria scores within ±1 standard deviation of the normative population, and a stereoscopic acuity of not less than 96 per cent on the Fry-Shepard scale. Visual tests were administered with a Bausch and Lomb orthorater (Model 71-21-31).

Apparatus. A number of specially designed apparatuses were employed. Those relating to training procedures are described in connection with reports of the experiments in which they were used. In the body of our work we used two kinds of stereoscopes. One was a prism stereoscope, and the other was a first-surface mirror stereoscope. The essential features of each are shown in Figs. 1.1 and 1.2, respectively.

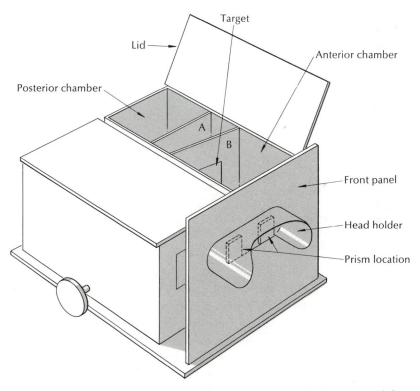

Fig. 1.1   Prism stereoscope. Prisms could be changed easily from rear of front panel, and the angle of partition B, which held the target, was variable. Panel A contained a diffusion screen for rear illumination of target. Both anterior and posterior chambers contained sources under separate control. Distance to the target could be changed by turning knob.

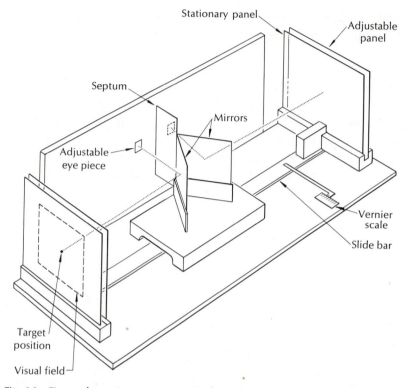

Fig. 1.2   First-surface mirror stereoscope. The slide bar ran in teflon tracks and was used to move the adjustable panels. The stationary and adjustable panels in each channel held different aspects of the target display, and their relative displacement introduced disparity calibrated with the vernier scale. Panels could be illuminated from in front or behind (not shown).

Our matrix targets typically were made by using a series of machine steel templates from which a wide variety of matrix patterns with precise control over dot size and inter-dot distance could be punched in paper. The paper templates were then mounted in a plastic frame or in glass and placed in the stereoscope, each channel of which had an independent light source for both front and rear illumination. Insofar as seemed reasonable, we have included in the book illustrations of the patterns actually used. The reader is encouraged to prepare facsimiles for display in a simple hand stereoscope, but it is necessary to caution that the perceptual effects thus obtained may, in some instances, deviate from those reported unless both luminance and angular subtense of the targets approximate those used in our experiments.

Plan of the Book

The formal treatment begins in the next chapter with a review of the important historical events of significance to the development of current thought on stereopsis. This is followed by a fairly detailed discussion of the geometrical horopter. Both Chapters 2 and 3 may be considered as introductions to the experiments that follow, and we believe they help set the stage for a more critical evaluation of our work. We think the chapter on geometry can serve also as a useful source in its own right, for we know of no other treatment like it.

The remainder of the book is organized in such a way that a full understanding of the material is best achieved if the chapters are taken in order. In general, the development of ideas is ordered, more or less, to parallel the course of our own thinking, although certain liberties have been taken for the sake of coherence.

Terms and symbols are defined in the glossary at the end of the book. References are cited by number in the text and they are listed alphabetically at the close of each chapter. A full list of names of the men and women whose work is cited appears in the author index.

2
Classical Theories
of Stereoscopic Vision

Early explanations of human visual perception focused primarily upon the optical and muscular properties of the eyes. This was particularly so for theories of depth perception put forth prior to the nineteenth century. This scientific focusing applies equally to the classical explanations of the perception of distance of objects located at varying physical distances from the perceiver and the synthetic but indistinguishable depth experience arising from perspective images of objects viewed with the aid of a stereoscopic instrument.

Originally, the human eye was conceptualized and studied as an optical instrument which behaved like the camera obscura, or pinhole camera, the focal power of which varies with the diameter of the pinhole and is therefore capable of focusing an object at infinity (*64*). This original conception of the eye was incomplete, but perhaps at the time was intuitively appealing because of the obvious variations in pupil size and the fact that the inside of the eye appears dark and obscure without the aid of an ophthalmoscope. Some of the earliest recorded investigations of human vision dating back to Alhazen (1000 A.D.) focused upon understanding and describing geometrically image formation in the human eye (*90*). Although the early investigators of the anatomy of the human visual system such as Galen (ca. 175 A.D.) devoted some of their writings to binocular vision and the singleness of the joint or combined visual field, systematic and empirical investigations of binocular vision began during the early part of the nineteenth century. However, despite

8

the late date of scientific interest in the problem, there were some important although unrelated artistic, philosophical, and physiological discoveries and conceptual developments across the centuries of time that helped to shape the nineteenth century investigations of vision with two eyes and particularly the phenomenon of stereoscopic depth perception. These molding forces arose from the artists who searched for the visual principles and techniques which would allow them to represent the three-dimensional properties of a scene upon a canvas, wall, or ceiling. In contrast, the philosophers studied the phenomenon of distance perception as partisans to a particular philosophical position or as a point of departure for a general theory of human knowledge (85). The physiologists attempted to integrate the empirical facts of optics, geometry, and the anatomy of the human visual system with the known facts of human depth perception. We turn now to a brief review of some of these artistic, philosophical, and physiological findings that have contributed directly to our understanding of human depth perception.

MONOCULAR AND BINOCULAR DISTANCE CUES

Although the Greeks and Romans employed visual cues that signaled depth in their paintings, it was the Renaissance painters who experimented with and articulated clearly the monocular *visual* cues to distance (4). The most influential of these painters for the study of depth perception was Leonardo da Vinci (1452-1519) who found that the depth of an object or scene could be represented in a painting by the appropriate combination of light and shadow (he spoke of attached and cast shadows) and perspective (he distinguished three kinds: linear, aerial, and detail perspective). He also discovered other *visual* depth cues that could not be employed in a painting, such as movement perspective in which a moving object appears to pass more slowly through the visual field than when the same moving object is closer to the stationary perceiver (91). More importantly, Leonardo da Vinci was the first to describe binocular parallax in which the two eyes can see around and behind a small spherical object and thus allow us to see more of the near object than under monocular regard and all of the more remote background not seen under monocular regard. The round object in Fig. 2.1 should appear transparent because nothing behind it is hidden from binocular regard, yet monocularly we cannot see all of the remote ground

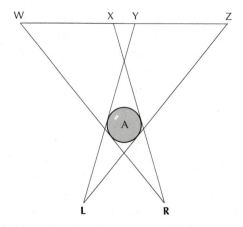

Fig. 2.1   Leonardo's Paradox. The left eye sees the background WY, and the right eye sees the background XZ. Inasmuch as the two eyes see all of the background WZ, the opaque object A should be transparent to binocular vision. After Boring (4).

behind the object requiring that the object must then be opaque. This paradox between binocular and monocular regard was resolved by da Vinci when he wrote that "a painting, though conducted with the greatest art, finished to the last perfection, both with regard to its contours, its lights, its shadows, and its colours, can never show a *relievo* equal to that of the natural objects, unless these be viewed at a distance and with a single eye. . . ." (*8*, p. 9). In short, perspective images can never generate the same depth experience resulting from viewing binocularly a three-dimensional object. We are indebted to the master painter for discovering and applying sublimely the monocular *visual* cues for depth perception and for identifying binocular parallax as one of the visual depth cues requiring two eyes. Some have argued that he also knew about the other binocular visual depth cue of retinal disparity even though he did not discuss it in his writings (*8*, p. 11).

There were many philosophers who contributed directly to our knowledge of human depth perception, and, in fact, it was they who first distinguished between *visual* and *nonvisual* cues to distance. Thus, Malebranche (*74*), whose theory of distance perception anticipated George Berkeley's epoch-making work, stated that man has available and employs a natural geometry when viewing binocularly an object based upon the triangulation arising from the two eyes and a point in the object where the visual axes meet. The appreciation of the distances of near objects by monocular viewing is thus inferior to binocular viewing inasmuch as one side and one base angle of the natural triangle are missing.

Continuing a similar theme, William Molyneux, in his *Dioptrika Nova,* the first text on optics published in the English language, stated that under binocular viewing, distance is perceived by the turn of the eyes or by the angle of the optic axis (*63*).

The influence of Molyneux and Malebranches' ideas are reflected in the works of George Berkeley who considered his predecessors authorities on the subject of vision. Unlike them, however, he did not confuse the visual experiences of distance with geometrical optics when he wrote in his *Essay Towards a New Theory of Vision* that lines and angles "have no real existence in nature, being only an hypothesis framed by the mathematicians" (*79*). He rejected an innate geometry and suggested in its place that when an object is placed at a near distance, a distance to which the interval between the eyes bears any sensible proportion (*79*), there arises "an habitual or customary connection" between the muscular sensations of convergence accompanying the different dispositions of the eyes with different distances of the object. For still closer distances, the nearer the object the more "confused" (blurred) it becomes and the more the eye "strains" (accommodates). In effect, Berkeley substituted two nonvisual cues and one visual cue in place of the lines and angles of geometry employed by his predecessors to explain the perception of near distances (*19*). Berkeley was the first to make plain that we do not perceive distances as a result of *only* visual impressions. In fact, exactly fifty years after Berkeley's *Essay* we find in Joseph Priestley's review of the historical developments in visual perception the following comment by W. Porterfield: "The most universal, and frequently the most sure means of judging the distance of objects is . . . the angle made by the optic axes" (*66*, p. 695).

Even though most of the cues for monocular and binocular distance perception were well identified by the beginning of the eighteenth century, it was the obvious singleness of binocular vision which implied to the sixteenth and seventeenth century physiologists that when the images of an object fall upon both retinas those images must stimulate corresponding retinal points in order to be seen as single. Thus, attempts to reconcile the fact that the two eyes yield a unified percept in depth intensified the investigation of retinal images and ultimately led to the discovery of the binocular distance cue of retinal disparity.

Binocular Vision and Retinal Images

Despite the fact that image formation by the camera obscura, the non-dioptrical pinhole camera, had been known and studied for almost a millenium, it was not until 1604 when Johannes Kepler stated in his *Ad vitellionem Paralipomena* the theoretical basis of the refracting or dioptrical properties of the cornea and lens, and again in 1619 when Pater Christopher Scheiner observed the retinal image at the fund of the eye and substantiated Kepler's position that it was abundantly made clear that the images of external objects are painted upon the retina (*64*).

The first systematic attempt to determine the principles that connect the direction and distance of binocularly viewed objects with their retinal impressions is found in the writings of Francis Aguillon or Aguilonius, a learned Jesuit, who published his *Optics* in 1613 (*72*). He introduced the term "horopter" to represent the locus of all points seen as single in the binocular field. Aguilonius considered the horopter a mental line rather than a real line that passed through the intersection of the optic axes (the fixation point), and he described a frontal (weak convergence) and a circular horopter (strong convergence). According to him, the retinal images from corresponding retinal points were always projected to the plane of the horopter and thus appeared single. He surmised that objects in front of or behind the plane of fixation or horopter stimulate noncorresponding retinal points, and these objects appear double. Some visual scientists have felt that the horopter serves the useful purpose of fosusing immediately an observer's attention upon the object of fixation at the expense of not attending to other objects that appear double and less distinct (*47*). Accordingly, the horopter is for both eyes what the fovea centralis is for one eye.

Although Aguilonius stated that retinal correspondence yields the singleness of binocular vision, he was well aware of the difficulty of reconciling the perceptual facts of a unified binocular visual field with the sensory facts of noncorresponding retinal images. Consequently, a number of theories were developed to explain the singleness of binocular vision.

One explanation of the singleness of binocular vision, suggested by Kepler to which Aguilonius was a partisan, is the projection theory of retinal images (*25*, p. 483). The theory states that each eye sees an object in a different direction along a line originating from an object that passes through the middle of the pupil to each retina, and there is only one point that the lines of visible direction have in common and that is the point in space where they intersect each other. According to Kepler's theory, the perceiver projects the retinal images of the object into space along the lines of visible direction to the intersection of the paths of projection. A binocularly viewed object is seen as single only at the intersecting point and at its proper distance, whereas if the object is seen as double, it is the result of an erroneous judgment of the *distance* of the object. For example, consider Fig. 2.2 in which *M* is the object that

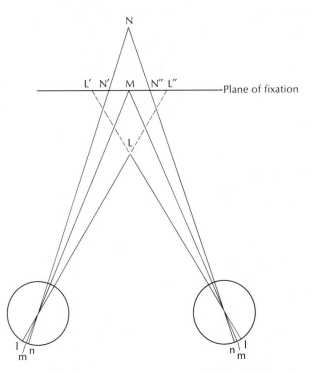

Fig. 2.2 According to the projection theory, retinal images are projected to the point of intersection of the lines of sight with the object in space thus appearing single and at the proper distance.

both eyes are looking at and L and N are in front of and behind the point of fixation, respectively. Now according to the theory, if the retinal images of L are projected as far as the plane of fixation (L', L'') they appear double because the point of intersection of the lines occurs at L. The only way L can be seen at the distance of M is if it actually were co-planar with M. Similarly, if the images of N are projected only as far as the plane of M, (N', N'') the object must appear double.

Unfortunately, one of the major liabilities of the projection theory is that it fails to explain why some images are projected correctly and seen as single, whereas others are projected incorrectly and seen as double even though the phenomenal index of inaccurate projection is an erroneous distance judgment. The theory stresses the importance of intersecting lines of sight for a unified binocular experience at the expense of ignoring the locus of retinal stimulation regardless of whether the retinal images fall upon corresponding or noncorresponding retinal loci. Despite these limitations, the projection theory is reflected in some more recent theories of stereoscopic depth perception with the modification of internalizing the projection to intersecting nervous pathways where the neural representations of disparate or noncorresponding retinal images "fuse" to yield both the singleness of binocular vision and spatial localization (3, 13).

An alternative explanation of the singleness of binocular vision is Johannes Müller's theory of identical retinal points (52). The essence of the identity theory is that images arising from corresponding retinal points lead to single vision, whereas retinal images from noncorresponding points should always give rise to double images in the binocular visual field. Even though Müller knew that each retina receives different perspective views of a fixated object and that nonfixated objects yield disparate retinal images, he did not connect these facts with binocular depth perception. He was more interested in describing the geometry of image formation and the singleness of binocular vision by establishing the geometrical rules of corresponding retinal points while ignoring a perceptual definition of correspondence. Unfortunately, this emphasis ignores the fact that not *all* disparate images give rise to doubling of objects in binocular vision. Thus, the major problem with identical points theory unlike the projection theory is that we obtain too few double images because only the binocularly fixated object should appear single.

We now know that an object that stimulates corresponding retinal points is seen single and can not be seen double, while an object that falls on noncorresponding areas is usually seen as single but also *can* be seen as double (*12*). If the identical points theory were true, we ought also to have an intuitive knowledge of the horopter as the plane of most distinct vision inasmuch as objects not in the horopter should appear double or at least blurred. A more detailed account of retinal correspondence including Müller's treatment of the problem is presented in Chapter 3.

CHARLES WHEATSTONE AND THE STEREOSCOPE

By the start of the nineteenth century there was growing recognition that "visual disparities" arose under binocular vision that were due in part to binocular parallax (da Vinci's perspective parallax) and that disparity information is related intimately to depth perception. For example, Joseph Harris came close to showing that disparate retinal images alone can be a robust stimulus for depth perception when he wrote in his *Treatise of Opticks:*

> We have other helps for distinguishing prominences of small parts besides those by which we distinguish distances in general, as their degrees of light and shade, and *the prospect we have round them*. And by the parallax, on account of the distance betwixt our eyes, we can distinguish besides the front part of the two sides of a near object not thicker than the said distance, and this gives a visible relievo to such objects, which helps greatly to raise or detach them from the plane in which they lie. Thus the nose on a face is the more remarkably raised by our seeing both sides of it at once. (*24*, p. 171).

Even earlier, Robert Smith provided a simple demonstration of depth perception of a unified image arising from the disparities between the retinal images.

In reference to Fig. 2.3, Smith wrote that:

> Having opened the points of a pair of compasses somewhat wider than the interval of your eyes; with your arm extended hold the head or joint in the ball of your hand, with the points outwards and equidistant from your eyes, and somewhat higher than the joint. Then fixing your eyes upon any remote object lying in the line that bisects the intervals of the points, you will first perceive two pair of compasses (each leg being doubled) with their inner

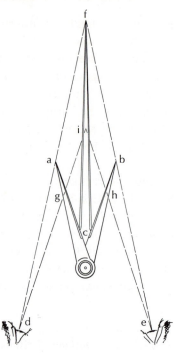

Fig. 2.3   Robert Smith's stereoscopic effect produced by fixating upon a more remote object and looking between the points and legs of a compass held in front of the eyes. From Smith (75).

legs crossing each other, not unlike the old shape of the letter W. But by compressing the legs with your hand, the two inner points will come nearer to each other; and when they unite (having stop[ped] the compression), the two inner legs will also entirely coincide and bisect the angle under the outward ones; *and will appear more vivid, thicker, and longer than they do,* so as to reach from your hand to the remotest object in view, even in the horizon itself, if the points be exactly coincident." (*75*, p. 388).

Smith stated that the third unified image was due to the fact that as the *legs* of the compass are compressed, the *points* of the compass eventually stimulate the same points of the retinas as those of the fixated object (f, Fig. 2.3), so that for the left eye, points d, a, and f are in one straight line, and for the right eye, points e, b, and f are in another (*75*, p. 389). Unfortunately, Smith failed to indicate that when the points of the compass are coincident with the more remote fixation point, the lower portions of each leg of the compass are not coincident with that point. Consequently, the images of the legs stimulate noncorresponding retinal loci even though one sees the third *unified* image with the points *and* legs extending continuously to the point of fixation. Had Smith gone a little further, he would have shown clearly that depth perception accompanied by an unified visual image can arise from noncorresponding retinal images.

The first unequivocal treatment of the subject that man can perceive an object in three dimensions solely as a result of the dissimilar retinal images of that object was made by Charles Wheatstone on June 21, 1838, before the Royal Society of London (*87*). Prior to this time, H. Mayo had mentioned briefly Wheatstone's discovery in his *Outlines of Physiology* (*49*, p. 288), which led E. G. Boring to conclude that the first stereoscope was probably constructed in 1833 by Wheatstone (*4*). In his Royal Society paper, Wheatstone indicates that previous investigators had limited their attention to substantiating the position that objects can be seen single *only* when their images fall upon corresponding points of the two retinas. Consequently, they ignored or explained away the fact that dissimilar retinal images can also yield perceptually a single object in three dimensions by concluding that the "differences" in retinal images were so small that they need not be taken into account (*87*). Wheatstone, however, set out to identify and define systematically the nature of the "visual disparities" produced by binocular viewing and how they relate to depth perception and the singleness of binocular vision. Toward this end, Wheatstone invented the mirror or reflecting stereoscope to analyze the elements of binocular vision and to afford recombination of these elements that can seldom be achieved by normal use of our eyes (*88*).

The principle elements of binocular vision that he considered were convergence of the optic axes, dissimilarity of retinal images, and size of the retinal images. He began with the normal binocular viewing condition in which a *fixated* object is seen at the intersection of the optic axes and therefore stimulates corresponding retinal loci, and, like Robert Smith (*75*), he observed that two similar objects can also stimulate identical retinal loci if each is placed in the direction of each optic axis and at equal distances *before* or *beyond* the point of fixation. These three

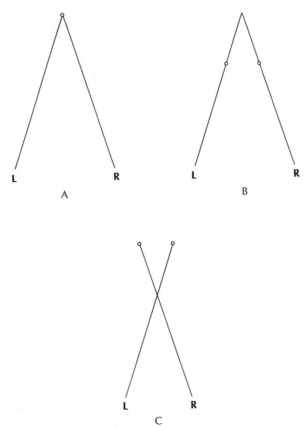

Fig. 2.4 Schematic representation of binocular viewing conditions in which monocular objects are at the point of fixation.(A), in front of the point of fixation (B), and behind the point of fixation (C).

viewing conditions are represented in Fig. 2.4, and it is important to note that all three configurations yield a single object seen at the intersection of the optic axes even though the association between convergence, perspective of the objects, accommodation, and the size of the retinal images have been uncoupled (B and C) from the normal condition represented in A. Obviously, the observer is required to converge at one point and to accommodate nearer (Fig. 2.4B) or farther (Fig. 2.4C) than the fixation point so that the images of the two objects will not unite readily, will appear blurred, or both. Wheatstone went on to show that if we substitute planar images of the two real objects, present them to each eye, and view them by converging our eyes in front of or behind the plane containing these images, we see a unified three-dimensional object indistinguishable from the solid object, and it is raised from the surface upon which the monocular images fall. Similarly, if we take two vertical lines at different distances from an observer and refer them to a common plane, we note that the lateral separation between the lines in each perspective image is different (Fig. 2.5). If we now view these half-images through a pair of tubes which allows us more readily to converge our eyes beyond the plane containing the images, we will see only two lines, one nearer to the observer than the other. In these

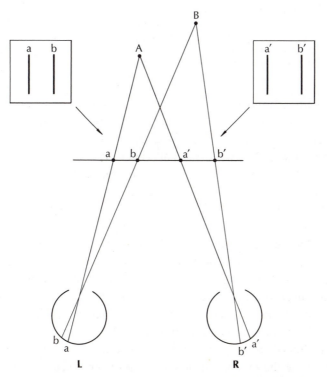

Fig. 2.5   An overhead view of two vertical lines (A and B) that have been referred to a common plane from which the left and right eye half-images have been constructed. Note that if the observer fixates upon A, then B stimulates noncorresponding retinal loci and vice versa.

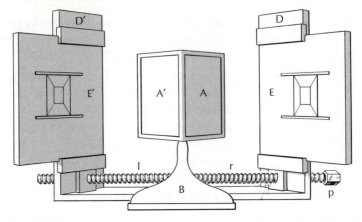

Fig. 2.6 The Wheatstone mirror stereoscope that was first mentioned in Mayo's *Outlines of Human Physiology* in 1833 (*49*, p. 288) with details of the instrument published in 1838 (*87*). The panels EE' bear the disparate drawings which are reflected by the mirrors AA', one into each eye as the observer faces the stereoscope. Adjustments are made by sliding EE' in the uprights DD', and changing the distance between DD' and AA' with the screw p. After Boring (*4*).

series of demonstrations, Wheatstone made plain that the visual disparity of binocular vision refers to the lateral separation between the retinal images of the fixated and nonfixated target. His basic rule of stereoscopic vision was that when the half-views of a stereogram are exact replicas of the monocular views of a solid object, then binocular combination of the half-views yields a percept of the solid object.

In order to make clear the view of this new visual world, Wheatstone constructed a mirror or reflecting stereoscope that eliminates the discordance between the planes in which the objects or perspective images are placed and the depth plane containing the point of fixation (Fig. 2.4B and C) so that a unified percept can be obtained readily and clearly by an untrained observer (Fig. 2.6). It is interesting to note that inasmuch as the chemically based photographic discoveries of Talbot, Niepee, and Daguerre were not known until the beginning of 1839, Wheatstone was forced to employ a variety of line-drawn configurations that were devoid of the monocular or visual cues to distance to demonstrate his stereoscopic effects (*88*). This advantageous fact made plain that stereoscopic depth perception is not dependent upon the learned monocular visual cues to distance.

Wheatstone concluded from his stereoscopic findings that the theory of identical retinal points of the singleness of binocular vision was inadequate because the retinal images of an object that do not fall on corresponding points of the two retinas yield an object that is single and tridimensional. In a broader sense, he went even further and concluded that a purely sensory or physiologically based theory of binocular vision was inadequate because of the following observations made by him (*87, 88*): If half-images that give rise to a line-drawn cube in the stereoscopic field are exchanged between the eyes, then a frustrum of a square pyramid with its base remote from the eye is perceived in stereoscopic space (conversion of relief or distance); if half-images differing only in size are viewed stereoscopically, then the binocular image appears intermediate in size between the two monocular images; if half-images that contain objects of different shape (*G* to the right eye and *L* to the left eye) are presented simultaneously to corresponding retinal regions, then the observer perceives a complete or fragmented *G* or *L* or a mixture of both over time in the stereoscopic field (binocular rivalry, *9*); if the half-images of Fig. 2.7 are viewed stereoscopically, one sees the upper portion of the darker (Wheatstone said stronger, *87*, p. 385) line titled behind and the lower portion titled in front of the apparent frontoparallel plane, while the fainter line appears in that plane even though it stimulates *identical* retinal loci of the left and right eyes. Finally, Wheatstone

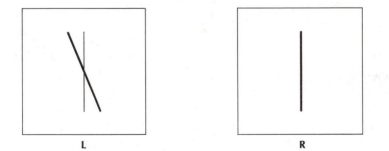

L   R

Fig. 2.7   Wheatstone's demonstration that objects falling upon corresponding retinal loci can appear double and in different stereoscopic positions. Under stereoscopic viewing, the two darker lines are combined and appear as a single line titled out of the apparent fronto-parallel plane with the lighter line appearing in that plane even though the latter and the dark line of the right eye stimulate corresponding retinal loci.

introduced the pseudoscope in which the left eye views what the right eye would normally view and vice versa. Thus, a bust viewed pseudoscopically from the front becomes a deep hollow mask while a framed picture hanging against a wall appears as an aperture in the wall.

Charles Wheatstone's observations had an important impact upon the early nineteenth century theories of binocular vision not only because they conflicted directly with the theory of identical retinal points, but because they conflicted with other existing explanations of binocular depth perception as well. Wheatstone rejected the theories of Gassendi (21, p. 395) and Porta (65, p. 142) that maintained that we see only with one eye at a given time even though both remain open. Such an explanation avoids the problem of noncorresponding retinal images, but it is inadequate according to Wheatstone because objects appear flat under monocular regard while they appear in relief under binocular inspection. Even though Wheatstone was the first to demonstrate systematically that dissimilar retinal images give rise to stereoscopic depth, he did not understand nor attempt to explain how the disparate images were coalesced into a unified tridimensionl percept. He concluded his investigations of human stereoscopic vision by stating simply that some new law of vision will be discovered that will include all the circumstances under which single vision by means of noncorresponding points occurs and is limited.

The Wheatstone-Brewster Controversy. Charles Wheatstone was a physicist by training and inclination, and his work in stereoscopy represented his only excursion into psychological problems. On the other hand, David Brewster of Edinburgh had investigated many more problems in physiological optics than Charles Wheatstone, and he challenged the propriety of Wheatstone's stereoscopic investigations. David Brewster, who outlined the principle of a refracting or prism stereoscope and who constructed one in 1849, argued that Charles Wheatstone was not the first to note that the dissimilarity of the two retinal images is not a new fact of vision nor was Wheatstone the first to conceptualize an instrument for uniting optically the two dissimilar images (8). According to Brewster, the former discovery belonged to da Vinci, Smith, and Harris and the latter to James Elliot who did not build a stereoscope until 1839 although Brewster claims that Elliot thought of the instrument in 1834

(*8*, pp. 19-21). Although Brewster was the first great authority on the optics of the stereoscope, he never understood the significance of Wheatstone's contribution, and he made no mention in his 1831 treatise on optics (*6*) concerning the fact that the retinas receive different perspective views of an object despite the fact that he took Wheatstone to task for claiming priority for this discovery when he later published *The Stereoscope* in 1856 (*8*).

In effect, the theoretical conflict between Brewster and Wheatstone centered around two separate aspects of analyzing stereoscopic vision: the direction of pointing the eyes (convergence) and the difference between the images formed on the retinas of the two eyes (disparity). Brewster championed the former position and Wheatstone the latter (*7, 8*). Essentially, Brewster believed that binocular depth perception was the result of changes of convergence when he wrote that:

> The successive convergence of the optics axes upon two points of an object at different distances, exhibits to us the difference of distance when we have no other possible means of perceiving it (*8*, pp. 50-51).

He stated that the same process operates under stereoscopic conditions, so that during rapid surveying of the stereoscopic object the whole of it appears distinctly solid even though every point of it is seen double and indistinct except for the point upon which the optic axes are for the instant converged. Brewster believed firmly that stereopsis operated on the basis of convergence by the successive combination of pairs of corresponding points in the half-images, and he never realized that it is the mere presence of the difference between the perspective views in each retinal image which in and of itself yields an impression of depth (*8*, pp. 76-89).

It is important to note that Brewster was not alone when challenging some of Wheatstone's findings and explanations of stereoscopic depth perception. For example, William Rogers supported Brewster's position that depth perception requires successive vision by corresponding points inasmuch as he found with some of his own stereograms that when he maintained convergence upon a given point, lines appearing behind or before it in the stereoscopic field first appear double and then lose their relief (*69*). Similarly, E. Brücke (*9*) proposed a theory of binocular vision in order to maintain the integrity of the theory of identical retinal points in light of Wheatstone's discovery that double images of an object arising from stimulation of noncorresponding retinal loci can be unified into a three-dimensional perception of that object. He suggested that when viewing stereoscopic half-images the axes of the eyes change their position constantly and rapidly, and that they thus pass through the various horopters of the stereoscopic image and these horoptic afterimages are *fused* into a unified perception. He demonstrated that very minor ocular movements would be necessary because the horopter intervals increase like the tangents of the angles of rotation of the eyes, and small vergence movements could occur quickly enough for the afterimages, which Brücke estimated to last about one-sixth of a second, to appear sequentially. Simultaneously, it was suggested that those portions of the object or image falling outside the instantaneous horopter are not seen as double because they are ignored. According to Brücke, depth perception was assigned to muscular sensations, and the tenability of the theory of identical points was maintained. However, this state of affairs was not long-lived because Dove (*14*) reported that stereoscopic depth perception could arise under illuminating conditions that lasted less than a millionth of a second which does not afford time for the eyes to move at all. Dove's finding was replicated by Volkmann (*81*), August (1), and Recklinghausen (*67*). The finding that stereoscopic depth perception occurs under extremely short stimulus durations has rendered convergence models of stereoscopy untenable.

BINOCULAR FUSION AND RETINAL CIRCLES OF SENSATION

According to P. L. Panum (*62*), the role of psychological processes in theoretical explanations of binocular space perception grew in prominence because they did not conflict with the identical points theory of the singleness of binocular vision, and Wheatstone himself had suggested that attention probably plays some part in stereoscopic depth perception. Accordingly, it was assumed that the perceiver does not attend to double images because they are indistinct and unclear. Speculations about the vagueness of the double images were based upon the assumptions that double images usually arise from stimulation of retinal regions outside the fovea which contains the images for the point of fixation, that the brightness of images falling upon identical retinal points is greater than for noncorresponding images, and that double images fall outside the plane of accommodation and therefore should appear blurred. However, Panum (62) rejected the position that psychological processes such as attention play a major functional role in stereoscopic vision, and instead he considered space perception an innate capacity thus moving the theoretical pendulum away from empiricism to nativism by advocating a purely sensory explanation of stereoscopic depth perception. Panum set out to demonstrate how the combined or joint binocular field is constructed solely out of sensory data, and in so doing he entrenched firmly the role of contours in subsequent models of stereoscopy (62, p. 138).

According to Panum, contours on the two retinas which neither intersect nor are tangent to each other predominate in the binocular field at the expense of monocular homogeneous grounds with the composite field arising from a uniform mosaic-like filling in of the binocular contours. However, not only are the compatible monocular contours carried into the combined visual field but also are their most contiguous grounds so that the half-images in Fig. 2.8 combine readily, whereas those in Fig. 2.9 do not and produce binocular rivalry at the intersection of the contours in the stereoscopic field.

For contours which did not strike corresponding retinal loci, Panum found that when the difference between the distances separating two of the contours in each half-image did not exceed 2 mm, at his viewing distance of 460 mm, the contours fused and depth was experienced without any double images of the lines (see Fig. 2.5). With a difference of 3 mm fusion was possible but not instantaneous, and with a 4 mm difference double images appeared even though the proper depth relationship was maintained. He determined that fusion of disparate contours could occur when the images fell within *retinal regions* (instead points) the diameters of which were 0.052 mm, or the width of 15 to 20 cones. He argued that a retinal portion of this diameter has a corresponding portion in the other eye and together they transmit a unitary (or fused) perception even though the contours may strike different retinal elements within these regions. He called these retinal areas "corresponding circles of sensation" and in so doing resurrected the identical points theory proposed by Johannes Müller. He went on to state that the horopter cannot be a flat plane from which all points are seen single with fixation constant

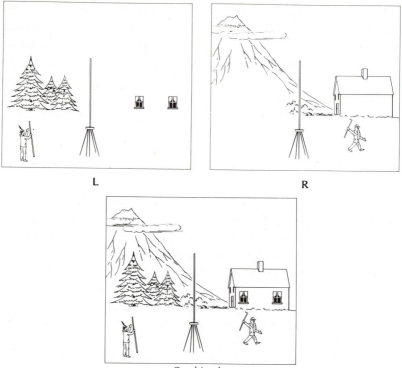

L   R

Combined

Fig. 2.8   A stereogram employed by P. L. Panum to demonstrate that the binocular visual field arises readily from the combination of monocular contours that do not intersect nor are tangent to each other. After Panum (62).

(Fig. 2.10), but rather it has a certain depth with the size of this region of binocular single vision surrounding the horopter growing larger the more the eyes approach a parallel position (62, p. 97).

Panum accepted the theory of identical retinal points first proposed by Johannes Müller, and he revitalized it by saying that for every point on one retina there is coordinated from the other not just an identical point, but rather a corresponding circle of sensation (*Emfindungskreis*). He stated that when identical retinal points are stimulated we *must* see single, whereas when corresponding circles of sensation are stimulated we *may* see single. The determining factors for fusion of contours that stimulate paired circles of sensation (but not identical retinal points) include the magnitude of spatial separation between the contours on the two retinas which cannot exceed 0.33° of visual angle according to Panum's earlier calculations and the similarity of contour orientation. Orthogonal contours yield strong binocular rivalry. Psychological processes such as attention played no part in the fusion of contour according to Panum. Different feelings of depth or distance would arise depending upon which retinal point of the one eye combined with this or that retinal point in the corresponding circle of sensation in the other eye. Panum concluded that stereoscopic depth perception is not the result of psychological processes or eye movements, but rather arises from innate processes including the specific nerve energies associated with the retina. According to Panum, the perception of depth is produced by means of a sensation or "synergy of the binocular parallax," while the fusion of disparate contours (contours which fall within corresponding sensory circles) results from the "binocular synergy of single

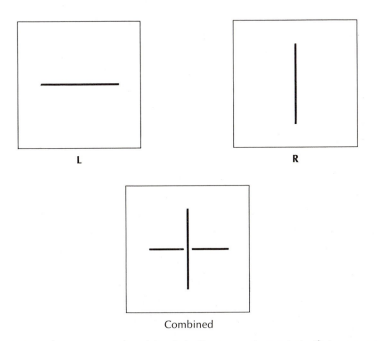

Combined

Fig. 2.9 A stereogram employed by P. L. Panum to demonstrate that monocular contours which intersect each other in the binocular visual field give rise to binocular rivalry and contour suppression. After Panum (62).

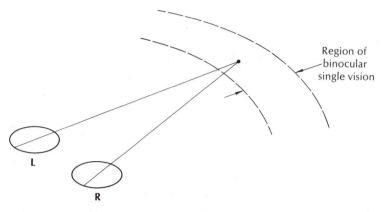

Fig. 2.10   Panum's conceptualization of the horopter which is surrounded by a region of binocular single vision based upon his discovery of corresponding retinal circles of sensation.

vision by corresponding circles of sensation." Even though Panum's nativistic theory excludes any role for experience as a contributing factor for stereoscopic depth perception and is itself vague and untestable, many of Panum's observations on the construction of the binocular field from monocular contour information still occupy a prominent position in contemporary models of human stereoscopic vision (73).

EWALD HERING: THE LAW OF IDENTICAL VISUAL DIRECTIONS
AND RETINAL MAPPING

Generally, we can distinguish between the nineteenth century visual scientists on the basis of their theoretical position regarding the mechanism for human space perceptions. The empiristic theorists included Volkmann (82, 83), Meyer (50), Lotze (48), Nagel (53), Wundt (92, 93), and Helmholtz (25), all of whom conceived of space perception as a gradual process of growth or acquisition given through experience. Contrariwise, the nativists stressed the instinctive dispositions and innate neural arrangements as the primary determinants of space perceptions; they included such notables as Johannes Müller (52), Brücke (9), Panum (62), and Ewald Hering (26, 27).

Hering's theory of binocular vision represented the ultimate refinement of nineteenth century nativistic or intuitive theories of space perception. He presented more clearly some of Panum's earlier views even though he did not cling as tenaciously to a strictly innate or nativistic explanation of space perception. Hering believed that our knowledge of space is an original and purely sensory experience that has to be refined and completed by elements of experience.

According to Hering (27), the human retina releases three kinds of "space feelings" when a retinal point is stimulated with the first two being the feeling of the altitude-value (*Hohenwert*) and the feeling of the azimuth-value (*Breitenwert*). Together these space values of height and breadth supplied the feeling of direction of the object in the visual field with these values identical for corresponding points on the two retinas. In addition to these two "space feelings" there was assumed to be a third, namely, the feeling of depth. The sensations of depth are identical at corresponding retinal points, with the space values of equal magnitude but *opposite* sign, whereas for any pair of retinal points that are symmetrically situated (images that fall upon the same hemi-retina), these values are equal and of the *same* sign. Accordingly, the depth feelings arising from points on the temporal halves of the two retinas were considered to be positive and corresponding with increases of depth, and those arising from points on the nasal halves of the two retinas as negative and corresponding with decreases of depth.

Every binocular perception of an object which is imaged on corresponding points has the *average* visual direction and the *average* depth value of all three of these space sensations. In the case of stimulation of corresponding retinal loci, the average depth value will always be zero because the depth sensations from each eye are of opposite sign. According to Hering, all such perceptions are localized by a simple act of sensation in a plane which Hering called the *nuclear plane or Kernfläche* of visual space which has no depth value at all. Hering stressed that the localization of an object or point relative to the nuclear plane must be conceived as a physiological process arising from a definite pair of retinal points. He ascribed to pairs of retinal points a space value, and he contended that this space value was stable and independent of the localization of the nuclear plane. Hering went further in constructing visual space and relating it to his conceptualization of retinal mapping and function when he proposed that the point in the nuclear plane that corresponds with the foveas serves as the center or *Kernpünkt* of a system

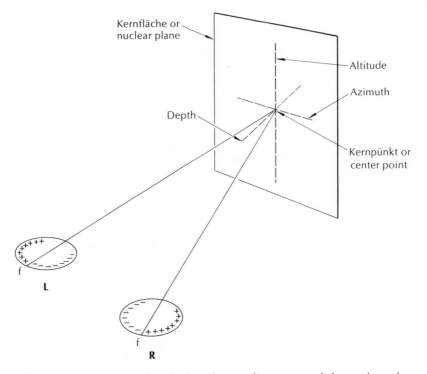

Fig. 2.11 Hering's visual space based upon the concept of the nuclear plane or Kernfläche. Images that stimulate identical retinal loci of each eye are projected to the nuclear plane which has zero depth value relative to the observer. The center point or Kernpünkt of the nuclear plane is the point of intersection of the foveal lines of visual direction from which the altitude, azimuth, and depth coordinates of visual space emanate. Notice that the temporal halves of the retina yield positive depth values while the nasal halves of the retina yield negative depth values.

of coordinates such that the height and breadth coordinates lie in the nuclear plane itself and the depth coordinate is orthogonal to it (Fig. 2.11).

Hering's nuclear plane was conceptualized by him as containing objects whose images fell on corresponding retinal points or whose images have only vertical disparity. It serves to differentiate in visual space all which is seen with crossed disparity from that seen with uncrossed disparity. The greater the horizontal disparity carried by the retinal images, the greater distance will the corresponding visual object appear to be behind (uncrossed disparity) or in front (crossed disparity) of this nuclear plane. All points or lines whose retinal images have equal amounts of uncrossed disparity will appear equidistant behind the nuclear plane and therefore will appear to be in a plane parallel to the nuclear plane. Likewise, the opposite applies to all points and lines whose images have equal crossed disparity (27).

The Kernfläche has at first no definite distance, and in this primitive visual space there is no reference to far and near. According to Hering, this elementary bifurcation of visual space arises only after the mental image (*Vorstellungsbild*) of our own body is on every occasion built into the visual space. This same recognition of the body as a starting point in visual space is the basis of the sense of absolute direction which Hering demonstrated as diverging or radiating from a point lying midway between the centers of the two eyes which Hering called the cyclopean eye.

Hering supported the doctrine of identical retinal points according to which stimuli acting on corresponding retinal points always excite only a single simple sensation. In order to demonstrate the stable and preformed relationships between corresponding retinal points, Hering postulated his *law of the identical visual direction of the two foveas which states that objects appear in the direction in space according to the parts of the retinas on which their images fall and are not seen in their real or actual directions.* The classic experiment demonstrating the validity of this law is as follows (Fig. 2.12). Assume you are about two feet in front of a window through which you have a view out-of-doors. With your hand steady and your right eye closed, direct your left eye to a distant object out-of-doors somewhat to your right. Assume this object is an evergreen tree, and the more salient this is from surrounding objects the more vivid will be the experiment. Now, while fixating the tree, make a small crayon mark on the window pane in line with your left eye and the tree. Now close the left eye and open the right eye and direct it to the same mark on the window pane, and out-of-doors in line with it identify a distant object, for example, a chimney. Finally, open both eyes and direct them to the mark on the pane. Immediately the images of this mark "fuse" and the mark appears as *one* straightforward direction (the principal visual direction) relative to the body. In effect, both of the foveas yield the same subjective direction inasmuch as the mark, the tree, and the chimney appear in the *same* subjective direction in spite of the widely separated difference in their actual directions relative to the observer. Objects

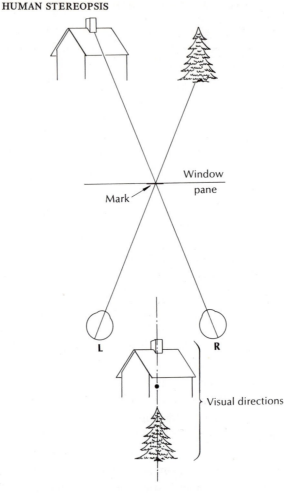

Fig. 2.12 The plan and results of the experiment which illustrate Hering's law of the identical visual direction of the two foveas. After Ogle (60).

appear in the direction in space according to the parts of the retinas upon which their images fall and are not seen in their actual directions. This fact was important to Hering's nativistic theory of space perception inasmuch as it demonstrated the consequences of retinal organization and neural correspondence upon the formation of the binocular field, and it supported the theory of identical retinal points. In fact, Hering wrote as follows:

The original idea represented by Mueller [J. Müller] which the correspondence of the retinas depends on an inborn arrangement, is widely opposed. It has been further declared that the correspondence of spatial values on both retinas is gained during the life of the individual, although the partial crossing of the optic nerve fibers at the chiasm, and the oft observed occurrence of corresponding partial incapability of the retinas, proves the correspondence is founded on an anatomical basis. Even though we may deny visual perception any original spatial attribute, and prefer to regard the spatial values of retinal points solely as a result of individual experience, we must give consideration to the facts and admit that there exists between corresponding points, an inborn, functional basis through which, whether it be sensory or motor, or both, the spatial interpretation of the sensations derived from cover points, follows a definite path (27, p. 19).

Inasmuch as corresponding retinal loci yield identical visual directions, it was incumbent upon Hering and his supporters to determine the perceptual and functional stability of this retinal organization for binocular vision. Accordingly, it was assumed that the mapping of corresponding retinal points would provide an accurate picture of how retinal organization was reflected in the organization of visual space. Recall that the horopter when determined experimentally for a given fixation point of the eyes represents all those points in space the images of which fall upon corresponding elements. On the basis of simple geometry and the concept of identical retinal points, the longitudinal horopter is a circle that passes through the centers of curvature of the two eyeballs and the fixation marker. This is the Vieth-Müller circle that remains the same as long as the point of fixation also is on it (Fig. 2.13). Both Hering and Helmholtz found that the empirical or actual horopter under viewing conditions of symmetrical convergence did not lie on the Vieth-Müller circle but actually between it and the objective frontoparallel plane. In fact, relative to the observer the horopter surface is concave at near distances becoming more and more flat as the fixation point recedes until finally for some observers it appears slightly convex at greater distances (60). The significance of this finding is that it suggests clearly that corresponding retinal elements were not as stable as Hering's theory demanded inasmuch as the shape of the horopter varied with viewing distance and even from one observer to another. However, Hillebrand (30) demonstrated that the deviation of the empirical longitudinal horopter

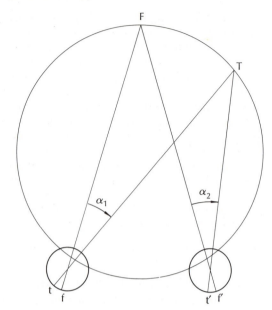

Fig. 2.13   The longitudinal horopter or Vieth-Müller circle in which the included angles α_1 and α_2 are equal. Note that F is the fixation point and T is another point on the Vieth-Müller circle. After Ogle (60).

from the Vieth-Müller circle could be accounted for by an asymmetry in the effective spatial positions of the corresponding elements in the two eyes. Consider Fig. 2.14 in which the object T outside the Vieth-Müller circle lies on the horopter. Note that the angular separations between the images of F and T is greater for the right eye than for the left. When T, however, falls on the Vieth-Müller circle, at T_o, the angular separations are equal. This so-called Hering-Hillebrand horopter deviation further prescribes that the shape of the horopter should change with changes of observation distance as previously mentioned which, in effect, is actually evidence in support of the stability of the corresponding retinal points (60).

According to Hering (27), the prevalence and conflict of contours which were first described by Meyer (51) and later studied by Panum (62) indicate that *differently* stimulated pairs of identical retinal points do not always yield a single fused sensation. Prevalence arises when contours which are presented only to one eye against contrasting backgrounds of the half-images remain clearly seen in the stereoscopic field indicating that the monocular contours themselves aid the portion of their adjacent background to suppress the contrasting background of the other half-image. Both Panum (62) and Hering (27) believed that the prevalence of contours was a function of the innate neural processes of the retina in that contours which strike the retina engender a different kind and a more robust nerve stimulus than that created by a plainly il-luminated surface. The conflict of contours or binocular rivalry (Fig. 2.9) indicates that each retina has a certain independence. When two contours are in conflict one must assume from Hering's theory that the dominant contour takes on the depth feeling of the victorious retina, thus precluding fusion of the depth feelings from each retina. Thus, it is diffi-cult to reconcile how the dominant monocular contour can appear with

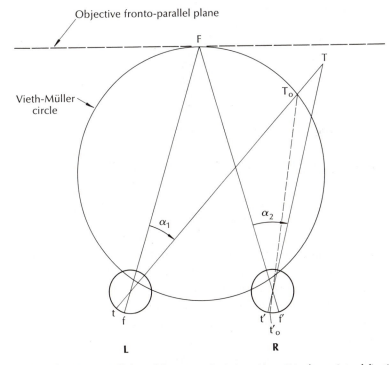

Fig. 2.14   The Hering-Hillebrand horopter deviation. Note F is the point of fixation and T is a point on a horopter that lies outside the Vieth-Müller circle. After Ogle (60).

a depth impression within the framework of Hering's concept of visual space which states that depth impressions are derived from a fusion of "depth feelings" from corresponding and or noncorresponding retinal loci. A related problem with Hering's theory comes from Wheatstone's demonstration that corresponding points of two retinal images can be shifted to two different places in visual space and appear double because Hering's theory stipulated that *only* one spatial localization and a single image must arise when corresponding points are stimulated (Fig. 2.7).

Hering stressed unequivocally that the singleness of binocular vision and identical visual direction are dependent solely upon the stimulation of corresponding retinal loci, and he took this as important proof of the validity of the theory of identical retinal points. However, in the last analysis it would be inaccurate to consider Hering as a pure nativist because he did not advocate a strict sensory basis of single vision arising from stimulation of disparate points on the two retinas, as Panum did, but rather a more psychological basis. He allowed a considerable part to the imagination as guided by past experience in the fusion of the impressions of disparate points. Also, he thought that the ability to recognize double images could be improved indefinitely by practice.

Hermann von Helmholtz and Unconscious Inference

The champion of nineteenth century empiristic theories of space perception is represented by the model put forth by H. von Helmholtz in his classic work on *Physiological Optics* (25). The fact that Hering and Helmholtz were contemporaries is indeed a fortunate circumstance even though they maintained opposing views on the nature of human space perception. They argued soundly and vigorously for their own separate views, and thus a comparison of their positions indicates clearly the assets and liabilities of the nativistic and empiristic theories of space perception with the usual outcome that the causes of science are advanced more by an amalgamation of apparently incompatible positions rather than by either alone.

According to Helmholtz, our sensations serve as signs for our consciousness, and their meaning is determined by our experience and subsequent understanding. In vision, these signs or tokens from our eyes may vary in intensity and quality, and in the case of space perception, there may be some further differences between the sensations depending on the place of retinal stimulation with the local signs in one eye being entirely different from those in the other eye. Through experience we learn what impressions an object which we see makes upon our eyes and the sum of all these sensations united is our idea (*Vorstellung*) of that particular object. The only psychological process required is the reproduction of associated ideas, and because the transition from sensation to associated idea can be expressed as an act of inference while at the same time there is no distinct consciousness of the elements of immediate sensation and mediate representation, Helmholtz referred to the above psychological process as an unconscious inference (*unbewusster Schluss*). In general, Helmholtz stated that,

> Such objects are always imagined as being present in the field of vision as would have to be there in order to produce the same impression on the nervous mechanism, the eyes being used under ordinary normal conditions (*25*, p. 2).

It is important to remember that Helmholtz spoke of conscious and unconscious inferences, the latter growing out of constant repetitions of the former that became so firmly entrenched in our experiences not to require our further conscious attention (*4*).

Unfortunately, Helmholtz did not elaborate upon the exact nature of the local retinal signs other than to say that they need not be arranged in a graduated system as Lotze (*48*) supposed, but rather they might be promiscuously distributed across the retina in any way whatever. According to Helmholtz, the fact that we always obtain the correct relief when viewing stereoscopic displays even for an instant indicated to him that the local signs from each retina are different, otherwise it should be possible to obtain the reverse relief just as easily and just as frequently as the correct stereoscopic organization. Inasmuch as the sensations of the two retinas are perfectly distinct from one another, they can combine into a single perception only when they stand as signs of single objects. This principle of the difference between the local signs for each retina can accommodate the facts of the normal coalescence of impressions of corresponding or identical points, the fusion of the impressions of disparate points for depth perception, and binocular rivalry.

According to Helmholtz, objects will appear double whenever their apparent positions with reference to the point of fixation in the visual fields of the two eyes are so different that this difference can be appreciated by the eyesight. When an object is seen single with two eyes, Helmholtz called it a total image or *Ganzbild*. When an object is not seen single by both eyes, the two images collectively were termed a double image. Helmholtz said the latter consisted of two half-images or *Halbbilde*. A total image usually results when corresponding retinal loci are stimulated or when disparate or noncorresponding retinal areas are stimulated providing the disparity is not too large.

He stated clearly that we do not always obtain a total image when corresponding points are stimulated as in the case of binocular rivalry (Fig. 2.9) and binocular lustre (Fig. 2.15) the latter having been discovered by Dove (*15*). These phenomena were considered by Helmholtz as important and unequivocal demonstrations that we can perceive separately each eye's image by *attending* to the target in one eye without being disturbed by the target in the other eye. In fact, Helmholtz stated that the prevalence and conflict of contours signified that:

> The content of each separate field comes to consciousness without being fused with that of the other field by means of organic mechanisms; and that, therefore, the fusion of the two fields in one common usage, when it does occur, is a psychic act (*25*, p. 499).

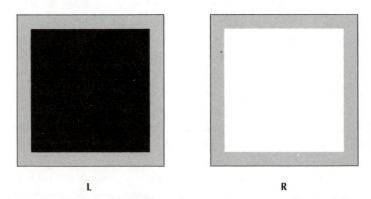

L   R

Fig. 2.15 An example of binocular lustre first reported by Dove (*15*). When the half-images are viewed stereoscopically, one sees a shiny metallic-like surface rather than either a black or white surface.

According to Helmholtz, the primary reason for the fusion of images falling upon disparate retinal points is the similarity between them to the two perspective images of one and the same object. The more perfect this kind of similarity is, the more difficult it will be for the observer to resist the fusion of the disparate images. He reported that when the disparity between the images is fairly large, fusion is not immediate and requires concentrated attention and some eye movements. Once the stereoscopic half-images are fused, however, it is very difficult and in most cases impossible to uncouple the half-images. Helmholtz stated that only by moving our eyes can we succeed in fusing retinal images that are very different. However, he makes plain that *all* perceptions of depth are not derived simply by movements of the eyes. Helmholtz observed that an object which stimulated corresponding retinal points could be seen as double and at different places in visual space just as Wheatstone (87) had reported (Fig. 2.7). Helmholtz attributed this to any condition which might be conducive to our making faulty comparisons between the different images in the two eyes which in the case of Wheatstone's stereogram refers to the fact that one of the vertical lines was much darker and wider than the other vertical line even though both images of the lines fell upon corresponding retinal points (25). In general, Helmholtz believed that images of similar contours and coloring are easier to fuse the nearer they are to identical retinal points.

Both Hering and Helmholtz stated that the fusion of disparate retinal images is not essential for stereoscopic depth perception. They felt that the recognition of double images is a function of the magnitude of the disparity carried by the retinal images and the attentional processes of an observer. Even though we are unaware of double images in our everyday visual experiences, we cannot conclude that the disparity causing the separation of the half-images is no longer the stimulus for stereoscopic depth perception. The depth experience does not depend upon any particular awareness of the doubling of the images inasmuch as both appear in depth and the depth can be clearly recognized without a distinct perception of the objects themselves.

In reviewing the problem of binocular rivalry, Helmholtz presented a stereogram that was intended primarily to demonstrate binocular lustre, but which also indicates clearly the critical importance of disparate contours for stereoscopic depth perception (59). When the half-images in

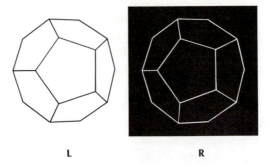

L   R

Fig. 2.16 Helmholtz's famous opposite-contrast stereogram which demonstrates that contours are the carriers of disparity information because these half-images differ in every way except that each contains contours. When the pattern is viewed stereoscopically, one sees against the lustrous ground the inner pentagon closer than the more radial outlines of the crystal. After Helmholtz (25).

Fig. 2.16 are combined stereoscopically, one sees against a metallic-like background a three-dimensional outline of a crystal with the enclosed pentagon appearing closer to the observer than the more radial outline. *Now the only common feature between these half-images is the contours, which means that the primary carrier of disparity information must be contours.* In fact, Ogle (59) has concluded on the basis of this stereogram, as well as other empirical findings, that the necessary and requisite stimulus for stereoscopic depth perception is the disparity between the retinal images of contours exclusive of the similarity or familiarity of the objects themselves.

A review of Helmholtz's contributions to the area of visual perception must out of necessity be limited because of the magnitude of his contributions. Helmholtz stated clearly that stereoscopic depth perception was primarily the result of experience. He concluded that stereoscopic depth represents an illusory phenomenon that results from the fact that when we view half-images we infer as a result of our past experience what object would have to be present in the stereoscopic field in order to produce the given patterns of retinal stimulation. In a more general sense, Helmholtz stated that binocular space perception rests entirely upon the fact that we are simultaneously aware of two different retinal images that arrive in consciousness without fusion. These sensations are combined in a simple representation when in consequence of repeated association they become signs of one and the same object (*68, 84*). Accordingly, the fusion of the sensations into a single notion of the external object is not achieved by any innate neural mechanisms but by a psychological process. Recently, Helmholtz's original concept of *unbewusster Schluss* has been modified and extended in order to account for the findings of stereoscopic depth perception arising from computer generated dot-matrix stereograms (*45, 46*). Even though Helmholtz was a man of the nineteenth century, his impact is still clearly evident in twentieth century visual science.

Gestalt Disparation and the Combination Zone

The contribution of Gestalt psychology to the area of stereoscopic depth perception is best represented by the writings of Kurt Koffka (*40, 41*) and the initial research findings of Lau (*43, 44*) and Dahlmann (*76*). The Gestalt psychologists emphasized that all visual perception is essentially tridimensional inasmuch as visual perception does not copy or grow primarily out of the bidimensional retinal image, but rather it approximately reconstitutes the three-dimensional stimulus object. Koffka (*41*) believed that the definitions of corresponding and disparate retinal points offered by Hering and Helmholtz were purely anatomical and geometrical facts which have very little to do with the "psychophysics of space." Essentially, the Gestalt approach focuses upon identifying the "forces of tridimensional organization" which result from the geometry of disparity.

Lau first attempted to define "Gestalt disparation" based upon his stereoscopic observations of modified geometrical illusory configurations such as the Zöllner and Poggendorf patterns (*43, 44*). An example of the stereoscopic patterns employed by Lau and others (*76*) is presented in Fig. 2.17 in which both half-images contain equally spaced vertical lines with crosshatched lines added to one of the half-images, thus inducing the appearance that those lines are nonparallel. Under stereoscopic viewing conditions, the lines have been reported to fuse momentarily and then appear *parallel and nearer* to the observer than the field of crosshatches (*76*). According to the Gestalt psychologists, this finding indicates that when the two eyes generate contour processes, which in spite of corresponding stimulation are as different from each other as

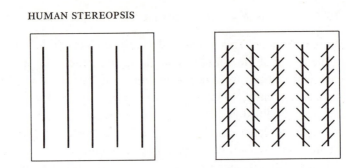

Fig. 2.17 An example of Gestalt disparation. The half-images contain equally spaced vertical lines so that the patterns do not carry any contour disparity even though one set of the vertical lines appears unequally spaced because of the cross-hatched lines. Stereoscopically, the vertical lines fuse momentarily and then appear parallel and nearer to the observer than the field of crosshatches.

the contour processes that would be produced by actual disparate stimulation, the same depth effect arises. Thus, Lau concluded that stereopsis is not produced by point for point stimulation, but rather the Gestalten as wholes are compared as configurational images, and divergencies between these very Gestalten yield the perception of depth. Later, Wilde concluded that:

> Binocular depth has nothing whatever to do with cross-disparation in the old sense of that term—depth is constructed in the first instance upon the ground of completed Gestalt units and is not possible without these (*89,* p. 259).

Tausch (77) later presented a very similar view that it is the *apparent* horizontal disparity between the configurations of each half-image which is the essential condition for stereoscopic depth perception.

A more refined version of the Gestalt explanation of depth perception is given by Koffka when he wrote that:

> . . . which pairs of points, or lines, on the two retinae will cooperate in determining the perceptual organization depends upon the two retinal patterns. This is not a geometrical or anatomical but a dynamical fact. In each case there must exist real forces which lead to one kind of coordination rather than another. The immediate origin of these forces cannot lie in the retinal patterns themselves, since they are separate and therefore unable to interact. Interaction can take place only where the *processes* started in the two optical tracts by the retinal patterns converge in the brain (*41,* p. 269).

According to Koffka (*40*), when we see a binocular object as single this reflects that the two organizational processes initiated in the retinas become united into one process in that part of the brain where the two optical tracts are brought together in what he called the "combination zone." The combination of organizational processes occurs for points that are projected on corresponding as well as noncorresponding points with fusion of disparate points resulting from a force of attraction between the two double images (*40*). However, as the disparity is increased, the fusional forces between the double images decreases so that eventually they grow so small that there is no displacement of the disparate points in the stereoscopic field, and thus the double images will appear in the same plane as the fixation point. Koffka generated the stereogram presented in Fig. 2.18 in order to demonstrate that the definition of disparity cannot be restricted solely to geometrical considerations based upon a point by point analysis of retinal images. The stereogram is said to carry a positive or crossed disparity, because the solid lines strike corresponding retinal points with less of a transverse separation between the dashed line and the solid line of the right half-image than the left half-image (*40*). The interesting feature of this pattern is that the dashes of one line are so arranged that they fall into the interstices between the dashes of the other line so that no *single* dash of either line has a corresponding element in the other line. In effect, there is no crossed disparate

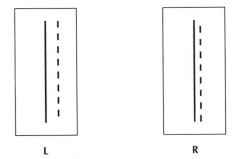

L   R

Fig. 2.18   A stereogram employed by Koffka to demonstrate stereoscopic depth in the absence of retinally disparate pairs of points. The dashes of one line are arranged so that no *single* dash of either line has a corresponding dash in the other line. When the pattern is viewed stereoscopically, the solid line appears in the plane of the paper and a broken line with small interstices appears closer to the observer. After Koffka (*40*).

pair of points. However, when Fig. 2.18 is viewed stereoscopically the solid line appears in the plane of the paper and a broken line with small interstices appears closer to the observer. Koffka concluded from this finding that even though there is no disparity of the elements of the dashed lines, the lines as wholes or Gestalten carry a disparity and, therefore, appear in depth.

It is quite obvious that the Gestalt contribution to our understanding of human space perception arises from and reflects their reaction to the elementism of nineteenth century German sensory psychology. Within the context of Gestalt psychology, space perception is considered the result of organized brain activity that can be understood only in terms of so called actual dynamic processes and not in terms of mere geometrical stimulus-sensation correlations. The Gestalt psychologists indicate that a strictly geometrical definition of the disparity of retinal images is inadequate, and that the definition must be extended to include *Gestalten* or forms. This extension of the concept of disparity implies that stereoscopic depth perception requires monocular contour recognition even though it does not require contour disparity as defined by a point for point comparison of retinal contours.

The major liability of the Gestalt approach to space perception is the difficulty of identifying and defining the so-called organizational processes of the human visual system and the paucity and the reliability of their stereoscopic depth findings from displays which carry only *apparent* transverse disparities of forms (*18, 57, 59*).

Kenneth Ogle's Theory of Stereoscopic Depth Perception

There is little question that the research of Kenneth N. Ogle represents some of the most significant contributions to the physiological and psychological explanation of human stereoscopy and that his manuscripts serve as the scientific link between nineteenth and twentieth century investigations of binocular depth perception. A major portion of Ogle's initial research in stereoscopic vision was conducted at the Dartmouth Eye Institute, a research organization under the direction of Adelbert Ames, Jr., that was devoted to studying problems in physiological optics, ophthalmology, and visual science in general (*10*).

According to Ogle, stereopsis is the single outstanding function of vision with two eyes, and it represents the fundamental functional difference between monocular and binocular vision (58). Ogle considers stereoscopic depth as a sensation because of the vividness of depth between objects. That is, the sense of space between the objects in depth implies that stereopsis must arise primarily as the result of a physiological process that may be enhanced, modified, or inhibited by psychological or experiential influences especially when the stereoscopic cue and the monocular cues to depth are at variance (57, 58). There are a number of facts that substantiate Ogle's position that stereopsis is primarily physiological in nature; they include the following: (a) the immediacy and compelling nature of the depth response to the stimulus of retinal disparity (58); (b) the positive correlation between stereoscopic acuity and visual acuity, especially for observers with visual acuities below 20/20 Snellen (20); (c) the fact that stereoscopic acuity toward the periphery of the retina appears to follow quantitatively the decrease of visual acuity with eccentric angle (11, 17, 23, 60); (d) the finding that different levels of stereopsis appear at different limits of transverse (54) and vertical (55) disparities; (e) the observation that stereoscopic acuity, like visual acuity, increases with increases in the luminance of the adapting ground (23); and (f) the fact that aftereffects occur in the third dimension as well as in only two-dimensional visual space (42).

Ogle states that disparity and disparity alone provides the necessary and sufficient stimulus condition for stereoscopic depth perception, and his research program focused upon determining the stability of the relationships between the experience of stereoscopic depth and the characteristics of the disparate stimuli (57, 58, 59, 60). He states that the physiological process underlying stereopsis (58, 70) responds to the disparity between the retinal images of objects in visual space, and the carrier of the disparity is monocularly recognizable contours or edges. In fact, Ogle states unequivocally that:

> We must stress the importance of contours, those lines of demarcation between the "figure" and the "background." In every case stereoscopic depth depends on the disparity between the images of identifiable contours (58, p. 380).

In order for contour disparity to exist there must be at least two objects in the binocular field of view. Thus, in Fig. 2.19 the difference in

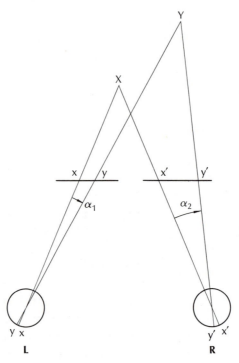

Fig. 2.19   Geometrical disparity. The difference in the angles α_1 and α_2, or the difference in angular separation of the two spatial objects X and Y subtended at the two eyes, is the geometrical disparity (η) which is expressed in minutes or seconds of arc.

angles α_1 and α_2, or the difference in angular separation of the two spatial objects X and Y subtended at the two eyes, is referred to as the *geometrical disparity* (η), and it is expressed in minutes or seconds of arc (59). This geometrical disparity must not be confused with *physiological disparity* which means that the retinal images of an object are seen in two different primary subjective visual directions according to Hering's law of identical visual direction (Fig. 2.12).

Ogle makes plain that we are dealing here with the problem of the precise definition of disparity. In addressing himself to this problem, Ogle cites the work of Panum (*62*) who demonstrated earlier that there is a region of binocular single vision surrounding the horopter. This finding indicates that the images of objects that fall within Panum's circles of sensation or Panum's fusional areas give rise to the perception of a single object with one primary subjective visual direction even though the images may fall upon different retinal loci within each eye (Fig. 2.10). Thus, we assume that in the fusion of disparate images within Panum's areas one of two alternatives occurs. Either one of the two monocular primary subjective directions disappears and the visual direction of the fused image is that of the other eye or both of the primary subjective visual directions of the monocular images are replaced by a new subjective direction lying between the two primary monocular directions (60). The transition from the subjective directions of the two monocular images to the subjective visual direction of the binocularly fused image has been referred to as a directional difference (78), a lateral displacement (80), or a functional displacement (86). In fact, Werner (86) has concluded that functional displacement, which refers only to a change of direction of an object in stereoscopic space without a change of the relative position of the object in one of the monocular retinal fields, is the only necessary perceptual condition for binocular depth perception. According to Werner (86), disparity of contours serves to release a dynamic perceptual process, and the behavioral reflection of this dynamic process is a real displacement of the visual direction of the object in the stereoscopic field. However, Ogle (58) concluded that when disparate images are fused, the new binocular direction is a compromise between the primary directions associated with the two noncorresponding retinal loci upon which the two disparate images fell and that the displacement accompanies but does not cause the depth. Ogle (60) has determined the extent of Panum's fusional areas (Fig. 2.20), and he states that within Panum's fusional areas the perception of doubling of all disparate images is masked with the subjective directions correlated with retinal elements representing only a two-dimensional elaboration of visual space.

In a classic paper, Ogle (54) determined the disparity values within which stereoscopic depth perception arises as a function of the magnitude of retinal eccentricity of the disparate images along the horizontal retinal meridian. The results of the experiment are presented in Fig. 2.21, and they suggest that the character of stereoscopic depth perception changes directly with the magnitude of disparity and that the range of disparity values for any given type of stereoscopic depth increases with increasing peripheral angle. Perceptually, as the magnitude of the un-

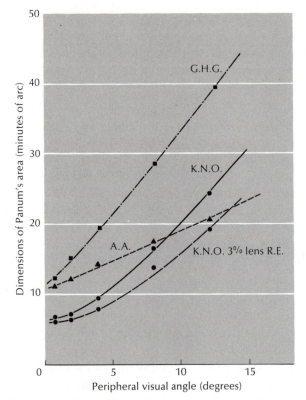

Fig. 2.20   The regional values of Panum's fusional areas along the horizontal retinal meridian. Note that with increasing peripheral angle the size of the fusional areas increases. After Ogle (59).

crossed disparity was increased, the observers reported that the disparate object was seen single and it appeared to move progressively behind the fixation point (fused patent stereopsis). As the disparity was increased still further, the observers reported a strong sense of depth even though the disparate object appeared double and the separation between the double images increased with increasing disparity (patent stereopsis with double images). With continued increases of disparity, the observers reported that the previously vivid depth impression disappeared, yet they could still report that the two images appeared unmistakably behind the fixation point (qualitative stereopsis). Essentially the same regions and regional values were identified when the disparity was crossed

(*54*). Thus, for patent or quantitative stereopsis the disparate images can appear fused or not fused with a depth experience that is vivid and compelling in either case. Within the range of patent stereopsis the magnitude of the depth response correlates with the magnitude of disparity. However, for larger disparities the depth experience is less obvious, the depth experience deteriorates with steady fixation, and the depth of both of the double images is apprehended qualitatively (that is, an observer can only report that the double images appear "nearer" or "farther" than the fixation point). According to Ogle, the finding that there are limiting disparity values for the different types of stereoscopic depth indicates clearly that stereopsis is not solely a psychological phenomenon and that there is a physiological basis for stereoscopic depth perception.

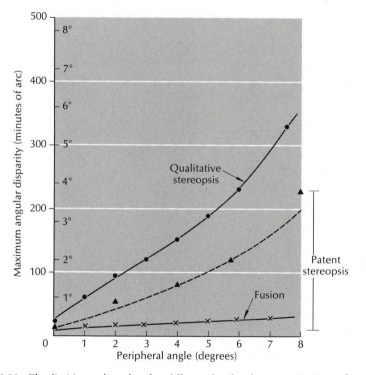

Fig. 2.21   The limiting values for the different levels of stereopsis. Note that for both patent and qualitative stereopsis the limits increase with increasing peripheral angle. After Ogle (*58*).

Unlike Hillibrand (31), Ogle (54) agrees with Hering (27) and Helmholtz (25) that fusion of disparate retinal images is not essential for the emergence of stereoscopic depth perception. However, he agrees with Hillebrand (28) and Hering (27) that vertical disparities alone do not give rise to stereoscopic depth perception. Ogle (55) found that when retinal images carry a transverse disparity, a large amount of vertical disparity (beyond 25 to 35 minutes of arc with foveal fixation) is essential before the stereoscopic depth response is abolished. Within these limits and even though the images are seen as vertically double, depth persists indicating the potency of transverse disparity and the fact that our binocular visual system is primarily sensitive to this direction of disparities.

Ogle (56, 58) states that convergence can enhance stereoscopic depth perception because eye movements provide bifoveal fixation with the result that the images of the objects fall upon retinal areas with the highest visual acuity. However, he agrees with others (2, 29, 34) that neither accommodation nor convergence alone can provide reliable and accurate cues to spatial localization.

In terms of the problem of defining corresponding retinal points, Ogle (58) concludes that we do not yet have a precise and reliable method of determining the horopter or the seen spatial counterparts of corresponding points. Although he discussed the potential inadequacies of the five criteria for determining the empirical horopter, we need only consider his treatment of two of the criteria inasmuch as they have been employed frequently. The first criterion, which was introduced by Hering (27), is the "apparent frontoparallel plane" which is based on the assumption that when objects (usually vertical threads viewed through a horizontal aperture) all appear at the same distance as the fixation point (nuclear plane, Fig. 2.11), then the horizontal disparity of the images of each object is zero. Some of the difficulties with this criterion are that it can be used only under restrictive experimental conditions such as only when black threads are seen against a white ground, with observation times longer than 0.8 seconds, and with symmetrical convergence (78). The second criterion of the "equating of primary visual directions" is the best of the five according to Ogle (58) inasmuch as it resembles the accepted definition of corresponding points, namely, that when an object appears to each eye in the same primary visual direction the images of that object fall on corresponding retinal points. Here, we are dealing with the "nonius horopter" in which the observer sees for example the upper-half of a thread with one eye against which he must align the lower-half of the thread presented to the other eye. Inasmuch as when the two portions of the thread are aligned they are seen in the same visual direction by each eye separately, the images are said to fall on corresponding retinal elements. This is a very difficult task, and the accuracy of the judgments is much less than the judgmental accuracy required in determining the apparent frontoparallel plane (58). Despite the difficulties inherent in trying to determine the empirical horopter, it is obvious that our subjective experience of stereoscopic depth does not depend upon our precise knowledge of the location of the horopter (for a more detailed discussion of the problem of determining retinal correspondence see Chapter 3).

In his last paper published a short time before his death in February 1968 (22), Ogle (61) discusses the problem of binocular rivalry and stereoscopic depth perception. This is an important manuscript inasmuch as after forty years of active research in visual space perception Ogle reaffirms the validity of the classical model of stereopsis dating back to Wheatstone and Helmholtz when he writes that "stereopsis depends only on the transverse disparities between the images in the two eyes of contours or borders, irrespective of the color of the details or difference in luminances of the background" (61, p. 89). In an interesting footnote in the same report, Ogle (61) speculates that even the Julesz results (35, 36) with random dot-matrix stereograms may not be contrary to the classical model of stereopsis although the disparate contours may be difficult to recognize monocularly. In terms of the relationship between stereopsis and rivalry, Ogle found, contrary to earlier reports (5, 32, 33), that the presence of stereoscopic depth perception tended to inhibit or stabilize binocular rivalry arising from the backgrounds against which the disparate contours were projected. This finding indicates that stereoscopic depth perception from transversely disparate contours is a robust and stable perceptual phenomenon even when the backgrounds of optical displays have the capacity to inhibit binocular registration of the monocular images.

The significance of Ogle's research in binocular vision is that he has attempted to clarify and quantify the basic concepts of the classical model of stereopsis. Accordingly, Ogle has stated repeatedly and un-equivocally that this model prescribes that the only necessary and suffi-cient stimulus condition for stereopsis is the retinal disparity between identifiable contours or edges. A corollary of this position is that the dis-parate contours must be recognizable monocularly. As a result of his rigorous experimentation, Ogle has concluded (58) that stereoscopic depth perception represents the unique functional difference between monocular and binocular vision, that it is a sensation, and that it arises primarily from a physiological process.

Up until now, it appeared that Ogle's statement of the classical model of stereopsis is sound and intact. However, since the early part of 1960 there has been a renewed and vigorous interest in stereoscopic vision that has been spurred by the findings from dot-matrix stereograms that sug-gest clearly that the traditional concept and definition of disparity must be modified and extended (36, 37, 38, 39, 45, 46, 71). In brief, these recent studies indicate that *instead of contours giving rise to depth, it is rather depth that gives rise to contours.* We will present in the remainder of this book an analytical treatment of the dot-matrix data in order to make clear and to substantiate our modification and extension of the classical model of stereoscopy.

Summary and Overview

Any attempt to telescope over a thousand years of philosophical and sci-entific inquiry into the problem of binocular space perception will neces-sarily be focalized and devoid, in part, of depth of treatment. However, from the outset it was abundantly clear that different cue systems medi-ated space perception under monocular and binocular vision. The early philosophers and artists studied most directly and clearly this issue, and their impact is still evident today when we speak of the unlearned and learned cues to distance.

Aguilonius (72) was the first to treat systematically the problem of the singleness of binocular vision arising from the two retinal images of an object. He introduced the concept of the horopter, the spatial locus of all points seen as single in the binocular field. This concept served as the impetus for two important theories of binocular vision.

Kepler's projection theory (25) stated that the spatial location of seen objects is at the point of intersection of the lines of sight of the projected retinal images. The theory accounts for the coalescence of retinal images but not for the fact of double vision. Müller's theory of identical retinal points (52) is the basis of subsequent nativistic theories of space perception. The theory holds that the retinal images of objects that strike corresponding retinal elements will appear single. Unfortunately, the theory fails to explain adequately single vision which results when disparate retinal points are stimulated.

Charles Wheatstone (87), physicist turned psychologist, was the first to demonstrate clearly that stereoscopic depth perception results directly from the "visual disparities" contained in the retinal images arising under binocular regard even though this important fact had been suggested partially by Joseph Harris and Robert Smith. Wheatstone's finding that single vision occurs when disparate retinal points are stimulated, and that it is precisely this kind of retinal stimulation that is responsible for depth, was a direct blow to the theory of identical points. Further damaging evidence against the theory was Wheatstone's demonstration that an object can be seen double and in two different places when identical retinal points are stimulated. Unfortunately, David Brewster (8) failed to recognize the significance of these findings, and he tried to explain stereopsis as the result of successive vergent eye movements.

Beginning with Brücke (9), nineteenth century sensory psychologists made steady contributions to our knowledge of stereoscopic vision. Brücke tried to resurrect the theory of identical retinal points when he claimed that the successive afterimages of the various points of fixation arising from a tridimensional object are fused into a unified percept. However, Dove (14) found that stereoscopy occurs with exposure durations sufficiently brief to prevent eye movements thus precluding any fusion of afterimages from successively fixated points. P. L. Panum (62) revised the theory of identity when he discovered the corresponding retinal circles of sensation. He stated that when identical retinal elements are stimulated we *must* see single, but when corresponding elements with the circles of sensation are stimulated we *may* see single. He made plain the importance of contours for binocular registration of half-images.

Ewald Hering (27) modified Panum's nativistic theory of space perception to allow a functional role for experience especially in the perception of depth from double images. Hering described the retina as possessing three space sensations of height, breadth, and depth. The first two values determine the visual direction of a seen object, and he formulated his law of identical visual direction which states that objects appear in the direction of space according to the locus of retinal stimulation and not their real or actual directions. He introduced the concept of the nuclear plane of visual space, and he adapted this as the criterion for determining the seen spatial counterparts of corresponding points.

The last of the great nineteenth century German sensory psychologists was Helmholtz (25). He stated that depth perception is the result of experience, and that stereoscopy arises from inferences that at first may be conscious and deliberate but through repetition become unconscious and automatic. He demonstrated that the contours in the half-images are the carriers of the "visual disparities" that Wheatstone discovered earlier. He made plain that the psychological process of attention influences binocular rivalry and binocular registration when identical and noncorresponding points are stimulated, respectively, which he considered as conclusive evidence against the theory of identical retinal points.

At the beginning of the twentieth century after almost 100 years of primarily a molecular and retinal approach to the study of space perception, we encounter the more global strategy and emphasis of Gestalt psychology. For Koffka (41) and other Gestalt psychologists, depth perception was the result of organizing processes within the brain. From them, we find empirical demonstrations that the geometrical and retinal analysis of the problem of space perception appeared to be inadequate. In effect, the Gestalt psychologists claimed that monocular form recognition was an essential condition for depth, and they concluded that stereoscopy could arise from an *apparent* as well as a *real* transverse disparity of contours.

Lastly, the classical or traditional model of stereopsis is best formulated in the work of Kenneth Ogle (58). He stated unequivocally that stereopsis depends solely upon the disparity of identifiable contours and that stereopsis is a sensory process with a specific physiological basis. However, he claims that the stereoscopic depth experience can be modified, especially when the stereoscopic cue of contour disparity conflicts with the learned cues to spatial localization. Ogle's work indicated that at the beginning of 1960, and after almost a thousand years of formulation, the classical model of stereopsis appeared valid and complete.

References

1. August, F. Über eine neue Art stereoskopischer Erscheinungen. *Pogg. Ann.*, 1860, *60*, 582-593.
2. Bappert, J. Neue Untersuchungen zum Problem des Verhaltnisses von Akkommodation und Konvergenz zur Wahrnehmung der Tiefe. *Z. Psychol.*, 1922, *90*, 167-203.
3. Boring, E. G. *The Physical Dimensions of Consciousness.* New York: London, 1933, pp. 118-119.
4. Boring, E. G. *Sensation and Perception in the History of Experimental Psychology.* New York: Appleton-Century-Crofts, 1942, p. 265.
5. Bower, T., and Goldsmith, W. Destruction of stereopsis. *Psychon. Sci.*, 1964, *1*, 287-288.
6. Brewster, D. *A Treatise on Optics.* 1831.
7. Brewster, D. On the knowledge of distance given by binocular vision. *The London, Edinburgh, and Dublin Phil. Mag. and J. of Sci.*, 1847, *30*, 305-318.
8. Brewster, D. *The Stereoscope.* London: John Murray, 1856.
9. Brücke, E. Über die stereoskopischen Erscheinungen. *J. Müller's Archiv fur Anat. und Physiol.*, 1841, p. 459.
10. Burian, H. M. The history of the Dartmouth Eye Institute. *Arch. Ophthal.*, 1945, *40*, 163-175.
11. Burian, H. M. Stereopsis. *Docum. Ophthal.*, 1951, *5-6*, 169-183.
12. Carr, H. A. *An Introduction to space perception.* New York: Longmans, Green & Co., 1935.
13. Dodwell, C. P., and Engel, G. R. A theory of binocular fusion. *Nature,* 1963, *198*, 39-74.
14. Dove, H. W. In the *Monatsberichte d. Berliner Akad.*, 1841, p. 251.
15. Dove, H. W. Über die Ursachen des Glanzes und der Irradiation, abgeleitet aus chromatischen Versuchen mit dem Stereoskop. *Ann. Phys.*, 1851, *83*, 169-183.
16. Du Tour, E. F. Discussion d'une question d'optique. *Memoirs de Mathematique et Physique d'Academie Royale Science Paris*, 1760, *3*, 514-530.
17. Ellerbrock, V. J. A comparison of peripheral stereoscopic and visual acuities. *Amer. J. Optom.*, 1949, *26*, 530-537.
18. Fleischer, B. Die Querdisparation als physiologische Grundlage des binokularen Tiefensehens. *Z tschr. f. Psychol. u. Physiol. d. Sinnesorg.* 1939, *147*, 65-132.
19. Fraser, A. C. *Selections from Berkeley.* New York: Macmillan & Co., 1884.
20. Frey, R. G. Die Beziehung zwischen Schschärfe und Tiefensehschärfe. *Wien. med. Wschr.*, 1953, *103*, 436-438.
21. Gassendi, P. *Opera omnia.* Vol. 2, Lugd., 1658, p. 395.
22. Graham, C. H. Kenneth Neil Ogle. *J. Opt. Soc. Amer.*, 1968, *58*, 860.

23. Guggenbühl, A. Das stereoskopische Sehen des hell- und dunkeladaptierten Auges. *Ophthalmologica*, 1948, *115*, 193-218.
24. Harris, J. *Treatise on Opticks*. 1775, p. 171.
25. Helmholtz, H. von. *Helmholtz's Treatise on Physiological Optics*. Vol. 3, J. P. C. Southall (Ed.), New York: Optical Society of America, 1925, p. 483.
26. Hering, E. *Beiträge zur Physiologie*. Leipzig: 1861-1864, Hefte 2 to 5.
27. Hering, E. Der Raumsinn und die Bewegungen der Auges. In Hermann, Ludimar: *Handbuch der Physiologie*, 3 (pt. 1). See English translation by C. A. Radde, *Spatial Sense and Movements of the Eyes*. Baltimore: The American Academy of Optometry, 1942.
28. Hillibrand, F. Die Stabilität der Raumwerte auf der Netzhaut. *Zeitschr. f. Psychol. u. Physiol. d. Sinnesorg.*, 1893, *5*, 1-60.
29. Hillebrand, F. Der Verhältnis von Akkommodation und Konvergenz zur Tiefenlokalisation. *Zeitschr. f. Psychol. u. Physiol. d. Sinnesorg.*, 1894, *7*, 97-151.
30. Hillebrand, F. *Lehre von den Gesichtsempfindungen*. Wein: J. Springer, 1929, p. 205.
31. Hillebrand, F. *Lehre von den Gesichtsempfindungen*. Wein: J. Springer, 1929.
32. Hochberg, J. Depth perception loss with local monocular suppression: A problem in the explanation of stereopsis. *Science*, 1964, *145*, 1334-1335.
33. Hochberg, J. Stereopsis suppression: addendum. *Science*, 1965, *146*, 800.
34. Irvine, S. R., and Ludvigh, E. J. Is ocular proprioceptive sense concerned in vision? *Arch. Ophthal. n. s.*, 1936, 1037-1049.
35. Julesz, B. Stereopsis and binocular rivalry of contours. *J. Opt. Soc. Amer.*, 1963, *53*, 994-999.
36. Julesz, B. Binocular depth perception without familiarity cues. *Science*, 1964, *145*, 356-362.
37. Julesz, B. *Foundations of Cyclopean Perception*. Chicago: Univ. Chicago Press, 1971.
38. Kaufman, L. On the nature of binocular disparity. *Amer. J. Psychol.*, 1964, *77*, 393-402.
39. Kaufman, L. Some new stereoscopic phenomena and their implications for the theory of stereopsis. *Amer. J. Psychol.*, 1965, *78*, 1-20.
40. Koffka, K. Some problems of space perception. In *Psychologies of 1930*, Worcester, Massachusetts: Clark Univ. Press, 1930, pp. 161-187.
41. Koffka, K. *Principles of Gestalt Psychology*. New York: Harcourt, Brace and Co., 1935.
42. Köhler, W., and Emery, D. A. Figural after-effects in the third dimension of visual space. *Amer. J. Psychol.*, 1947, *60*, 159-201.
43. Lau, E. Über das stereoskopische Sehen. *Psychol. Forsch.*, 1922, *2*, 1-5.
44. Lau, E. Über das stereoskopische Sehen. *Psychol. Forsch.*, 1925, *6*, 122-126.

45. Lawson, R. B., and Gulick, W. L. Stereopsis and anomalous contour. *Vision Res.*, 1967, *7*, 271-297.
46. Lawson, R. B., and Gulick, W. L. Apparent size and distance in stereoscopic vision. In Human Space Perception: Proceedings of the Dartmouth Conference. *Psychonomic Monog. Suppl.*, 1970, *3*, 193-200.
47. Le Conte, J. *Sight: An expression of the principles of monocular and binocular vision.* New York: D. Appleton & Co., 1881.
48. Lotze, H. *Medizinische Psychologie.* Leipzig: 1832, pp. 325-371.
49. Mayo, H. *Outlines of Human Physiology.* London: Burgess and Hill, 1833, p. 288.
50. Meyer, H. Beitrag zur Lehre von der Schätzung der Entfernung aus der Konvergenz der Augensachen. *Archiv für Ophthalmologie,* 1856, *2*, 92-94.
51. Meyer, H. Über den Einfluss der Aufmerksamkeit auf die Bildung des Gesichtsfeldes überhaupt und die Bildung des gemeinschaftlichen Gesichtsfeldes beider Augen im besondern. *Archiv für Ophthalmologie,* 1856, *2*, 77-92.
52. Müller, Johannes. *Zur vergleichenden Physiologie des gesichtssinnes des Menschen und der Thiere.* Leipzig: Cnoblock, 1826.
53. Nagel, A. *Das Sehen mit zwei Augen und die Lehre von den identischen Netzhautstellen.* Leipzig: C. F. Winter, 1861.
54. Ogle, K. N. On the limits of stereoscopic vision. *J. Exper. Psychol.,* 1952, *44*, 252-259.
55. Ogle, K. N. Stereopsis and vertical disparity. *A.M.A. Arch. Ophthal.,* 1955, *53*, 495-504.
56. Ogle, K. N. Stereoscopic acuity and the role of convergence. *J. Opt. Soc. Amer.,* 1956, *46*, 269-273.
57. Ogle, K. N. Present status of our knowledge of stereoscopic vision. *Arch. Ophthal.,* 1958, *60*, 755-774.
58. Ogle, K. N. Theory of stereoscopic vision. In *Psychology: A Study of a Science,* Vol. 1, S. Koch (Ed.), New York: McGraw-Hill, 1959, pp. 362-394.
59. Ogle, K. N. The optical space sense. In *The Eye,* Vol. IV, Hugh Davson (Ed.), New York: Academic Press, 1962, pp. 209-417.
60. Ogle, K. N. *Researches In Binocular Vision.* New York: Hafner, 1964.
61. Ogle, K. N., and Wakefield, J. Stereoscopic depth and binocular rivalry. *Vision Res.,* 1967, *7*, 89-98.
62. Panum, P. L. *Physiological investigations concerning vision with two eyes.* Kiel: Schwering's Bookstore, 1858. Translated by Camilla Hübscher, Dartmouth Eye Institute, Hanover, N.H., 1940.
63. Pastore, N. Locke and Molyneux, Chapter 4 in *Selective History of Theories of Visual Perception 1650-1950,* New York: Oxford, 1951.
64. Polyak, S. *The Vertebrate Visual System.* Chicago: Univ. Chicago Press, 1957.

65. Porta, J. B. *De Refractione.* 1593, p. 142.
66. Priestley, J. *The History and Present State of Discoveries Relating to Vision, Light, and Colours.* London: J. Johnson, 1772, p. 695.
67. Recklinghausen, F. v. Zum korperlichen Sehen. *Pogg. Ann.,* 1861, *64,* 170-173.
68. Ribot, T. A. *German Psychology of Today: The Empirical School.* Translated by J. M. Baldwin. New York: C. Scribner's Sons, 1886.
69. Rogers, W. B. Observations on Binocular Vision. Part III. *Amer. J. Sci. and Arts,* 1856, *21,* 80-95, 173-189.
70. Rønne, G. The physiological basis of sensory fusion. *Acta Ophthal.,* 1956, *34,* 1-26.
71. Shipley, T. Visual contours in homogeneous space. *Science,* 1965, *150,* 348-350.
72. Shipley, T., and Rawlings, S. The nonius horopter—I. History and theory. *Vision Res.,* 1970, *10,* 1225-1262.
73. Shipley, T., and Hyson, M. The stereoscopic sense of order—A classification of stereograms. *Amer. J. Opt. and Archiv. Amer. Acad. Opt.,* 1972, *49,* 83-96.
74. Smith, N. Malebranche's theory of the perception of distance and magnitude. *Brit. J. Psychol.,* 1905, *1,* 13-203.
75. Smith, R. *A Compleat System of Opticks.* Vol. 2, 1738, pp. 388-389.
76. Squires, P. Stereopsis produced without horizontally disparate stimulus loci. *J. Exper. Psychol.,* 1956, *52,* 199-203.
77. Tausch, R. Die beidaugige Raumwahrnehmung. *Z. angewand. Psychol.,* 1953, *3,* 394-421.
78. Tschermak, A. Beiträge zur physiologischen Optik III; Raumsinn. In Bethe, A., Bergmann, G. V., Embden, G., and Ellinger, A. *Handbuch der normalen und pathologischen Physiologie,* Vol. 12, Berlin: J. Springer, 1930, pp. 833-1000.
79. Turbayne, C. Berkeley and Molyneux on retinal images. *J. of the Hist. of Ideas,* 1955, *16,* 339-355.
80. Verhoeff, F. H. A new theory of binocular vision. *Arch. Ophthal. n. s.,* 1935, *13,* 151-175.
81. Volkmann, A. W. Das Tachistoskop, ein Instrument, welchis bir Untersuchung des momentanen Schans den Gebrauch des elektrischen Funkens ersetzt. *Leipz. Ber.,* 1859, 90-98.
82. Volkmann, A. W. Die stereokopischen Erscheinungen in ihrer Beziehung zu der Lehre von den identischen Netzhautstellen. *Archiv für Ophthalmologie,* 1859, *2,* 1-100.
83. Volkmann, A. W. Über identische Netzhautstellen. *Berliner Monatsber.,* August, 1863.
84. Warren, R. M., and Warren, R. P. *Helmholtz on Perception: Its Physiology and Development.* New York: Wiley, 1968.
85. Watson, R. *The Great Psychologists: Aristotle to Freud.* New York: J. B. Lippincott, 1968.

86. Werner, H. Dynamics of binocular depth perception. *Psychol. Monog.*, 1937, *49*, 1-127.
87. Wheatstone, C. Contributions to the physiology of vision. Part I. On some remarkable, and hitherto unobserved, phenomena of binocular vision. *Royal Soc. London Philos. Trans.*, 1838, *128*, 371-394.
88. Wheatstone, C. Contributions to the physiology of vision. Part II. On some remarkable, and hitherto unobserved, phenomena of binocular vision (continued). *The London, Edinburgh, and Dublin Phil. Mag. and J. of Sci.*, 1852, ser. 4, *3*, 504-523.
89. Wilde, K. Der Punktreiheneffekt und die Rolle der binok. Querdisparation beim Tiefensehen. *Psychol. Forsch.*, 1950, *23*, 223-262.
90. Winter, H. J. J. The optical researches of Ibn Al-Haitham. *Centaurus*, 1954, *3*, 190-210.
91. Woodworth, R. S. Visual space, Chapter 26 in *Experimental Psychology*, New York: Henry Holt and Co., 1938.
92. Wundt, W. *Beitrage zur Theorie der Sinneswahrnehmung.* Leipzig and Heidelberg, 1862.
93. Wundt, W. Zur Theorie der räumlichen Gesichtswahrnehmungen. *Phil. Stud.*, 1898, *14*, 1-118.

3

Retinal Correspondence

In the previous chapter on the history of ideas about the perception of visual space, some mention of retinal correspondence found its way into the treatment because of its obvious relationship to disparity, a topic central to an understanding of depth perception. Inasmuch as interpretations of disparity depend upon the concept of retinal correspondence, it is essential to know thoroughly both the value and the limitations of this concept.

Retinal correspondence has a long and lively history nurtured by the important role given to it in theories of stereopsis. One of the reasons for the liveliness has been a failure by those who have advanced the concept to agree upon and make plain what correspondence means and what ends it serves.

The origin of the idea of correspondence probably had its roots in a dilemma. Because man has two eyes forward in the head, much of what is seen with one eye also is seen with the other. While the lateral peripheries of vision are monocular, the nose serving as occluder, the region of central vision is not only binocular, it is with certain limitations redundant. Yet, despite image duality, percepts are of single objects.

Based upon the writing of Empedocles in the middle of the fifth century B.C., the belief was widely held that knowing was mediated by the sense organs in that they somehow mirrored the external world. Perception of the visual world was believed to arise when activity in the external environment was met by similar activity within the eyes: *like is perceived by like.*

The heritage from Empedocles was that man thought of his *eyes* as perceivers, and the inertia of this belief helped to set the stage for the development many centuries later of the idea of correspondence. Inasmuch as a single object in binocular space stimulates two agents of perception, singleness of vision was claimed to arise because the eyes were redundant. Only much later, in the 1500's, did advances in optics lead to a refinement in the concept of correspondence from one of simple redundancy to one of sophisticated geometry.

One might suppose that, had the eyes of man been lateralized fully in the manner of so many creatures, the concept of geometrical correspondence never would have arisen. Yet, suppositions aside, the development of geometrical descriptions of the relationships between external space and ocular space lent force to the concept of correspondence. For each locus on one retina, one could argue that there was a geometrically corresponding locus on the other retina, with the two matched loci serving as the means to achieve redundancy and, therefore, singleness of vision from two eyes. Of course, it is obvious to us now that binocular inspection of a single object in space provides image redundancy only of a sort, for in many particulars the images fail to show complete retinal correspondence. Indeed, it was the growing appreciation of this fact that led to the idea of retinal disparity; and from an idea of such importance, it was not long before geometry became an important tool to study disparity and stereopsis. Nonetheless, what has not always been appreciated is that geometrical analyses, for the most part, tell us very little about *visual* space. Although physical space may be conveniently described as a Euclidean space, there is no particular reason *a priori* to assume that *perceived* space can also be described conveniently by the same metric rules.

Our primary purpose here is to review some of the important ways in which the concept of retinal correspondence has been employed to account for stereoscopic space perception. The treatment begins with an overview of two major interpretations of correspondence. Most current elaborations can be considered as representative of one or the other of these two interpretations.

TWO INTERPRETATIONS: GEOMETRICAL AND VISUAL

The first interpretation considers correspondence strictly in the *terms of geometry*. When one compares geometrical models of correspondence, they are seen to differ only in the means through which geometrical facts are supposed to relate to the facts of binocular vision, particularly to stereoscopic depth perception. The nature of the relationship between geometry and vision is often beclouded by other concepts like fusion, and most extensions of geometry into models of binocular vision show a logical lapse, as we shall demonstrate presently.

The second kind of interpretation defines correspondence strictly in the *terms of visual perception,* with particular emphasis upon the visual criterion of *singleness of vision.* The extent to which retinal geometry is incorporated as being relevant to singleness of vision varies, but in the extreme, geometry is disregarded.

Here, then, we have two different interpretations of correspondence. The first of them assumes that a model based upon a common geometry is adequate to describe the facts of stereoscopic vision, presumably because the visual system behaves as though it knows the rules of common geometry. The second of them avoids such an assumption, and by so doing, it suggests that if geometry is to be of use, it is ultimately the facts of visual perception that will describe the geometry rather than the other way around. These two interpretations are not always exclusive one from the other; rather, it is often more a matter of emphasis.

Geometrical Correspondence: Classical Views

Geometrical correspondence requires that one thing be compared to another. In the context of binocular vision, the comparison has dealt with the location of the retinal image in one eye to its location in the other eye. To serve simplicity, we here shall confine the discussion to the case of images of a point source. In order to make a comparison meaningful, it is necessary first to establish a means whereby the location of an image on each retina can be specified. Let us consider how this has been accomplished.

Assume that the eye is a sphere and that the retina can be fairly represented by the zone (surface) of a hemisphere determined by the intersection of the sphere by a vertical plane that includes the spherical center. If, to this original plane, two orthogonal planes are added, as shown in Fig. 3.1, then the latter two planes intersect the retinal surface to form vertical and horizontal coordinates. These coordinates can be

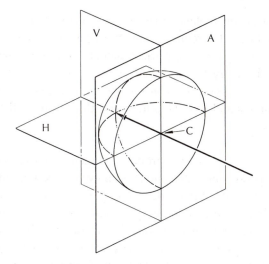

Fig. 3.1   The retina represented as a hemisphere. Plane *A*, a coronal plane, defines the hemisphere, and planes *V* and *H* determine the vertical and horizontal axes of the retina, respectively. All planes are orthogonal to one another and each includes the spherical center, *C*. The arrow indicates the path of light falling on the axis intersection.

used to specify the location of any point that lies on the zone. Accordingly, geometrical correspondence occurs when a point on one hemisphere has the same coordinates as a point on another identical hemisphere.

PROBLEMS OF APPLICATION: MONOCULAR

Although the definition of geometrical correspondence just given is simple enough, a number of difficulties are encountered when one attempts to establish the location of the coordinates for the eye. Let us review the more serious of them.

Determination of Coronal Plane. The first difficulty is the establishment of a suitable coronal plane. Because the eye moves relative to the head, some aspect of the eye that is easily identified must be used as a frame of reference. Suppose one establishes the reference coronal plane as that one that best fits the points representing the peripheral boundary of the retina. The intersection of the vertical and horizontal coordinates thus formed by the orthogonal planes then is given without regard to any identifiable properties of the retina except its peripheral boundary. While such coordinates satisfy the geometrical model, they are believed by many to be unsatisfactory because they do not intersect at the fovea. Here we encounter a classic confusion surrounding the concept of correspondence, and an example will help to clarify the nature of the confusion.

The Fovea and Geometry. With appropriate vergence and accommodation, light from a point source that enters each eye can be imaged on the fovea, and despite the fact of binocular viewing, the point of light is seen as single. According to our second interpretation of correspondence, singleness of vision, the foveas may be said to correspond. However, they may, or may not, correspond geometrically, depending only upon the structural referents that determine the location of the retinal coordinates. Nothing in the geometrical model *requires* that the foveas be at the intersection of the coordinates. It is rather that the utility of the model is believed to be enhanced when it is adjusted to accommodate the criterion of singleness of vision. One cannot claim that singleness of vision occurs because corresponding points are stimulated. It must always be the other way around.

The confusion often is implicit, as in the following: "Theoretically, corresponding points are those that would be coincident if one retina could be placed over the other with vertical and horizontal axes through the foveas superimposed" (*7*, pp. 522, 523). This typical definition of correspondence is, of course, more than a simple statement of geometry because the foveas are made to correspond, by definition.

The fact that the foveal region can be distinguished from the surrounding retina on the basis of identifiable characteristics like receptor orientation, cellular morphology, and neural innervation, should mean that the foveas "correspond" in those characteristics and only those characteristics. Yet, one finds frequently the arguments that the foveas correspond *geometrically* either because they are structurally similar or because images from a fixated point of light may fall upon them. If the foveas are to correspond geometrically, then that fact can be established only by the methods of geometry. Apparently structural similarity and singleness of vision together have unwittingly lent geometrical significance to the foveas. One cannot but wonder what form the geometrical model would have taken had the retinal mosaic been devoid of an identifiable fovea.

It is important to our present purposes to recognize the following: It has been assumed that a functional map of correspondence, determined perceptually according to a criterion of singleness of vision, would be exactly congruent with a geometrical map of correspondence. What we should like most to know, of course, is whether or not the loci of points on the two retinas that result in singleness of vision always bear identical geometries relative to their respective foveas, regardless of visual direction.

Determination of Axis Orientation. A second difficulty encountered when a geometrical model is applied to the eye is the establishment of the direction of the axes. If we conclude that a two-coordinate system is a useful means by which to specify the location of retinal points, then we are still left to determine precisely the course of these axes along the retinal surface. We have so far referred to them as being in vertical and horizontal planes; but with regard only to geometry, any two axes in orthogonal planes would allow the specification of retinal loci. Yet, just as singleness of vision at the foveas suggested the locus of axis intersection, there are structural and functional properties of the eye that have dictated axis orientations. These properties have led to a second adjustment in a strict geometrical model.

It has been common practice to establish one axis as vertical because the nasal and temporal portions of the retina project differently. Thus, the second axis is horizontal. Needless to say, the words *vertical* and *horizontal* are not especially precise in this connection because there is ocular rotation in the coronal plane with vergence, as well as movement of the head; and surely a geometrical scheme to establish correspondence would require that the coordinates remain invariant relative to the retinal mosaic. Furthermore, many who apply geometry to vision incorrectly assume that there is an invariance between retinal axes and the true vertical rather than retinal axes and the retinal mosaic.

Limitations of Assumptions. If to these general problems arising from the application of geometry to the eye we add that the retinal surface is itself not quite spherical and that one eye is not anatomically symmetrical to the other, we are left to wonder just how useful a tool geometry can be as a frame of reference within which the facts of binocular vision are to be arranged.

So far, of course, our discussion has been limited to problems that arise from a geometrical model applied to one eye, even though our ultimate purpose is to compare the locus of stimulation in one eye with that in the other. Let us, therefore, turn our attention to some additional observations specifically involving binocular vision.

PROBLEMS OF APPLICATION: BINOCULAR

The assumed locations of the *optical node* and the *center of rotation* around which horizontal eye movements occur both have important consequences for binocular geometry. In the treatment that follows sufficient detail is provided to make clear the major consequences of their locations.

Müller's Horopter. Aware of earlier work by Vieth (*24*) in 1818 on the application of geometry to binocular vision, Johannes Müller (*18*) set forth a very complete treatment of the topic in 1826. His analysis continues to influence theoretical developments in binocular vision although credit is usually granted to more recent statements for which his earlier analysis served as the foundation.

According to Müller (*18*, p. 46), a point of light in space appears as single during binocular vision whenever imaginary straight lines from the source through the optical node of each eye intersect the retinas at corresponding loci. Taken by itself, Müller's view is ambiguous because it does not make clear which of our two criteria he took to be primary. In the context of his treatment of the geometry of binocular vision, one can suppose that he intended to apply both a geometrical and a perceptual criterion to establish the origin of his coordinate system because he took the fovea as the intersection of the orthogonal axes. Nevertheless, it is probably fair to state that, for him, singleness of vision resulted from stimulation of geometrically congruent loci on the retinas.

Müller assumed, like so many others, that each retina could be likened to the zone of a sphere. Accordingly, if the eyes remain converged upon a single point in space, then the construction of straight lines from many pairs of geometrically congruent loci that pass through the optical nodes would lead to as many points in space, each one of which would be determined by the intersection of the lines drawn from a pair of congruent loci. In theory there are an infinite number of such points in space, and the surface upon which they lie is known as the *geometrical horopter*. If it be true that geometrical correspondence results in singleness of vision, then for a given attitude of the eyes, any point that lies on the geometrical horopter should be seen as single whether or not it is imaged at the foveas.

In order to examine the implications of Müller's position, it is necessary to consider a few facts of geometry. To provide both emphasis and clarity, here we shall treat of a simple instance from plane geometry and take for this purpose the horizontal plane, as shown in Fig. 3.2. The eyes, represented as spheres, are converged symmetrically on a near fixation point *F*. This point and the centers of both spheres (*C* and *C'*) define a horizontal plane that intersects the eyes to define their horizontal

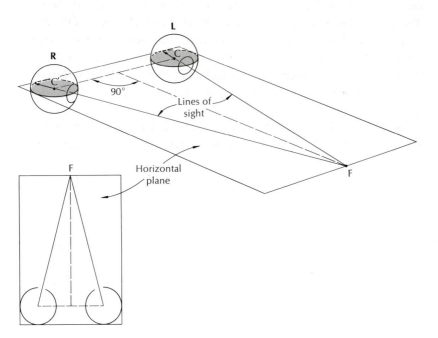

Fig. 3.2   The eyes, represented as spheres, are shown converged symmetrically upon a near fixation point, *F*.

axes, shown in the figure as the perimeters of the shaded circles. The primary lines of sight are assumed to intersect the axes exactly at the center of the foveas. The insert shows the same geometrical arrangement in top view, one which we shall use henceforth to consider Müller's case.

The geometrical facts required to understand Müller's horopter are summarized in Fig. 3.3. On the left of the figure are shown five straight lines that diverge from point C to intersect the circumference of a circle the center of which is also at C. Inasmuch as angles *1, 2, 3,* and *4* all equal 30°, the arcs *de, ef, fg,* and *gh* are equal. *Equal angles with coincident vertices define equal arcs on any circle whose center is also coincident.*

In the center of Fig. 3.3, the same arrangement of lines is maintained, but the position of the circle is changed so that the coincident vertices fall on its circumference at N rather than at its center, C. Inasmuch as angles, *1, 2, 3,* and *4* are equal, so also are the arcs DE, EF, FG, and GH. Here, then, is a second principle: *Equal angles within a circle define equal arcs on that circle when their vertices lie on its circumference.* Whereas the first principle stated that the vertices had to lie at the center of the circle, thereby requiring coincidence, the second principle states only that the vertices lie on the circumference. While the central portion of Fig. 3.3 shows the vertices as coincident at N, it may be demonstrated easily, for example, that arc EF subtends the same angle at H as it does at N.

On the right of Fig. 3.3, the two principles just given are shown combined in simple fashion. A single point N lies both at the center of the

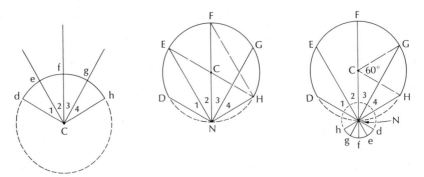

Fig. 3.3 Geometrical facts necessary to an understanding of Müller's horopter. See text for explanation.

smaller circle and on the circumference of the larger one. Our two principles tell us of the equality of the arcs within each of the circles. Note,
however, that arcs *gh* and *GH* are not equal. Lines *hH* and *gG* intersect
at *N* to form angle *4* and its vertical angle (*gNh*), both of which equal
30°. Whereas *N* is the appropriate point of reference to measure arc *gh*
(30°), *C* rather than *N* must be used to measure arc *GH* (60°). We
will consider this inequality later when we develop a more complex
geometrical statement of correspondence. For the present, we need only
recall the equalities illustrated in Fig. 3.3.

According to Müller's analysis, the optical node, the center of rotation, and the center of the spherical eye all are coincident. Accordingly,
the smaller circle of Fig. 3.3 may be identified as a horizontal section
of the eye. When a second eye is added, as shown in Fig. 3.4, the implications for binocular vision become apparent. In Fig. 3.4 the eyes are
converged symmetrically upon a near fixation point *F* located in the mid-
saggital plane. Accordingly, *f* and *f'* represent the foveas of the left and
right eye, respectively. The angles (*φ*) formed at *C* and *C'* by arc *EF*
are equal because their vertices lie on the circumference of the same circle. Therefore, it follows that arc *fe* equals arc *f'e'*. If *f* and *f'* are *defined*
as geometrically corresponding points, then *e* and *e'* also correspond.
Indeed, straight lines drawn through *C* and *C'* from corresponding loci
will always intersect at a point that lies on a circle that contains the point
of fixation and *C* and *C'*. Such a circle is often referred to as *Müller's
circle,* or the *Vieth-Müller circle,* and it has been taken to represent the
general case of the horizontal *geometrical horopter*. In the analysis depicted in Fig. 3.4, it is not essential that convergence be symmetrical
provided that *C* and *C'* are assumed to be the locations of both the optical nodes and the centers of rotation. Had the eyes been converged asymmetrically upon point *E,* point *F* would continue to fall on corresponding
loci. Finally, note that the angle of convergence (*γ*) is invariant for all
possible fixation points on any given horopter circle. There is, of course,
a different horopter circle for each value of *γ*.

The simplicity of Müller's treatment is cause for admiration, but the
successful application of his analysis hinges critically upon two assumptions: first, that the optical node of the eye falls at its geometrical center;
and, second, that the center of rotation (defined as the point of zero
velocity during horizontal eye movements) is coincident with the node.

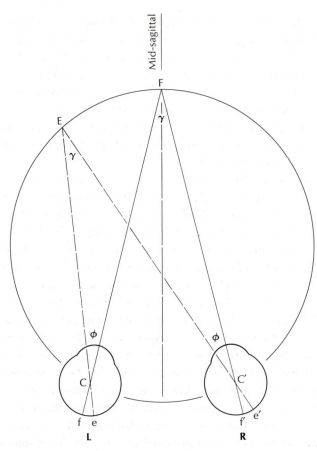

Fig. 3.4   Müller's geometrical horopter circle for the horizontal plane. With the eyes converged at *F*, all point sources that lie on a circle containing *F* and the optical nodes (*C* and *C'*) may be shown to stimulate corresponding retinal loci. Moreover, fixation at any point on the circle leaves the angle of convergence (γ) invariant. Because Müller believed that the eyes rotated about their spherical centers, where he also located the optical nodes, his horizontal horopter applies equally well to conditions of asymmetrical convergence.

In 1861 Hering (*8*) began a series of published works that advanced a different interpretation of the horopter. His conception of the horopter emphasized visual rather than geometrical criteria, and it stemmed directly from his law of *identical visual directions* (*9*, p. 38). Mention of Hering is made here simply to indicate that it did not take very long for scepticism about Müller's geometrical horopter to show itself. Hering's scepticism took its thrust both from his persuasion that visual criteria were superordinate to geometry and from his growing doubt about the validity of Müller's two assumptions. In the ensuing years, despite the accumulation of data to indicate that the assumptions of Müller were wrong, it is a remarkable curiosity that one cannot find in the literature a simple statement of the influence of changes in the locations of the optical node and rotation center upon the geometry of binocular vision. Recognition of the importance of these locations to studies of the horopter is given by Shipley and Rawlings (*21, 22*), but the *specific* consequences for geometrical models are wanting.

What one does find in the literature are frequent admissions of the oversimplification of Müller's geometrical horopter along side statements that it is a good approximation of retinal correspondence. To admit that a model is oversimplified may be to admit that it is wrong, at least in some of its particulars, and perhaps in its entirety. If so, then attempts to reconcile differences among sets of data obtained on the horopter according to different criteria are intellectual exercises that probably serve fancy too well. Let us, therefore, consider the ways in which Müller's conception is too simple so that the extent of the utility of the geometrical horopter in understanding binocular vision can be clarified. We begin with a modern statement by Graham.

Graham's Horopter. Whereas Graham accepted Müller's assumption of the coincidence of the optical node with the center of rotation when he wrote, "The centers [of rotation] may be considered nearly coincident with the nodal points," he located the "point" of coincidence anterior to the geometrical center of the eye (*7*, p. 523). Accordingly, the geometrical relations earlier given in connection with Müller's conception need to be re-examined.

In the upper left of Fig. 3.5 five straight lines are shown diverging from point *O* in such a way as to make angles *1, 2, 3,* and *4* equal (30°). However, in contrast to Fig. 3.3, here the point of coincidence of the vertices of these angles lies neither at the center nor on the circumference of the surrounding circle. Under this condition the arcs *de, ef, fg,* and *gh* are no longer equal. The shaded areas show what would have to be added to angles *1* and *4* in order to achieve equality among the arcs. In the

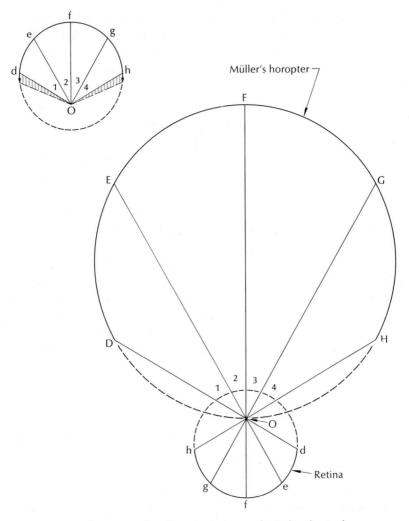

Fig. 3.5   An illustration of nonlinearity between physical and retinal space as a consequence of an anterior location of the optical node. See text for discussion.

remainder of Fig. 3.5 may be seen the geometrical relations for two circles where *O* is eccentric but on the circumference of one of them. We know from our discussion of Müller's horopter that the arcs *DE, EF, FG,* and *GH* are equal because their angles are equal and the vertex of each lies on the circumference of the same circle. If we assume that the smaller circle is a horizontal section of an eye, with *O* as its optical node, then it is apparent that point sources arranged on the larger circle (Müller's horopter) so as to be separated by equal arcs would stimulate retinal points separated by *unequal* arcs. Moreover, *each successive arc from the fovea (f) is progressively attenuated as the periphery of the retina is approached.*

The effects of relocation of the optical node upon the positions of retinal images is shown in Fig. 3.6 where the geometries according to

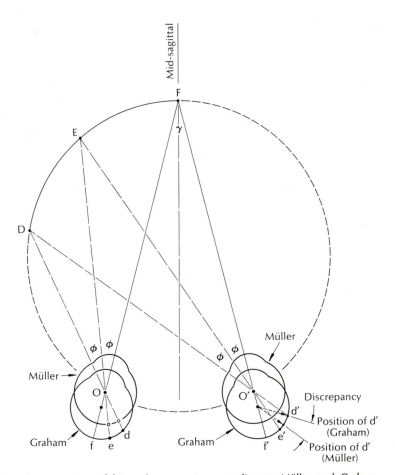

Fig. 3.6 A comparison of binocular geometry according to Müller and Graham. See text for discussion.

Müller and Graham are compared. The lines from *D, E,* and *F* through the optical nodes *O* and *O'* indicate the positions of the images of these points on the retina when the node is in the center of the eye (Müller) as well as when the node is anterior to the center (Graham). In the diagram of the left eye, the open circles show the position of the images of *D* and *E* according to Müller, while the solid circles show their positions according to Graham. The dashed arrows in the right eye diagram indicate the discrepancy between the two geometries in the location of the image of *D,* as measured relative to the center of the retinal curvature.

Let us determine now whether or not the differences in the binocular geometries noted in Fig. 3.6 change the horopter circle. Some of the effects of an anterior nodal position are most easily described with reference to Fig. 3.7 where the eyes are depicted as converged (solid lines) upon a near point *F* that lies in the mid-saggital plane. As before, the large circle includes the fixation point as well as the optical nodes *O* and *O'*. Because arcs *DE* and *EF* are equal, so are their angles of subtense (ϕ) at each node. The similarly shaded areas represent congruence, so that if *f* and *f'* represent the central foveas and are defined as corresponding, then *e* and *d* on the left retina correspond to *e'* and *d'* on the right retina. Even though the angles of subtense (ϕ) for arcs *DE* and *EF* are equal at each node, with the result that their vertical angles are also equal, the arc *fe* (*f'e'*) is larger than the arc *ed* (*e'd'*) because the latter is more peripheral relative to the fovea. Nevertheless, lines drawn from geometrically corresponding loci on the retinas through the optical nodes continue to intersect at points in space that lie on Müller's circle.

Suppose now that the eyes fixated point *E* rather than *F,* and that in doing so, they rotated about their optical nodes, in the manner stated by Graham. In this case *E* would be imaged on the foveas while the images of *F* and *D* would be located symmetrically about each fovea. This image symmetry then would make all retinal arcs equal inasmuch as the defining limits are symmetrically displaced toward the peripheries. That is, with *e* now at the fovea, *f* would lie as far toward the temporal periphery as does *d* toward the nasal periphery. Hence, the arcs between each of them and the fovea would be equal since attenuation brought about by the anterior nodal location would also be equal. For this reason, geometrical congruence occurs even when convergence is asymmetrical. From this discussion we may conclude that Müller's circle continues to satisfy

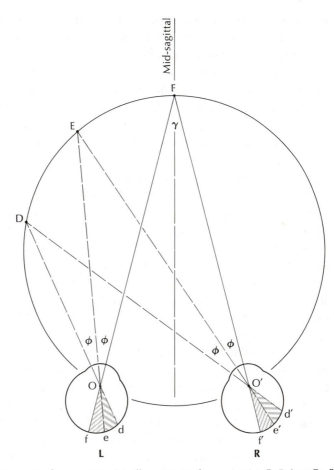

Fig. 3.7 The eyes are shown symmetrically converged upon point *F*. Points *D*, *E*, and *F*, and the optical nodes *O* and *O'*, all lie on Müller's horopter. Inasmuch as arcs *DE* and *EF* are equal, so also are their angles of subtense (φ) at each node. Nevertheless, with the nodes anterior to the center of the eyes, the arc *fe* (*f'e'*) is larger than the arc *ed* (*e'd'*). Because similarly shaded areas are congruent, if the foveal centers (*f* and *f'*) are defined as corresponding, then so also do *e* and *d* correspond to *e'* and *d'*, respectively.

the requirements of the geometrical horopter. However, this is true only if the eyes rotate about their nodes.

Before considering the effects of a separation of the optical node from the rotation center, there is one final observation to make about the geometry of Graham. As described, Graham's model results in a nonlinear transformation between physical and retinal space. In addition, asymmetrical convergence interacts with the transformation in a complex fashion that may not be obvious from the treatment so far. For example, with reference to Fig. 3.7, when the left eye fixates F, the retinal arc fd is smaller than it is when the eye fixates E. This is so, of course, because in the former instance d lies farther from the fovea. Hence, there is greater attenuation. The same relationship applies to the other eye.

While the interaction of the nonlinear transformation with levels of asymmetrical convergence does not influence retinal correspondence insofar as geometry is concerned, the interaction has important implications for neural models of stereopsis. Whereas in Müller's model the spatial properties of a retinal matrix to code points on any single horopter could remain invariant across levels of asymmetrical convergence, this would not be possible under the conditions suggested by Graham.

An illustration of this important difference is provided in Fig. 3.8. At the top of the figure is shown a Müller circle that includes three points in space (X, Y, and Z) and the optical node of an eye (O). The arcs XY and YZ are equal because their angles of subtense (ϕ) are equal. The geometry according to Müller is shown on the left for fixation to each of the three points in space. The arrow on each retina indicates the fovea. The rectangles are simple maps of the retina under each condition of fixation, and on each is given the separations of z from y and of y from x by the symbols α and β, respectively. Note that $\alpha = \beta$ regardless of fixation. When the node (O) lies at the center of the eye (C), then equal arcs on the horopter give equal arcs on the retina, and the latter are always proportional to the former. If the concept of geometrical correspondence is to have functional significance for vision, then the linear transformation from external space to retinal space would allow us to conceive of a relatively simple neural model to code horizontal retinal distances, and in such a model we could disregard visual direction.

By contrast, consider the geometry according to Graham shown on the right of Fig. 3.8. With the node in an anterior location and fixation at Z, note first that the retinal arc zy is greater than it is under the same viewing conditions in Müller's model. This, of course, reflects the fact that O lies farther from the retina. Were it the case that all we had to do to compare the two models was to add a constant to Graham's retinal

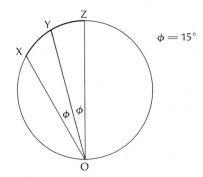

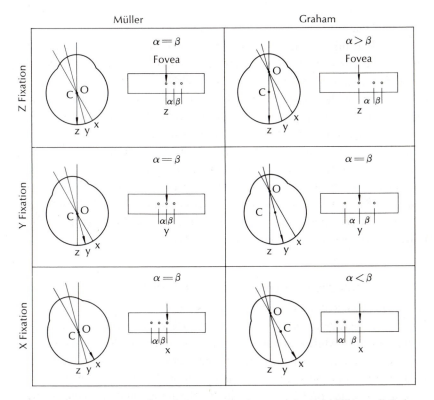

Fig. 3.8   A comparison of single eye geometries according to Müller and Graham, showing the nonlinear transformation in Graham's model and the influence upon it of changes in fixation. See text for discussion.

arcs, then both models would be linear and our remarks about neural coding would apply equally well to both models. Unfortunately, as we know, the case is otherwise.

The relative sizes of the separations α and β may be seen to differ, depending only upon which of the three points is taken for fixation. The nonlinearity of Graham's model stands in sharp contrast to the simpler linear one of Müller. With fixation constant, say at Z, then retinal arcs separating the images of a series of points equally separated on the horopter circle would show progressive attenuation as they fell ever more peripherally on the retina. Moreover, both the absolute and relative values of these arcs change as a function of fixation. Therefore, in the case of Graham, a neural model to code horizontal retinal distance could be neither linear nor invariant with reference to points in space. Recall, however, that this complexity arises only when the geometry is made to serve as the basis for models of binocular *vision*. As long as the geometry serves its own ends without regard to physiological or psychological criteria, then the horizontal geometrical horopter continues to be a circle that contains the point of fixation and the optical nodes, wherever situated, whether or not convergence is symmetrical or asymmetrical.

In all instances treated so far, points on the horopter circle always are imaged on geometrically corresponding retinal loci. However, we have not yet considered what specific consequences follow when the optical node is separated from the center of ocular rotation. To this matter we now turn, after which we shall be able to draw some conclusions on the utility of the concept of retinal correspondence.

Geometrical Correspondence Reconsidered

SEPARATION OF NODE AND ROTATION CENTER

We alluded earlier to the fact that current data require us to reject the assumptions of Müller about the locations of the nodes and rotation centers. So, too, must we reject the assumptions of Graham. In the treatment that follows, we shall locate the optical node on the primary visual axis at a distance of 17 mm anterior to the fovea, and we shall locate the center of rotation on the same axis at a distance of 11 mm anterior to the fovea. These values represent mean locations taken from several sources (*1, 5, 13, 20*). The values adopted here place the optical node approximately 7 mm behind the cornea whereas the center of rotation lies virtually at the geometrical center of the eye.

In order to establish the effects upon binocular geometry of the separation of the center of rotation from the optical node, two additional relationships need to be brought to attention. Both are illustrated in Fig. 3.9. On the top is shown a Müller circle on which fall the optical nodes of the eyes (O and O') and two points in space (F and G). The arc FG subtends the same angle (ϕ) at O and O', as we know already. However, if the optical node for the right eye were relocated inside the Müller circle, then the arc FG would no longer subtend the same angle at the two nodes. As shown in the figure, the angle of subtense would be greater at the right node. Conversely, if the optical node of the right eye were located outside Müller's circle, then the angle at the right node would be smaller than that one at the left node.

The second relationship of importance is made clear in the bottom portion of Fig. 3.9. Here the right eye is shown converged slightly as if fixed upon a point in the mid-saggital plane 50 cm away. Müller's horopter circle is drawn so as to include the node O' and the fixation point. Because the eye rotates around its center (C'), the location of the node must always lie on an arc of 6 mm radius with C' as its center. When the line of sight changes as a consequence of a 20° rotation to the left, the node falls within Müller's circle at s. On the other hand, a 20° rotation to the right places the node outside Müller's circle at t.

The specific effects upon binocular geometry of shifting the optical node in the manner described might reasonably be expected to be so small as to be inconsequential. Yet a careful study of these effects indicates quite the contrary. What is required, of course, is to determine the location of the retinal images of a point source first when the node and center of rotation are assumed to be congruent and then when they are assumed not to be congruent. Before we consider this matter we shall state several general principles that derive from the facts shown in Fig. 3.9.

Assume that the eyes are converged symmetrically upon a near fixation point 50 cm away in the mid-saggital plane, and that a circle can be drawn that will include the fixation point and the optical node of each eye. Under these conditions, any point that lies on the circle will be imaged on geometrically corresponding loci on the retinas. A different

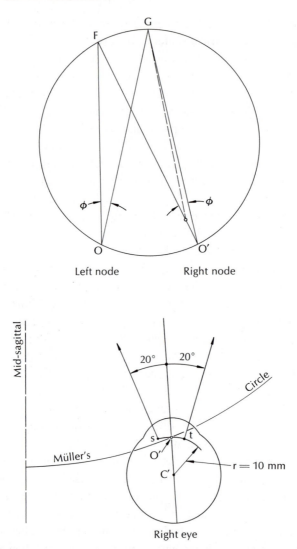

Fig. 3.9 At the top is shown the effects upon the angle of subtense (φ) for arc FG of movement of the right optical node (O) from the horopter circle to a location within the circle. At the bottom, the node O' is shown to move about an arc of 6 mm radius with C' as its center. Rotation 20° leftward and rightward moves the node to s and t, respectively.

circle is required for each possible fixation point along a horizontal line in the mid-saggital plane, and each circle must take into account *both the new distance of the fixation point and the new locations of the optical nodes* brought about by altered vergence. As long as convergence is symmetrical, a Müller circle represents the geometrical horopter despite the fact that the optical nodes do not lie at the centers of rotation. Furthermore, as long as the fixation point lies on the mid-saggital line, the center of the horopter circle always will fall on the same line. The reason is clear from our earlier treatment of binocular geometry. When a fixation point F lies in the mid-saggital plane, for example at 50 cm, then a point L located 20° to the left (relative to the center of the inter-ocular axis) and on Müller's circle has its image on corresponding loci because the arc FL subtends equal angles at both optical nodes. Accordingly, if F is imaged at the foveal centers, then the images of L correspond geometrically.

The geometry becomes altered with asymmetrical convergence. Suppose, in the example just cited, the eyes fixed upon L rather than F. Not only is convergence asymmetrical, but in addition the optical node of the left eye now falls outside the Müller circle whereas the opposite is true for the right node. As a consequence, straight lines from the two points of light in the visual field (F and L) to each node now form different angles at each node. Therefore, if L is imaged at the foveal centers, then F *cannot* be imaged on geometrically corresponding loci. Moreover, there is no new circle that can include points F and L and the two optical nodes.

We are led to conclude that *two invariant point sources in visual space may on one occasion stimulate geometrically corresponding places on the retinas and on another occasion stimulate noncorresponding places, with the difference determined only by which of the two is fixated.* Stated differently, L falls on the horopter for F, but F does not fall on the horopter for L.

The general case is illustrated in Fig. 3.10, and from an examination of it one can observe why points F and L cannot lie on the same horopter circle when fixation changes from F to L. Let us consider, first, the geometry for an instance of symmetrical convergence. When the eyes fixate point F, the primary lines of sight include the centers of rotation (C and C') and the optical nodes (O and O' for F). Accordingly, a circle drawn

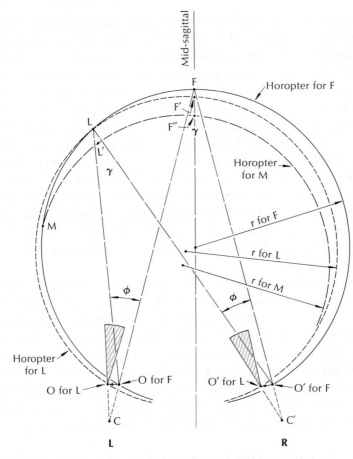

Fig. 3.10 An analysis of binocular geometry showing that there is a unique horopter circle for every fixation point in the horizontal plane despite the fact that the angle of convergence (γ) is held constant. See text for details.

so as to include *F, O,* and *O′* is the horopter for *F,* and it is shown in the figure as the solid circle. Because point *L* lies on the *F*-horopter, the angle of subtense (ϕ) of the arc *FL* is equal at both nodes. If point *F* is imaged at the center of each fovea and the centers are defined as corresponding loci, then *L* also is imaged on geometrically corresponding loci.

When fixation changes from *F* to *L,* then the optical nodes are relocated leftward on arcs of 6 mm radii with their centers at *C* and *C′*. As shown in the figure, the node of the left eye now falls outside the F-horopter, whereas the right one falls inside. The angles of subtense of the arc FL at the new nodal locations, indicated by shaded wedges, are no longer equal, the left one being the smaller. Therefore, when L is imaged at the foveal centers, F does not represent a point in space that would stimulate geometrically corresponding loci.

The horopter for L, shown as the dashed circle in Fig. 3.10, includes L and the appropriate optical nodes. To achieve retinal correspondence for point F during fixation of L, point F would have to be moved toward the observer so that it fell on the L-horopter. One such position is given as F'. Conversely, M would have to be moved away from the observer to achieve retinal correspondence.

Let us consider the implications of the facts depicted in Fig. 3.10. First, symmetrical convergence allows us to establish a *null horopter* that includes the fixation point and the optical nodes. As long as convergence remains symmetrical, all points on the null horopter are imaged on corresponding places. However, as soon as convergence becomes asymmetrical, no points on the null horopter are imaged at corresponding places except for the new fixation point. Accordingly, *there is a unique horopter circle for every possible point of fixation in the horizontal plane.* A single geometrical horopter cannot accommodate eye movements, and for this reason the geometrical horopter has no generality at all.

Second, when convergence is asymmetrical with the fixation point to the left of the mid-saggital plane, then all points on the null horopter that are to the left of fixation fall inside the new horopter and therefore carry a *crossed* disparity, while those to the right of fixation fall outside the new horopter and thus carry an *uncrossed* disparity. In contrast, when fixation is to the right, then all points that are to the right of fixation carry a crossed disparity while those to the left of it carry an uncrossed disparity.

Third, the disparity of any particular point varies in magnitude, and in certain circumstances in direction, as a function of the extent of the asymmetry of convergence. With regard once again to Fig. 3.10, suppose now that point M on the F-horopter were a fixation point located to the extreme left of the binocular field of vision. The dashed arc denoted as the M-horopter is so drawn that the full circle would include M and the appropriate nodal positions (not shown in the figure). To achieve retinal correspondence for points F and L during fixation at M, F and L would have to move toward the observer to F'' and L', respectively. Both F and L carry an uncrossed disparity, but in different amounts. Moreover, the change in fixation from L to M leads to a larger increment in the disparity of F than does the change in fixation from F to L. This is most easily seen in the figure by the fact that while M has twice the displacement of L relative to the center of the null horopter, the distance between F' and F'' is more than twice that which separates F and F'. Needless to say, the angular disparities cannot be accurately determined in so simple a manner, but the major conclusion stands. All points on the F-horopter carry zero disparity when F is the fixation point, but as the level of asymmetrical convergence increases as a consequence of taking up new fixations to the left (right), the uncrossed disparity of any single point to the right (left) of fixation grows with positive acceleration, with the absolute value determined by the angular separation between the point of fixation and the particular point in question.

Let us consider now the results of calculations of the retinal disparities that accompany a number of specific viewing conditions. In this way the limitation of the geometrical horopter will become even more evident.

DISPARITY AND THE NULL HOROPTER

The general plan of the analysis that follows is most easily grasped by reference to Fig. 3.11. In the manner of all previous discussion in this chapter, the analysis was limited to points in a horizontal plane. Accordingly, the location of the point sources in question and the location of their respective images on the retinas could be given by reference to two orthogonal linear axes. The x axis included the centers of the eyes (C and C'), and the y axis was the mid-saggital line. The point of origin was the midpoint (CC) of the interocular axis that connects the centers of the eyes. Inasmuch as the eyes rotate about their centers during horizontal movements, the position of CC remains invariant relative to all stable points in space even when fixation changes from one point to another. This invariance, of course, would not obtain had we used the center of the internodal axis.

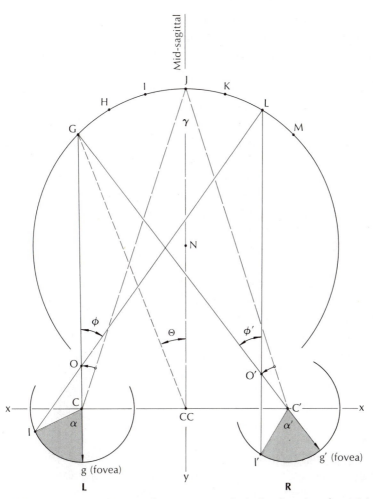

Fig. 3.11   A diagram to illustrate the manner in which the disparity of point *L* on the null horopter was determined when fixation was at point *G* on the null horopter. See text for discussion.

For each of three fixation distances (0.5, 1.0, and 3.0 m), the disparity of each of seven locations (*G* through *M*) was calculated under conditions of fixation to each location. Although not required by the analysis we employed, we chose for convenience to measure fixation distance from *CC* along the mid-saggital line to point *J*. The interocular axis (CC') equaled 6.5 cm, and with J, C, and C' thus located in our two-dimensional space, we could then determine the angle of convergence (γ) at J as well as the locations of the two optical nodes during fixation of J. The nodes were assumed to move on an arc of 6 mm radius relative to the center of the eye. Thereafter, an imaginary null-horopter was constructed that included these nodal locations and J (symmetrical convergence). The remaining six locations on the null-horopter, each separated by 15° arcs measured from N, were then given coordinate values in our space.

The positions of the seven points in space may be described in terms of their *binocular visual directions* (Θ). The direction of each point was expressed as the angle of inclination from the mid-saggital line of an imaginary straight line drawn between each point and CC. Visual directions (Θ) carried negative signs for points to the left of J and positive signs for points to the right of J.

Based upon our earlier treatment, we know already that when the eyes are converged asymmetrically at point G in Fig. 3.11, then the remaining points, all located to the right of fixation, carry an uncrossed disparity. The figure suggests schematically how the disparity of one of these points was determined. With fixation at G, the appropriate nodal locations (O and O') were determined. We took the retinal curvature to have a radius of 11 mm. Accordingly, we could determine the location of the retinal images g and g'. Taking account of the nodal locations during fixation of G, we could also determine the locations l and l'. The distances along the retinal curvature between l and g in the left eye and l' and g' in the right were converted to angles α and α' relative to the center of the eyes. Disparity (η) was expressed as the absolute angular difference between α and α'. In like manner, the disparity of each point was determined for all conditions of fixation at each of the three viewing distances. We chose to measure disparity in angular terms relative to the center of the eyes so as to take full account of the nonlinear transformation of physical space at the retinas.

Although conception of the problem of null horopter disparities is relatively simple, the solution of the problem was complex. For the interested reader, a sample solution is given in Appendix A, along with our computer program.

The results of the analysis are given in Table III-I in the form of

Table III-I   The angular disparities in minutes and seconds of arc for each of seven locations on the null horopter as a function of visual direction. The first entry in each cell is for a fixation distance of 0.5 m, the second for 1.0 m. Parentheses indicate crossed disparity.

Visual direction (θ)	Point fixated	Point location						
		G	H	I	J	K	L	M
−22.5°	G	0-0	0-59	1-47	2-30	3-16	3-51	4-26
		0-0	0-14	0-27	0-41	0-48	0-57	1-4
−15°	H	(0-35)	0-0	0-33	1-9	1-35	2-3	2-33
		(0-10)	0-0	0-11	0-20	0-25	0-31	0-38
−7.5°	I	(0-37)	(0-17)	0-0	0-17	0-26	0-46	1-5
		(0-8)	(0-5)	0-0	0-6	0-8	0-12	0-18
0°	J	0-0	0-0	0-0	0-0	0-0	0-0	0-0
		0-0	0-0	0-0	0-0	0-0	0-0	0-0
7.5°	K	1-5	0-46	0-26	0-17	0-0	(0-17)	(0-37)
		0-18	0-12	0-8	0-6	0-0	(0-5)	(0-8)
15°	L	2-33	2-3	1-35	1-9	0-33	0-0	(0-35)
		0-38	0-31	0-25	0-20	0-11	0-0	(0-10)
22.5°	M	4-26	3-51	3-16	2-30	1-47	0-59	0-0
		1-4	0-57	0-48	0-41	0-27	0-14	0-0

angular disparities in minutes and seconds of arc for each of the seven locations on the null horopter under each condition of fixation. The first entry in each cell gives disparity for a fixation distance of 0.5 m, whereas the second entry gives disparity for a fixation distance of 1 m. Data for the 3 m condition are considered later.

It is obvious, of course, that the point under fixation never carried any disparity. Furthermore, because all points fell on the null horopter, defined by symmetrical convergence at J ($\theta = 0°$), no points carried disparity when J was fixated. Entries in parentheses indicate that the disparity was in the crossed direction. All others were uncrossed.

The results for the 0.5 m condition also are presented in graphic form in Fig. 3.12. Here disparity is plotted in minutes of arc with uncrossed and crossed directions plotted above and below the reference plane, respectively. In the figure, fixation at each point on the null horopter is expressed in terms of binocular visual direction (θ), previously defined.

When convergence was symmetrical at J ($\Theta = 0°$), no points carried disparity. On the other hand, when convergence was asymmetrical, every point except the fixation point carried a different level of disparity.

The curved surface representing disparity has a symmetry to it in that the right half, were it rotated 180° around R, would be exactly congruent with the left half. For clarity, then, contour lines describing this surface appear only on the left half of the surface.

Surfaces plotted in identical manner for the 1.0 and 3.0 m conditions differ from the one shown only in one respect. The curvature of the disparity surface is reduced as distance to the fixation point increases. When J is 3.0 m away, the curvature of the surface is so slight as to be almost congruent with the reference plane that represents no disparity. The surface for the 1.0 m condition lies between these two. Bear in mind that, had we accepted the assumptions of Müller or Graham, all disparity surfaces would have been coincident planes.

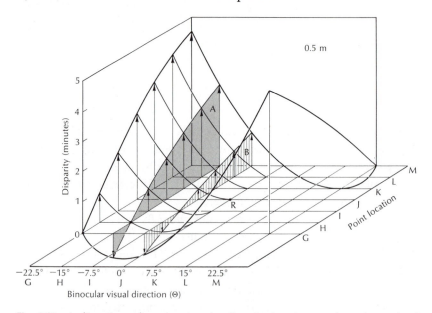

Fig. 3.12 A disparity surface showing the disparity in minutes of arc for each of seven point locations on the null horopter as a function of fixation of each of them. Direction of the fixation point from the center of the cyclopean eye is given in degrees (Θ) relative to straight ahead. Negative and positive values of Θ denote fixation leftward and rightward, respectively. Upward arrows indicate uncrossed disparity; downward arrows, crossed disparity. For absolute values, see Table III-I. See text for discussion.

The influence of viewing distance upon disparity is easily understood when it is recalled that the origin of the disparity is a relative movement of the optical nodes in or out of the null horopter circle. Nodal movements effect progressively smaller influence on the angle of subtense (ϕ) as they represent smaller and smaller proportions of the total viewing distance, so that for objects of 3.0 m or beyond, the influence becomes inconsequential.

In Fig. 3.12 the shaded area A indicates the disparities for each of the point locations during fixation of point H ($\Theta = -15°$). The upward and downward arrows indicate uncrossed and crossed disparities, respectively. When H is fixated, for example, the direction of the disparity of the other points depends only on which side of H they lie while the amount of disparity for any given point is nearly a linear function of the distance of the point in question from that one fixated. The vertically striped surface (B), representing fixation at I, allows us to draw the same general conclusions. Observe, however, that while the disparity is, more or less, a linear function of point location when visual direction is constant, the disparity of a particular point, for example J, is not a linear function of binocular visual direction.

The values of Θ given in Table III-I and in Fig. 3.12 are subject to slight modification because the geometrical conditions that would have left Θ invariant across our three viewing distances were not fulfilled exactly. If the three null horopter circles (0.5, 1.0, 3.0 m) shown in Fig. 3.13 had had a single common point coincident with the center of the cyclopean eye (CC), then binocular visual direction would have been constant for each of the seven locations, regardless of the distance of J from CC. This invariance is apparent from inspection of the figure. Straight lines from CC intersect each of the three horopter circles at points that bear constant angular displacements relative to their horopter centers.

Inasmuch as the null horopter, by definition, must include the fixation point and the optical nodes, none of the circles we used could include CC. Moreover, because the nodal positions and the curvature of the horopter change with convergence, there was no point on the mid-line common to the three horopters. Failure to meet the strict geometrical requirement that would have kept the seven visual directions independent of viewing distance did not influence the calculated disparities already given in Table III-I. It means only that Θ values for each of the seven

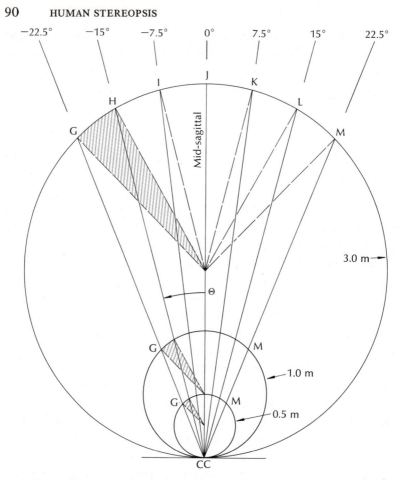

Fig. 3.13   An ideal arrangement of three horopter circles (0.5, 1.0, 3.0 m) that have a common point CC. Under the conditions shown, each binocular visual direction (solid straight line), measured as angle of inclination from mid-sagittal plane (Θ), leaves the points of intersection with each circle invariant relative to the center of the same circle. The shaded areas are geometrically similar. As shown, visual direction is independent of fixation distance.

points changed slightly with viewing distance. The actual values are presented in Table III-II.

IMPLICATIONS OF HOROPTER DISPARITIES

When the binocular geometry is worked out according to the conditions applied in the analysis just described, it is apparent that the geometrical horopter loses a good deal of its significance. Whereas the models of Müller and Graham lead to a horopter of considerable generality, our treatment indicates that their models are in serious error, particularly for objects that are near an observer. Inasmuch as the vast majority of empirical studies of the horopter and retinal correspondence have been undertaken with viewing distances of less than 2 m, the results of these studies necessarily must be open to question whenever the geometrical model employed to determine correspondence assumed that a single horopter could be applied regardless of binocular visual direction.

Quite apart from the array of problems earlier mentioned in connection with the application of geometry to the binocular system, perhaps the most significant observation now to be made is that *the geometrical horopter cannot accommodate the facts of binocular vision when fixation changes;* and this limitation remains even when the angle of convergence goes unaltered.

The major purpose of our treatment in this chapter was to make plain the exact nature of the limitations of geometrical descriptions of the relationship between physical and retinal space. Although specific reference was made to some of the implications of these limitations for physiological and psychological theories of binocular vision, it is important to un-

Table III-II   Binocular visual directions (Θ) to each of seven points (G-M) on each of three null horopters. Direction is measured as the angle of inclination between the mid-sagittal plane and a straight line connecting the point in question and the center of the cyclopean eye. Negative values are left of straight ahead (J) and positive values are right of straight ahead.

	0.5 m	Distance to J 1.0 m	3.0 m
G	−22°07′29″	−22°17′17″	−22°25′26″
H	−14°45′26″	−14°51′47″	−14°57′03″
I	− 7°22′51″	− 7°25′59″	− 7°28′33″
J	0°	0°	0°
K	7°22′51″	7°25′59″	7°28′33″
L	14°45′26″	14°51′47″	14°57′03″
M	22°07′29″	22°17′17″	22°25′26″

derstand that the utility of geometrical models is compromised seriously by the narrowness of their scope.

Horopter Disparities and Stereoscopic Acuity. When fixation distance is 0.5 m, we know from Table III-I that the disparity of some points on the null horopter can exceed 4' of arc, as measured from the center of the retinal curvature. We need to consider whether or not a disparity of this magnitude makes a difference in the phenomenal location of a target in space.

Stereoscopic Acuity. Determinations of stereoscopic acuity have been obtained under a variety of experimental conditions. Howard (*10*) employed an apparatus that presented two vertical rods of 1 cm diameter at a viewing distance of 6 m. His criterion was the least depth difference from the observer to the rods that could be discriminated 75 per cent of the time. Disparity was measured as the difference in the angle of subtense (ϕ) at the left and right nodes. His more sensitive observers had thresholds of about 2" of arc.

With the apparatus Howard used, retinal image size varied inversely with the distance of the movable rod. While Howard addressed himself indirectly to this problem, and concluded that size was not a factor of influence in his stereoscopic threshold determinations, this matter was later studied directly by Woodburne (*25*). Woodburne developed an apparatus that kept retinal image size constant. Despite the fact that he used a different viewing distance (2 m), he found the threshold to be of the same order of magnitude (2.12" of arc).

In the late 1930's Matsubayashi (*14, 15, 16*) published a series of ten papers on factors that influence stereoscopic acuity. Target size, angular separation between the stationary and movable rods, distance of observation, and monocular acuity all influenced the threshold. The range of values was 1.5 to 6" of arc.

Luminance has been shown to influence stereoscopic acuity inversely (*2, 17*). At photopic levels the threshold was found to be nearly constant over five log steps at about 5" of arc, whereas at scotopic levels sensitivity declines to about 22" of arc.

Langlands (*11, 12*) studied the effects of target shape and retinal location on stereoscopic acuity and established that acuity at the fovea was independent of shape, but that sensitivity generally declined with extra-foveal stimulation. Nevertheless, in the latter instance his threshold values were within the range established by Matsubayashi. Unfortunately, he did not study acuity for locations beyond 4° from the fovea.

In 1949 Ellerbrock reported an investigation of the relationship between peripheral stereoscopic and visual acuities (4). He employed meridional size differences in the manner described by Ogle (19) in order to obtain stereoscopic thresholds. To facilitate the comparison of the two types of acuities, both were expressed as reciprocals of sensitivity. However, when his stereoscopic threshold data are expressed directly in angular units of measure, then the amount of disparity required for threshold judgments of "nearer" or "farther" increases linearly as a function of the angular displacement of the test target from the fovea. The insert in Fig. 3.14 depicts his results and shows the relationship between stereoscopic acuity in seconds of arc as a function of peripheral angle in degrees. Peripheral angle refers to the inclination of the test target (comparison) relative to the standard, as measured at the observer. Accordingly, it is more or less equivalent to binocular visual direction; but the angular values are relative rather than absolute in that his *peripheral angle* is the *difference* between two visual directions, one being to the comparison and one being to the standard target.

In Ellerbrock's study, stereoscopic acuity was measured as the difference in the angles of subtense at the optical nodes (more specifically, at the pupillary entrance). Therefore, if we are to ascertain whether or not the null horopter disparities exceed those that obtain at stereoscopic threshold, then we must modify his threshold values and express them with reference to the center of the retinal curvature, just as we did in the case of the null horopter. This adjustment is made easily by dividing his acuity data by a constant of 0.59. The constant was determined trigonometrically and, in effect, swells the threshold values because a particular retinal arc subtends a larger angle at the center of the eye than it does at a more anterior point like the node or pupillary entrance. The adjusted function (η_t) is shown both in the insert and, in modified form, in the main portion of Fig. 3.14.

The shaded area (η_t) in Fig. 3.14 is derived from the adjusted data of Ellerbrock, and it represents the region within which disparity is too small to allow judgments of "nearer" or "farther" except on the basis of chance. In a way, then, it represents an area of uncertainty with the

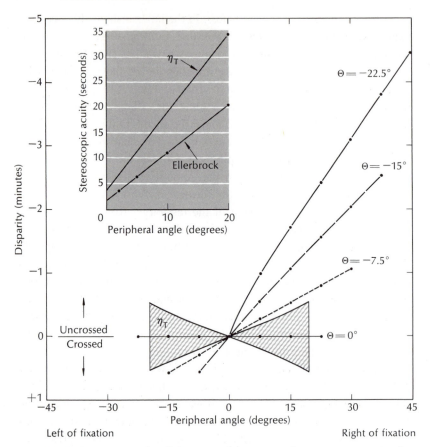

Fig. 3.14 A comparison of null horopter disparities and stereoscopic acuity for each of four binocular visual directions (Θ). Fixation distance is 0.5 m. See text for explanation and discussion. Stereoscopic acuity data from Ellerbrock (4).

more typical interval of uncertainty represented as the vertical height between the limiting boundaries at any particular peripheral angle.

As shown, the area is symmetrical both around the zero disparity line and the zero peripheral angle line. Given the psychophysical procedure that Ellerbrock used, there is no justification on the basis of his data for the assumption that stereoscopic acuity differs significantly for uncrossed (−) and crossed (+) conditions. The symmetry around a peripheral angle of zero is predicated on the assumption that stereoscopic acuity is independent of right and left halves of the visual field. When fixation is to a target on the mid-saggital line, then a second target, located to the right of fixation and at a distance appropriate for the production of disparity, would be imaged on the nasal side of the right retina and on the temporal side of the left retina. The converse is true for a similar target located to the left of fixation. While these two target locations obviously lead to different pairings of hemiretinas, there are no data to indicate, or even suggest, that the pairings themselves influence stereoscopic acuity. While some data indicate that the nasal and temporal retinas differ in terms of curvature (23), cortical receptive fields (3), and receptor density (6), these differences ought not to influence stereoscopic acuity provided that the coding of disparity, at whatever neural level, is based upon interocular comparisons across opposite hemiretinas.

The functions shown in Fig. 3.14 indicate the amount of disparity (from Table III-I, 0.5 m) for each of the seven locations on the null horopter for each of four binocular visual directions ($\odot$). Note that the functions are so drawn as to place the point of fixation at a peripheral angle of zero. The location of the seven points on the null horopter are specified with reference to the binocular visual direction of the fixation point. For example, a peripheral angle of 15° always means that the point in question had a binocular visual direction 15° rightward of fixation. Negative values denote leftward from fixation.

The important conclusion to be drawn from Fig. 3.14 is that asymmetrical convergence, according to our analysis, produces disparities for points on the null horopter that exceed stereoscopic acuity, sometimes by a factor of 4. The excess grows with the degree of asymmetry. When fixation distance equals 0.5 m, we have calculated that null-horopter disparities do not exceed stereoscopic acuity as long as the point of fixation lies between ±5.2° ($\odot$). A comparable value for a fixation distance of 1 m is ±19.8°. As previously noted, the null-horopter disparities are close to zero when fixation distance is 3 m. Accordingly, asymmetrical convergence to objects at 3 m or beyond does not lead to disparities that exceed stereoscopic acuity.

Empirical Horopter. Amigo gathered data on the empirical horopter by the nonius method and graciously provided us with his raw data. In one

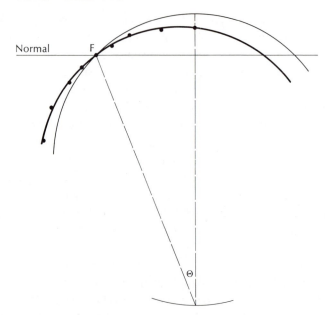

Fig. 3.15   Observers used the nonius method to establish an empirical horopter. Fixation was asymmetrical to F (Θ = 20°). Data points fell on the horopter calculated by our method rather than on the *null*-horopter of Müller or Graham. Data from G. Amigo, The stereoscopic frame of reference in asymmetric convergence of the eyes, *Vision Res.*, 1967, 7, 785-799.

condition observers viewed binocularly a fixation point 40 cm away under the condition of asymmetrical convergence (Θ = 20°). A comparison of·our geometrical model with his parameters (heavy line) and the null-horopter (light line), as given in Fig. 3.15, shows ours to be the better predictor of his data.

References

1. Alpern, M. Specification of the direction of regard, Chapter 2 in *The Eye*, Vol. III, Hugh Davson (Ed.), New York: Academic Press, 1962.
2. Berry, R. N., Riggs, L. A., and Duncan, C. P. The relation of vernier and depth discrimination to field brightness. *J. Exper. Psychol.*, 1950, *40*, 349-354.
3. Blakemore, C. B. Binocular interaction in animals and man. Unpublished doctoral dissertation, Univ. California (Berkeley), Berkeley, Calif., 1968.

4. Ellerbrock, V. J. A comparison of peripheral stereoscopic and visual acuities. *Amer. J. Optom.,* 1949, *26,* 530-537.
5. Emsley, H. H. *Visual Optics,* Vol. I, 5th Ed., London: Halton Press, 1955, p. 360.
6. Glaser, J. S. The nasal visual field. *Arch. Ophthal.,* 1967, *77,* 358-360.
7. Graham, C. H. Visual space perception, Chapter 18 in *Vision and Visual Perception,* C. H. Graham (Ed.), New York: Wiley, 1965.
8. Hering, E. *Beiträge zur Physiologie.* Leipzig: W. Engelmann, 1861-1864.
9. Hering, E. *Spatial Sense and Movements of the Eyes.* First Ed., Baltimore: The American Academy of Optometry, 1942.
10. Howard, H. J. A test for the judgment of distance. *Amer. J. Ophthal.,* 1919, *2,* 656-675.
11. Langlands, N. M. S. Experiments in binocular vision. *Trans. Opt. Soc.* (London), 1927, *28,* 45-82.
12. Langlands, N. M. S. Experiments on binocular vision, IV. In *Reports of the Committee upon Physiology of Vision,* Medical Res. Council, Spec. Rep. Ser. No. 133. London: His Majesty's Stationery Office, 1929.
13. Le Grand, Yves. *Form and Space Vision.* Rev. Ed., Trans. M. Millodot and G. G. Heath, Bloomington, Indiana: Indiana Univ. Press, 1967, p. 162.
14. Matsubayashi, A. Forschung über die Tiefenwarhnehmung. II., *Acta Soc. Ophthal. Jap.,* 1937, *41,* 2055-2074.
15. Matsubayashi, A. Forschung über die Tiefenwarhnehmung. V., *Acta Soc. Ophthal. Jap.,* 1938, *42,* 2-21.
16. Matsubayashi, A. Forschung über die Tiefenwarhnehmung. VIII., *Acta Soc. Ophthal. Jap.,* 1938, *42,* 480-491.
17. Mueller, C. G., and Lloyd, V. V. Stereoscopic acuity for various levels of illumination. *Proc. Natl. Acad. Sci.,* 1948, *34,* 223-227.
18. Müller, Johannes. *Beiträge zur vergleichenden Physiologie des Gesichtsinnes.* Leipzig: Cnoblock, 1826.
19. Ogle, K. N. Perception of distance and of size, Chapter 14 in *The Eye,* Vol. IV, Hugh Davson (Ed.), New York: Academic Press, 1962.
20. Riggs, L. A., Armington, J. C., and Ratliff, F. Motions of the retinal image during fixation. *J. Opt. Soc. Amer.,* 1954, *44,* 315-321.
21. Shipley, T., and Rawlings, S. C. The Nonius horopter. I. History and theory. *Vision Res.,* 1970, *10,* 1225-1262.
22. Shipley, T., and Rawlings, S. C. The Nonius horopter. II. An experimental report. *Vision Res.,* 1970, *10,* 1263-1299.
23. Tschermak, A. von. *Introduction to Physiological Optics.* Trans. by P. Boeder, Springfield, Illinois: Thomas, 1952.
24. Vieth, G. A. U. Über die Richtung der Augen. *Ann. Phys.,* 1818, *58,* 233-251.
25. Woodburne, L. S. The effect of a constant visual angle upon the binocular discrimination of depth differences. *Amer. J. Psychol.,* 1934, *46,* 273-286.

4
Form Disparity

Our review of the major historical developments in stereoscopy and bin-ocular vision makes plain the strong conceptual union between retinal disparity and edges. Disparity itself derives from a failure of strict geo-metrical congruence between the correlated images of a visual target, and until recently the method of its measurement has been specification of the analogous but noncorresponding displacement of imaged edges in angular notation or some derivative thereof. This classical view of dis-parity found modern expression in 1959 when Ogle wrote, ". . . in every case stereoscopic depth depends on the disparity between images of identifiable contours" (9, p. 380). The wide and generally uncritical acceptance of this view was essentially *doctrine* long before Ogle pre-sented his theory of stereopsis. There were occasional challenges to the doctrine, advanced particularly by some participants in the Gestalt movement, but the challenges never culminated in a serious doubt about the doctrine because simple laboratory demonstrations that suggested a denial of the necessity of disparate edges to depth perception were taken more as curiosities than as science. This was due to the lack of favor in which phenomenology was held at the time, the difficulties sur-rounding ways of measuring the Gestalt principles of perceptual organi-zation, and a failure to provide a truly compelling example of stereo-scopic depth perception in the absence of edge disparities.

One year after Ogle had summarized the evidence in favor of edge disparities and six years after Aschenbrenner produced the first random texture stereogram (*10*), Julesz (*5*) published a paper in which he described a technique for the production of monocular patterns that gave rise to depth perception when viewed stereoscopically even though they contained no disparate edges in the traditional sense. It soon became clear that an important challenge to classical theory was at hand.

RANDOM DOT STEREOGRAMS

The technique of Julesz consisted of using a computer to generate a textured pattern of dots within a two-dimensional matrix. Whether or not a given cell in the matrix had a dot within it was determined randomly according to some overall probability. A random dot pattern thus generated served as a monocular target for the right eye. The pattern for the left eye was identical except that all those dots that fell within a central sub-matrix were shifted one column to the right. For example, assume that the right eye random pattern fit in an overall matrix of 60 × 60 cells, with a dot appearing in 80 per cent of them. If the central sub-matrix were 20 × 20 cells, then, counting from left to right, the left eye pattern would be obtained by moving the dots of the 21st column that fell in the sub-matrix to the 22nd column, those of the 22nd to the 23rd column, and so on until the 40th, which, rather than being displaced to the 41st, instead would be used to occupy the vacant 21st column. This manipulation leaves unaltered the relational properties of the dots within the sub-matrix and within the surrounding matrix, but it gives all the dots of the sub-matrix a one-column crossed disparity.

When compared to line drawn stereograms and those comprised of photographs of objects, the random dot technique has several advantages. First, the monocular displays are devoid of all depth and familiarity cues, provided that the horizontal shift of the sub-matrix always is kept an integral multiple of matrix cell size. The stereogram half-image does not allow an observer to recognize any global forms or extended linear contours.

Second, utilization of the computer, coupled with appropriate output displays, allows the generation of an infinite variety of patterns with different textures and differently shaped sub-matrices, all accomplished with relative ease and great precision.

Julesz (*6*) suggested a third advantage. In traditional stereograms, disparity information is carried only by the edges of targets and never by their homogeneous surfaces. However, in random dot stereograms, the "surfaces" of displaced sub-matrices are textured by dots so that, in a general way, the "surface" itself may be said to carry disparity inasmuch as every dot in one half-image has an analogous dot in the other. For this reason Julesz describes his targets as *efficient;* but one could also argue that they are highly inefficient in that the amount of redundant information about disparity far exceeds what the visual system normally needs to produce veridical judgments of stereoscopic depth.

The Texture Dimension. While the percepts of random dot stereograms differ in important respects from those arising from line drawings, it is important to recognize that these two kinds of stereograms differ primarily along a texture dimension.

When the whole matrix of a random dot stereogram subtends a large solid visual angle and it also contains but a few cells, then the filling of some of its cells randomly, according to some probability, will result in a pattern of such coarseness that each filled cell will be recognized as a global form, such as a square or a circle, with continuous boundaries and a surface of homogeneous brightness. Shifting the location in one half-image of a one-celled sub-matrix is to do no more than construct a standard stereogram, and the disparity is carried by the lateral edges of the monocularly recognizable form.

On the other hand, if the solid angle is held constant while the number of cells in the matrix is increased by a thousandfold, then the texture of the matrix becomes so fine that it is no longer possible for the visual system under monocular or binocular viewing conditions to keep track of particular cells. Somewhere between the extremes of coarse and fine textures, the monocular recognition of *global* forms with edges fails, even though the individual entries in the cells of the matrix may continue to be recognized on the basis of acuity. The critical aspect of the Julesz technique is to achieve *a texture that is fine enough to eliminate the monocular cues of global form and global edges without being so fine as to prohibit binocular abstraction of correlated patterns.* When these conditions are met, Julesz refers to the percept of stereoscopic depth as *cyclopean* because it is the result of some central process of abstraction based on the comparison of the stimulation of the separate eyes.

PERCEPTION OF A RANDOM DOT STEREOGRAM

A typical random dot stereogram is shown in Fig. 4.1. Within the overall matrix (64 × 64 cells) lies a centered square sub-matrix (32 × 32 cells) that has been shifted one column rightward in the left eye half-image, thus giving the sub-matrix a small crossed disparity. Without the aid of a stereoscope to achieve binocular fusion of the half-images, the patterns appear only as randomly textured surfaces, and the global form of the central sub-matrix cannot be discerned. However, stereoscopic presentation changes the percept in three ways. First, as expected, the analogous but disparate dots of the central sub-matrix appear in a plane closer to the observer than the plane of dots comprising the surround. Second, and more remarkable, the background against which the central closer dots are seen also is shifted into depth in like manner. Finally, and most remarkable, the square surface of the shifted central sub-matrix appears to have sharp contours on all four sides, and these contours are located *between* the rows and columns of dots.

When contour perception occurs in the presence of abrupt gradients, it is not limited to stereoscopic sight. However, with random dot stereograms, the perception of global contours (extended linear contours) *requires* binocular viewing of half-image matrices that involve retinal disparity of an inner matrix. Clearly, Ogle's position on the *necessity* of disparate contours to patent stereopsis is untenable. As we wrote in 1967, ". . . *instead of contours giving rise to depth, it is rather depth that gives rise to contours*" (8, p. 272).

If monocularly recognized global contours are not necessary to stereopsis, then we need to consider how the analogous but disparate dots of a central sub-matrix cause the surface against which they are seen to appear in depth.

Form Disparity and Depth

Not every dot stereogram with a shift in the location of its sub-matrix leads to surface depth and binocularly induced contour. Whether or not the surface of the sub-matrix is perceived in depth depends upon the extent to which the patterning of the dots defines a form. Of course, it is obvious that whenever identical dots comprise the matrix texture, then

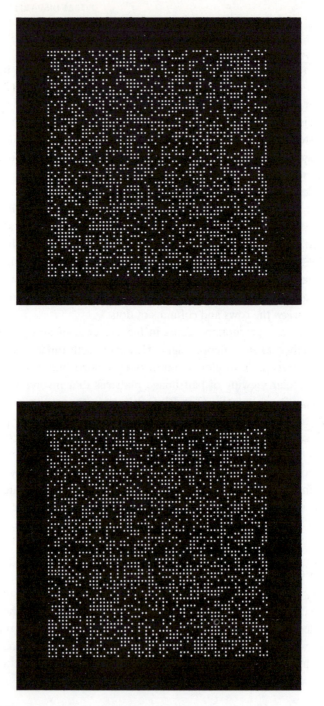

Fig. 4.1   A typical random dot stereogram with a matrix 64 x 64 cells and a central sub-matrix 32 x 32.

the probability of each cell entry must be less than one and greater than zero because in both of these limiting cases the shift of a central matrix fails to achieve any difference in the half-images.

What is less obvious is that the perception of surfaces in depth with random dot stereograms is influenced heavily by the number of matrix cells per unit solid visual angle and by the percentage of cells filled. The former parameter we shall refer to as *global density,* whereas the latter we shall refer to as *matrix density.*

ROLE OF DENSITIES

To determine the effects of global and matrix densities on the perception of surface depth, we had each of twelve observers view each of twenty-one random dot stereograms five times, with the order of presentation random for each observer with the restriction that each of the twenty-one stereograms had to be seen once before any was seen twice, and so on. The observers met strict visual criteria for acuity (20/25 or better), phoria, and stereopsis acuity (90 per cent Fry-Shepard, or better). Their task was to report the presence or absence of depth, first, of the dots in the central disparate sub-matrix and, then, of the surface against which they were seen.

The matrix and the central sub-matrix in all half-images were squares with sides subtending 2° and 1°, respectively, and the central matrix was displaced so as to give a crossed disparity of 6′ of arc. Dot diameter was constant at 4′ of arc, and the dots had a luminance of 2.5 ft-L and were seen against a background of 8.6 ft-L.

There were three levels of *global* density achieved by 20 × 20, 40 × 40, and 60 × 60 overall matrices, all with the same solid visual angle subtense (2° × 2°). These three matrices had 400, 1600, and 3600 cells, or global densities of 100, 400, and 900 cells per 1° solid angle. The 6′ disparity was achieved by shifting the central matrix 1, 2, and 3 columns, respectively, in the three global density conditions.

For each level of global density there were seven levels of *matrix density* (20, 30, 40, 50, 60, 70, and 80 per cent of the cells filled with dots). The experiment followed a 3 × 7 factorial design with repeated measures.

The effects of global and matrix densities on the frequency with which observers saw the surface of the central matrix in depth are shown in Fig. 4.2. Inasmuch as the dots themselves always were seen in depth, the data shown are limited to surfaces. Note that for any given matrix density, the emergence of a square surface in depth is made more likely as global density rises. It is clear from our earlier consideration of the limiting cases of 0 and 100 per cent matrix density that each of the functions shown has to be inflected because depth is not seen with either limiting case. The high and medium global density functions begin to show a decline in their effectiveness for surface depth at the higher matrix densities. Apparently, once global density reaches some moderate level, the binocularly recognized pattern carried by the displaced dots of the central sub-matrix reaches its maximum with matrix densities between 50 and 60 per cent. This is not surprising to us. If one thinks of the patterning as involving the random *presence* of dots in some cells

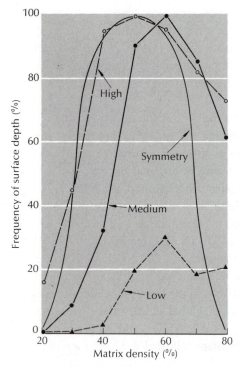

Fig. 4.2　Frequency of seen surface depth (%) of the sub-matrix for each of three global densities (Low = 100, Medium = 400, High = 900 matrix cells per 1° solid visual angle) as a function of matrix densities. N = 60 for each point plotted.

as well as the random *absence* of dots in others, then levels of density that exceed 50 per cent, in effect, leave the patterning increasingly to the vacant cells. Indeed, one could argue for the presence of a symmetry of patterning around the 50 per cent condition. For example, 20 and 80 per cent matrix densities are equivalent insofar as patterning is concerned because in the former case the sub-matrix is defined by the shift of dots and in the latter by the shift of spaces. Considered in this way, both the 20 and 80 per cent conditions have identical levels of patterning.

If this symmetry of patterning were utilized by the binocular visual system, then one would expect the functions of Fig. 4.2 to be symmetrical around the 50 per cent matrix density condition, as shown by the symmetry line. Clearly, such symmetry is absent, although it is suggested. We suppose that failure of symmetry is due to the fact that we kept the angular size of the dots constant even as matrix cell size varied across the global density conditions. It appears, therefore, that in this experiment the dots always were better carriers of patterning than were the spaces. This is especially apparent in the low global density condition where the preponderance of the target area was comprised of background. Had we utilized square elements rather than circular dots, and had they always exactly filled the matrix cells, then perhaps better symmetry would have been achieved. After all, a matrix of the sort just described that had 20 per cent matrix density would be identical in density to one of 80 per cent if one simply reversed the brightnesses of the cell entries and their background. This points up a danger we have noted elsewhere (*8*), namely, it is too easy to think of targets in experiments with matrices in terms of the particular operations that the experimenter makes upon them. Stated differently, we could as easily refer to the Julesz kind of stereogram as a random-space stereogram.

Our view, then, is that patterning reaches a maximum usefulness for surface depth at a matrix density of 50 per cent, provided that each element present always fills the cell of the matrix in which it appears. Furthermore, the perception of depth of a surface depends on the extent to which the patterning within the sub-matrix defines its form through binocular processing. The low global density condition in this experiment never was sufficient to the perception of surface depth. From this experiment we conclude that moderate global densities (400 cells per 1° solid angle, or higher) in conjunction with matrix densities of 50 per cent comprise optimal targets for the perception of surfaces in depth. The depth of the surface is achieved through binocular abstraction of the form of the sub-matrix, and the form thus abstracted always carries a disparity equal to that of the dots that define it.

ROLE OF BINOCULAR CORRELATION

Perfect binocular correlation in random dot stereograms means that for each dot in one half-image there is an analogous dot in the other. In its simplest conception, perfect correlation occurs when the half-images are identical. However, the introduction of disparity in a sub-matrix by the lateral shift of the dots it contains need not alter binocular correlation provided that each dot in one half-image continues to have a dot in the other half-image with which to form a pair. In a random dot stereogram like those earlier described, the pairs comprising the surrounding matrix all are without disparity while the pairs comprising the central sub-matrix all are with identical disparity. Nevertheless, binocular correlation is preserved. The Julesz technique does, in fact, introduce some difficulties for correlation, but for now we shall ignore them and treat them fully later in the chapter.

In our experiment on global and matrix densities we followed the procedure of shifting all of the dots within the central matrix so that each carried disparity alike. The binocular abstraction of form was shown to depend upon both of these densities. Suppose, however, that for a given global and matrix density condition, the binocular correlation of the sub-matrix in the half-images was systematically reduced. One could then determine the importance of correlation to the binocular process of form abstraction and surface depth, its perceptual corollary.

We chose a moderate global density of 400 cells per 1° of solid visual angle and a matrix density of 50 per cent. As before, the total half-image matrix (40 × 40) was a square 2° on a side and the central square matrix, 1° on a side, was shifted for the left eye so as to produce a 6' crossed disparity.

Seven stereograms were used, and each was viewed five times in random order by each of ten naive observers asked to report the presence or absence first of dot depth and then of surface depth. One stereogram consisted of identical half-images. The remaining six all had a shift in the sub-matrix, but the percentage of dots within the sub-matrix that were shifted ranged from 100 to 50 per cent. In this experiment we operationally defined the level of binocular correlation as the percentage of dots in the sub-matrix actually displaced.

The observers were increasingly unable to report surface depth as binocular correlation declined. The identical half-image stereogram, of course, resulted in a two-dimensional percept. The most stable surface occurred with 100 per cent correlation, and in this stereogram the surface carried sharp stereoscopically induced contours. A reduction of the correlation to 80 per cent had a severe influence on surface depth, as shown in Fig. 4.3. While the observers could report that the central matrix was a square, the form thus recognized generally had no surface properties and never had stereoscopic contours. Despite the absence of

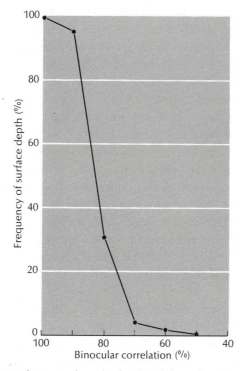

Fig. 4.3   Frequency of seen surface depth (%) of the sub-matrix as a function of the level of binocular correlation defined as the percentage of sub-matrix dots shifted in the left half-image.

surface depth, many of the dots were seen in depth, as would be expected.

The fact that we always shifted dots so as to give them a crossed disparity does not mean that they were always *coded* as having a crossed disparity because whenever binocular correlation is less than perfect, the binocular system can code particular dots either as crossed or uncrossed, depending only upon the random juxtapositions that our manipulation achieved. This effect was most pronounced in the 50 per cent correlation condition. When viewing it, observers reported that most dots appeared to lie in one of three planes; that is, in front of, within, or behind the plane of the surrounding matrix. In effect, then, one could consider that portions of the total of the sub-matrix dots were coded as *crossed, zero,* and *uncrossed* in disparity with the result that three different planes were simultaneously defined, each by approximately one-third of the total number of dots in the sub-matrix. Apparently, the lowered binocular correlation did not allow the perception of surface depth because the density of dots *within each of the three planes* was too low to define the form. With perfect binocular correlation all of the dots of the sub-matrix appear in a single closer plane because they are all coded as having a single level of crossed disparity. As a consequence, the density of dots within the single plane apparently was sufficient to allow the system to abstract a square form and thereby facilitate the perception of surface depth. However, with low binocular correlation, the sub-matrix dots became spread in depth to appear in three planes, each of which had a dot density of about one-third of the former case. Bear in mind that in cases of perfect and of low binocular correlation, the density of dots when imaged on the retina was unaltered. *Retinal density,* therefore, remained constant across levels of binocular correlation while the number of dots per depth plane changed. We have referred to the number of dots per depth plane as *cyclopean density.*

Cyclopean Density. We believe that failure to obtain surface depth with reduced binocular correlation is an observation of major significance because it suggests that *retinal density* is not as important as *cyclopean density.* Even though we utilized global and matrix densities sufficient to the perception of surface depth and stereoscopic contours, the reduction of binocular correlation allowed the visual system enough options in the coding of the disparity of the individual dots to spread the two-dimensional density of the matrix target into a three-dimensional space. Despite the fact that retinal density was sufficient to define a surface in depth when binocular correlation was perfect, it was insufficient when lower correlations were used. In the former instance the retinal density and the cyclopean density remain the same. That is, all the dots that comprise the sub-matrix are perceived in a single closer plane. However, changes in binocular correlation always reduce the density of dots in perceived planes (cyclopean density) whenever the dots of the sub-matrix appear in more than one plane. Reductions in binocular correlation actually reduce cyclopean density by adding ambiguity to the coding of dot disparities. It is our view that *surface depth,* therefore, ultimately *depends upon the density of dots in a given stereoscopic plane rather than upon retinal density itself.* Cyclopean density is determined by global and matrix densities interacting with the level of binocular correlation.

The results of our experiment confirm the earlier work of Lawrence (7) who studied surface depth and stereoscopic contours as a function of binocular correlation. In discussing the results of her experiment she noted that the ". . . surface (sub-matrix) came either forward as a whole or was completely continuous with the surface of the surround. The perception of depth of the surface broke down before the perception of dot depth disappeared." Like us, she found that surface depth and stereoscopic contours were severely affected when binocular correlation dropped to 80 per cent; and further, she reported that the dots of the sub-matrix came to be seen in multiple planes as binocular correlation was reduced.

FORM DISPARITY AND HOMOGENEITY

With the Julesz technique of generating random dot stereograms, the sub-matrix defines a form stereoscopically provided that the random but disparate pattern of dots is sufficient in density and binocular correlation. Under optimal conditions both surface depth and stereoscopic contours are perceived. In our early experiments on density we happened upon a pattern that consisted of a surround matrix with 100 per cent density and a shifted central matrix with 0 per cent density. Such a pattern is shown in Fig. 4.4. Stereoscopic inspection of this stereogram leads to the

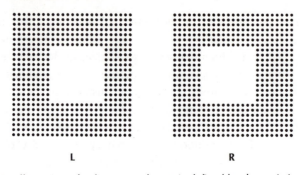

L   R

Fig. 4.4   An illustration of a disparate sub-matrix defined by the omission of dots so as to achieve its definition through homogeneity.

perception of the central homogeneous square as a sharply contoured surface interposed between the observer and the more distant surrounding matrix. While the square form can be recognized monocularly, we found that the perception of the sub-matrix surface in depth depended upon its disparate location within the surrounding matrix. As in the Julesz patterns, depth occurred in the absence of disparate contours in the classical sense. Moreover, surface depth always was accompanied by sharp stereoscopic contours that were located inside the bounding rows and columns of dots. It appears, then, that disparity can be carried by homogeneous regions of a matrix as well as by random patterning.

With patterns similar to the one shown in Fig. 4.4, we again studied both global and matrix density effects on surface depth perception. The results for global density were the same as before in that the higher the density, the more frequently was depth reported. However, the matrix density results were different. With random dot stereograms, a 100 per cent matrix density cannot define the sub-matrix. However, when the sub-matrix is defined by the absence of dots (homogeneity), then the matrix is best defined by the 100 per cent density condition in the surround. Accordingly, decreasing the matrix density of the dots in the surround lowered the frequency with which the surface of the sub-matrix was seen in depth. By contrast, recall that surface depth was most frequently reported with a 50 per cent matrix density in the random dot experiment.

It is our contention that a form defined by a homogeneous region made so by the omission of dots is a simpler way to conceptualize the construct of form in matrix stereograms comprised of dots. One could begin with a stereogram like the one shown in Fig. 4.4, where the central square carries a crossed disparity, and proceed to add a random pattern of dots within the homogeneous central areas of the half-images. If the pattern of dots is of low density, as in Fig. 4.5, then the dots are seen in depth because they carry a disparity relative to the surround, while the surface against which they are viewed is seen in depth because the square form is also disparate with reference to the surround. In this instance the random pattern of sub-matrix dots does not define the form because sub-matrix density is too low. Yet, it is precisely the low density that allows the definition of the square form based on its relative homogeneity. Clearly, as more and more dots are added to the sub-matrix, the monocularly recognizable homogeneous form becomes lost. Whether or not surface depth is seen during stereoscopic viewing depends on the extent to which the binocular system is able to abstract the form of the sub-matrix from the random yet correlated pattern of dots.

Target Comparisons. The Julesz random dot stereograms are suited ideally to the study of cyclopean abstraction because neither classical contours nor monocular cues to form are present in the half-images. However, while it is clearly possible to study stereoscopic contour processes with random dot stereograms like the one shown in Fig. 4.1, we think targets like the one shown in Fig. 4.4 are better suited to this purpose.

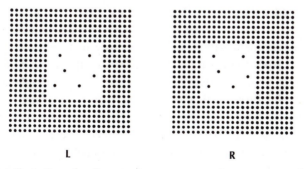

L   R

Fig. 4.5   An illustration of a disparate homogeneous sub-matrix upon which a random pattern of equally disparate dots has been superimposed.

There are two liabilities with the random dot stereogram that work against optimal conditions for the perception of stereoscopically contoured surfaces in depth. The first relates to the particular technique used to generate the half-images. For example, when the last shifted column of the sub-matrix, considered from left to right, is used to fill the vacant first column, then ambiguity is added to the stereoscopically defined form at both of its lateral boundaries. This is due to the fact that this particular column does not match either the identically numbered column in the right eye matrix or the column immediately to its right. A similar difficulty arises at the other lateral boundary. The Julesz technique, therefore, achieves a perfect binocular correlation both for the surrounding matrix and for the sub-matrix *except at the two lateral boundaries where the correlation drops to a chance level.* Certainly, if there were any columns where perfect correlation is desired for unambiguous form abstraction, it is in those columns that represent the transition from matrix to sub-matrix at the lateral boundaries; and yet it is precisely in these columns that correlation fails. The perceptual effect is that some of the dots in these columns are coded as having a disparity and thus are seen in the plane of the sub-matrix, while others are coded as having no disparity (with reference to the surround) and thus are seen in the plane of the surrounding matrix. Even when global and matrix densities are adequate to the perception of surface depth in the sub-matrix, the vertical stereoscopic contours of the right and left sub-matrix boundary lose clarity because the surface in these critical regions is not unambiguously in a single plane. This difficulty is removed when the sub-matrix is defined by its homogeneity, as in Fig. 4.4.

Another advantage of the homogeneous sub-matrix is that homogeneity is a better way to define forms than is random patterning. Superposition of a random pattern on a previously homogeneous region can only detract from the clarity of the definition. If one wished to determine whether or not random correlated patterns were sufficient to define a binocular form, as they clearly are, then random dot stereograms are appropriate targets. On the other hand, if one wished to determine the general conditions that are necessary to stereoscopic contours, then homogeneous sub-matrices are superior inasmuch as one can then directly degrade the surrounding and defining matrix to assess the roles of global and matrix densities and the role of binocular correlation.

OTHER METHODS OF PATTERNING

Random yet binocularly correlated patterns comprised of identical elements like dots, with or without regions of surface homogeneity brought about by a selective omission of matrix elements, do not constitute the only means whereby disparate forms can be achieved in matrix targets.

Matrix Element Differences. In the Julesz patterns, the binocular abstraction of the form of a sub-matrix requires a matrix density less than 100 per cent because the elements comprising the matrix are alike. However, Kaufman (2) has shown that stereoscopic depth can occur with matrix targets with 100 per cent density provided the patterning of the correlated sub-matrix is carried by the variety of shapes among the elements in the matrix. Simply, Kaufman generated a matrix of typed alphabet characters in which every cell contained a letter chosen at random. A shift of a sub-matrix in one half-image, according to the method of Julesz, achieved a crossed disparity, and this led to the perception of the sub-matrix letters in a plane closer to the observer than the surrounding matrix.

Unfortunately, no details were provided that would allow the computation of global densities. He reported only the presence of a "depth-effect" (2, p. 396). Our inspection of his and similar patterns persuades us that surface depth and stereoscopic contours are absent even though the sub-matrix letters themselves are seen in depth. Even their depth is abolished when the viewing distance becomes too great to allow the shapes of the individual entries to be coded. For example, to reach a global density of 400 cells per 1° solid visual angle, a moderate level with random dot stereograms, the viewing distance of the typed matrix is about 3 m, and at such a distance acuity fails or is too marginal. Photographic reduction does not solve this problem. Accordingly, at moderate global densities (or higher) the typed matrix becomes functionally a dot matrix with 100 per cent matrix density, and of course, no depth experience results from its stereoscopic inspection. In summary, then, one must conclude that the Kaufman letter patterns are sufficient to give rise to element (alphabet letter) depth according to classical theory only when their shapes are discernible, and further, that the letters under such circumstances provide too coarse a texture to generate surface depth with stereoscopic contours.

Brightness. Kaufman (*2*) also provided two demonstrations of brightness patterning within a sub-matrix. In the first example, the matrices were of typed letters with every cell filled with a letter chosen randomly except that the sub-matrix contained within each cell an iterated letter, for example, *e.* The half-images were identical except for a brightness pattern imposed upon the sub-matrix by making some of the *e*'s lighter than others. This brightness pattern carried a one column crossed disparity. Kaufman reports that a "depth-effect" occurred upon viewing these half-images stereoscopically. The point of the demonstration was to show that brightness patterning can lead to stereoscopic depth even while the elements, in this case the letter *e,* had no contour disparities because the positions of the elements in each half-image were identical.

Our observations of similar stereograms suggest that low and high global densities lead to different percepts. When global density is low, only the letters of discrepant brightness appear in depth, whereas at high global density the entire sub-matrix appears in depth and it brings its surface along with it. In the latter instance, as noted earlier, acuity for the shapes of the letters fails, but it does not matter because the disparate brightness pattern remains discernible. It is as though one had a dot-matrix of 100 per cent density with a shifted brightness pattern. This being so, it does not matter what particular letter is used in the sub-matrix to carry the brightness pattern. Indeed, they could even be different letters in the half-image, as Kaufman showed in his second demonstration.

Patterning in matrix targets can be achieved by different but distinguishable shapes within cells that carry a disparity and by disparate brightness patterns superimposed on nondisparate shapes. When global densities are low, which means that the angular subtense of a single matrix cell be large, then the shape dimension leads to the perception in depth of the disparate shapes themselves, and neither surface depth nor stereoscopic contours are present. However, when global densities are high, which means that the angular subtense of a single matrix cell be very small, then shape becomes functionally irrelevant, and whether or not surface depth and stereoscopic contours are perceived depends upon the same factors that apply to random dot stereograms.

Under conditions of high global density, brightness patterns are sufficient to produce well-defined binocular forms that lead to surface depth and stereoscopic contours, and the patterning can be independent of the shape of the elementary carriers. However, when global density is low, brightness patterns require shape correlations as well. Otherwise, binocular rivalry or failure of fusion occurs, either of which makes the stability of the percept wanting.

Brightness Disparity. In a series of experiments and demonstrations Kaufman (*1, 2, 3*) and Kaufman and Pitblado (*4*) have concluded that brightness disparities represent an invariant in stereopsis. Kaufman's conclusion that brightness disparity is both necessary and sufficient for stereopsis and that ". . . contour is essentially irrelevant" (*4*, p. 391) needs to be examined.

When brightness disparity is considered at a molecular level, thereby necessitating multiple comparisons of the brightnesses present at corresponding loci within two half-images, one cannot predict the resultant stereoscopic percept. At the top of Fig. 4.6 there appears a stereogram analogous to one used by Kaufman. Ignore the circles for the moment. The central sub-matrix is defined by square elements, in contrast to the circular dots of the surround. None of the squares is disparate, but there is a superimposed brightness pattern that is disparate. The random brightness pattern shown does not produce brightness disparity for each element carrying the brightness pattern. The cells of the sub-matrix which have brightness disparity at corresponding loci are encircled. If brightness disparity is necessary and sufficient for stereopsis, then only the encircled squares should appear in a different depth plane from the remainder of the target. Yet observations of this stereogram lead to the perception in depth of all the darker squares and none of the lighter ones. Inasmuch as some of the darker squares seen in depth did not have brightness disparity while some of the lighter squares not seen in depth did have brightness disparity, we conclude that brightness disparity, considered by point-for-point comparisons, is neither necessary nor sufficient for stereopsis.

One could, of course, consider brightness disparities in a more global manner, as Kaufman and Pitblado also have suggested. At the bottom of Fig. 4.6 is shown a stereogram that results in the perception of the darker squares in depth. With a point-for-point comparison, it is clear

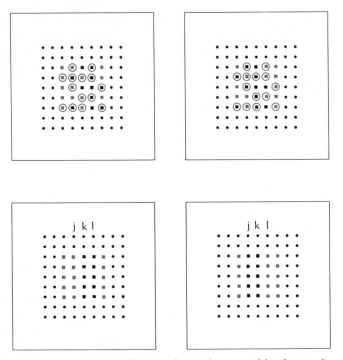

Fig. 4.6 Two stereograms that illustrate the inadequacy of brightness disparity at corresponding retinal loci to predict depth. The circles in the top pattern indicate those cells in which brightness disparity is present. In the bottom pattern only columns *j* and *l* carry a brightness disparity. In both stereograms all the darker squares appear in depth.

that brightness disparity is present in columns *j* and *l* and absent in column *k*. The fact that column *k* appears in depth seems better accounted for if the rectangular forms defined by the darker squares are thought of as carrying the disparity. In this stereogram the matrix density is low so that, while the dark squares suggest a rectangular form, it is insufficient to be seen in depth; that is, the dark squares do not also bring into depth the surface against which they are seen. However, an increase in global density does lead to surface depth and stereoscopic contours (6) because the texture that carries the brightness is finer. Apparently, reliance upon global form abstraction in stereopsis is slight when texture is coarse.

References

1. Kaufman, L. Suppression and fusion in viewing complex stereograms. *Amer. J. Psychol.,* 1964, *77,* 193-205.
2. Kaufman, L. On the nature of binocular disparity. *Amer. J. Psychol.,* 1964, *77,* 393-402.
3. Kaufman, L. Some new stereoscopic phenomena and their implications for the theory of stereopsis. *Amer. J. Psychol.,* 1965, *78,* 1-20.
4. Kaufman, L., and Pitblado, C. Further observations on the nature of effective binocular disparities. *Amer. J. Psychol.,* 1965, *78,* 379-391.
5. Julesz, B. Binocular depth perception of computer-generated patterns. *Bell Syst. Tech. J.,* 1960, *39,* 1125-1161.
6. Julesz, B. *Foundations of Cyclopean Perception.* Chicago: Univ. of Chicago Press, 1971.
7. Lawrence, Sharon McH. Perception of contour in stereoscopically presented random dot patterns. Unpublished thesis, Tufts Univ., Medford, Mass., 1965.
8. Lawson, R. B. and Gulick, W. L. Stereopsis and anomalous contours. *Vision Res.,* 1967, *7,* 271-297.
9. Ogle, K. N. Theory of stereoscopic vision. In *Psychology: A Study of a Science,* Vol. 1, S. Koch (Ed.), New York: McGraw-Hill, 1959.
10. Shipley, T. The first random-dot texture stereogram. *Vision Res.,* 1971, *11,* 1491-1492.

5

Stereoscopic Contours

Contour refers to the perception of a clearly defined edge attributed to an object or surface in visual space. While abrupt changes in hue or saturation alone can serve as stimuli for the perception of contour, the more common correlate is an abrupt luminance change at the surface of the retina. The perceived sharpness of a contour depends directly on the abruptness (rate of change) of the luminance gradient at the imaged edge and on the magnitude of the difference in the luminance levels of the adjacent surfaces separated by the edge.

An early view of contour held that the visual system is comprised of many parallel channels connecting receptors to cortical cells, and that contour is coded by different response rates between the channels coding two contiguous surfaces of unlike luminance. According to this view, retinal images become transformed into spatial cortical patterns defined by different neural response rates. Two-dimensional visual space and cortical space were assumed to be related topologically if not topographically.

In retrospect it would appear that the visual scientist believed himself when he said that the eye was like a camera; but the fundamental passivity of this long-held view of contour could not accommodate new lines of evidence. In 1942 Marshall and Talbot (*14*) published a theory of visual contour and acuity processes that took into account the concept of lateral inhibition and the then recent evidence on response patterning in ganglion cell activity. Central to their theory was the role of physio-

118

logical nystagmus as a means of sharpening perceived contours through the integrated action of "on-off" ganglion cells. At that time "on-off" discharge patterns were taken to be essentially invariant properties of particular ganglion cells, and they were classified as a kind.

While many of the essential tenets of the Marshall and Talbot statistical theory have failed of support in the years since 1942, the theory nevertheless served us well, primarily as an important challenge to what had gone before. Even though the results of experiments on stabilized retinal images (17, 18) made it clear that the role attributed to physiological nystagmus by Marshall and Talbot was open to serious question, their effort to incorporate some complex retinal processes into a general theory probably helped set the stage for an impressive series of new discoveries pertaining to the functional organization of the retina and the higher neural levels of the visual projection system. In particular, the unfolding of principles of organization such as receptive fields (8, 9, 11) and feature detectors (8, 9, 13) proved to have important relevance for our current understanding of contour perception. Moreover, some of the quantitative aspects of lateral inhibition became known (6, 15, 16) and thereby advanced the sophistication of contour models. From these few landmark studies have grown some very active lines of research that together make it fair to state that we now consider the physiological basis of contour perception that occurs with abrupt luminance gradients to be rather different than earlier imagined.

At present there continues to prevail a general notion that the retina codes edges directly in terms of local processes at or near the site of the imaged edge. Furthermore, the history of visual science suggests that there is an inherently compelling reason to think so. First, direct and local coding of edges is consistent with topology and with older views of the retina as a sort of film upon which images of objects are projected; and, second, even if one abandons the concept of the eye as a passive receptor, the realness of objects is somehow felt to be enhanced if one assumes a direct spatial correlation between the edges of an object in space and the neural space that codes them.

There is an alternative to the doctrine of isomorphism which does not assume a spatial correlation between object edges and their neural representation. Through a Fourier analysis, any luminance gradient can be described mathematically as a unique combination of sine waves of particular frequencies and amplitudes. An extremely abrupt gradient, one like the side of a square wave, requires in its Fourier description the presence of high frequency sine components. One could propose, then, that the sharpness of a perceived contour depends on the extent to which a luminance gradient contains high frequency components, assuming, of course, that the eye is directly sensitive to these different frequencies.

Research in physiological acoustics has demonstrated clearly that many first-order neurons in the acoustic nerve are selectively tuned to *temporal* frequencies (*4*). What is required in vision is a class of cells selectively tuned to *spatial* frequencies. In recent years evidence of selective tuning in cortical cells to particular spatial frequencies has been established (*5*). Such cells as have been found show themselves to be maximally active to retinal stimulation with grid targets of unique spatial frequency and specific grid orientation. Whether or not spatial frequency detectors account for the perception of contours remains to be determined, but the possibility is present (*1, 2, 3, 22*). Shapley and Tolhurst (*20*) argue for their *edge detector hypothesis* (*21*), and in support of it they present some consistent and compelling psychophysical data.

Most studies of the physiological basis of contour perception have involved some sort of manipulation of luminance gradients, and perhaps because of this, many experimenters have been disposed to think of the contours arising from such gradients as *objective* contours. On the other hand, contours which occur in the absence of luminance gradients often are referred to as *subjective* contours, as if to remind the unwary that some contours occur without any "real" stimulus correlates (*19*). This distinction between objective and subjective contours seems to us to be unjustified. We take the view that any conditions, subject to specification, that lead to the perception of a sharp boundary meet the criterion for contour, and that no further distinction *in the percept* is necessary.

The fact that abrupt gradients are usually present when contour perception occurs does not, by itself, make the contours objective. Instead, it makes the contours predictable. The objectivity of contour perception is neither dependent upon our ability to explain contour satisfactorily in terms of physiological processes nor our own intuitions about the proper characteristics of the proximal stimulus. What is required is the establishment of invariant relationships between conditions of stimulation and contour perception.

The sharp stereoscopic contours that sometimes accompany surface depth in matrix targets represent an important challenge to our present understanding of contour processes because these contours occur in the absence of abrupt luminance gradients that for so long had been assumed to be necessary to contour. In this chapter we shall consider a number of experiments that were directed toward establishing the conditions leading to contour perception in the absence of abrupt luminance gradients.

Stereoscopic Contours and Form Disparity

In our discussion of form disparity in the previous chapter, we stated that matrix targets occasionally led to the perception of well-defined contours that served to delimit the surfaces of sub-matrices seen in stereoscopic depth. These contours occurred in the absence of a continuous abrupt luminance gradient, and they seemed to depend on the perception of surface depth brought about by the binocular abstraction of a disparate form. The form itself could be defined in a random dot stereogram by a horizontal shift of a sub-matrix, but the level of form definition depended upon the global and matrix densities of the patterns and the amount of binocular correlation between the half-images. We implied that stereoscopic contours were limited to conditions wherein the form of the sub-matrix could be abstracted unambiguously through binocular processing. Evidence for this implication comes from experiments in which stereoscopic contour was studied first as a function of density and then as a function of binocular correlation.

THE ROLE OF DENSITIES

Random dot stereograms like those previously described were employed in the first experiment. The matrix in each half-image subtended 2° visual angle on a side and had one of three global densities (100, 400, or 900 cells per 1° solid visual angle). For each global density there were seven levels of matrix density (20, 30, 40, 50, 60, 70, and 80 per cent). Seen against a background luminance of 8.6 ft-L, the dots had a luminance of 2.5 ft-L and each dot subtended 4' of arc. In each of the 21 experimental stereograms (3 global densities × 7 matrix densities) the dots in a central matrix (1 × 1°) had a 6' crossed disparity.

Ten observers saw each of the experimental stereograms three times, and on each occasion they reported the presence or absence of surface depth for the sub-matrix. In addition, observers assigned a number to the contours of that surface to reflect its sharpness.

The assignment of numbers to the contours was done according to a scale developed independently by each observer in preliminary sessions. The observer viewed a five channel optical device that appeared to him as a horizontal row of five rectangular screens. The surface of the left most screen (channel 1) was homogeneous and had a luminance of 8.3 ft-L. The right most screen (channel 5) was bipartite with the upper and lower halves set at 12 and 4 ft-L. The horizontal boundary thus produced was sharply defined. The observer then adjusted the optics of channel 3 so as to produce an edge that appeared to him to bisect the interval of contour clarity present in channels 1 and 5. After eight settings, the experimenter set channel 3 at the mean, after which in like manner the observer bisected the intervals between channels 1 and 3 and then 3 and 5. In the end, each observer had available to him a 5-point contour scale that went from 1 (no contour) to 5 (sharp contour). During the main experiment the observer was asked to assign the numbers 1, 2, 3, 4, or 5 independently to each of the four sides of the sub-matrix. His standard scale was available for reference.

Inasmuch as there were no significant differences in the numbers assigned separately to the four sides of the sub-matrix within each of the twenty-one experimental stereograms, the data were collapsed so that the perceived contour of the sub-matrix in any given stereogram for any given observer was denoted by a single number, the mean of the four sides.

Summary data are shown in Fig. 5.1, where the mean contour judgment is given for each of the three global density conditions as a function of matrix density. Recall from the previous chapter that the frequency of seeing surface depth was a function of global and matrix densities (see Fig. 4.2). With regard to the present experiment, observers never reported contour in the absence of surface depth, although they did sometimes report surface depth in the absence of contour.

The results of this experiment indicate that stereoscopic contour is facilitated by increases in global and matrix densities. In this experiment a low global density (100 cells per 1° solid visual angle) never was sufficient to the perception of a sharp stereoscopic contour, no matter the

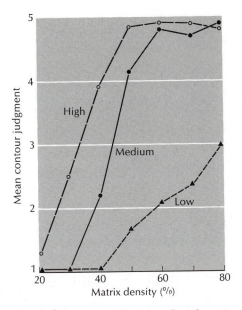

Fig. 5.1   Mean contour judgment on a 5-point scale, where 1 = no contour and 5 = sharp contour, as a function of matrix density for each of three global densities. High = 900, Medium = 400, Low = 100 matrix cells per 1° solid visual angle.

level of matrix density. Further, when matrix density was 50 per cent or higher, both medium and high global densities allowed the perception of very sharp contours.

From our experiments with random dot stereograms there appears to be a strong relationship between stereoscopically defined forms and stereoscopically induced contours. When the defining properties are weak, the disparate *dots* of the sub-matrix appear in depth, but surface depth and stereoscopic contours are absent. However, when the defining properties are made stronger by higher densities, then the elements of the sub-matrix and the surface upon which they appear both are shifted into a single stereoscopic plane different from the surround. *The concomitant shift of the surface is a necessary condition to stereoscopic contour,* but our results show clearly that it is not sufficient. Rather, the clarity of the stereoscopic contour grows as ambiguity to the binocular process of matching global patterns diminishes. Failure to obtain instances of stereoscopic contour with control stereograms (identical half-images) makes it clear that disparity is necessary to these contours.

Density and Homogeneous Forms. As we mentioned earlier in connection with our discussion of form disparity, random dot stereograms lead to surface depth and stereoscopic contour only when the form of the sub-matrix is abstracted through binocular processing. The form of the sub-matrix cannot be detected monocularly. However, when the sub-matrix is defined by homogeneity (0 per cent density), as shown at the top of Fig. 5.2, then the form of the sub-matrix is already apparent, and, therefore, its contours might not depend so critically upon binocular form abstraction and surface depth.

Inspection of either half-image at the top of Fig. 5.2 leaves one with an impression of a contoured square within the matrix because global density is fairly high and matrix density in the surround is 100 per cent. If global density were increased greatly, then the pattern shown at the

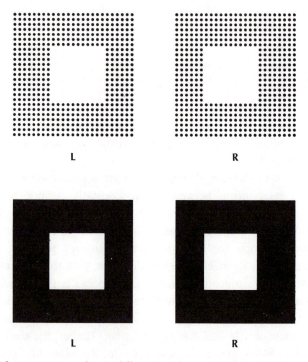

L   R

L   R

Fig. 5.2   The stereograms shown differ primarily in global density. The coarser texture of the surround in the upper one degrades the contour of the central squares, but stereoscopic viewing sharpens them.

bottom of Fig. 5.2 would result. In this case, of course, the perceived contour would result from an abrupt gradient. Clearly, one can upgrade an edge by altering the texture of one of the bounding surfaces, in this case the surround.

Both of the stereograms shown in Fig. 5.2 lead to depth perception of the inner square when they are presented stereoscopically. In the case of the solid surround, the crossed disparity shifts the location of the edges of the inner white square as well as the surface they enclose. Here, then, we may describe the target as having both form and edge disparity in identical magnitudes. In the case of the matrix surround, there is also form disparity and, perhaps, degraded disparate edges.

If the contours of the inner surface in the matrix target are no sharper when the surface is brought into depth during stereoscopic viewing than they are in monocular viewing, then we would have to conclude that there is no such thing as a class of contours that derive a sharpening from stereoscopic processes. Instead, we would have to consider the role of form disparity simply as important to the localization of contours in visual space.

We argue, of course, that there is a distinct class of contours that is generated centrally; otherwise there would be no obvious way to account for the contours reported by observers when they viewed random dot stereograms. On the other hand, the local retinal coding of edges could conceivably occur in random dot stereograms if the boundaries of the sub-matrix were defined as regions of change in global pattern matching rather than in terms of density changes or luminance gradients.

In order to determine whether or not the processes underlying stereopsis influenced the clarity of contours surrounding homogeneous submatrices, we had observers judge the sharpness of these contours in each of three global density conditions both in the presence and absence of sub-matrix form disparity.

The half-images always consisted of square matrices $4° - 20'$ on a side in which each matrix cell contained a dark dot except for a square central region in which dots were omitted. The surround, therefore, always had a matrix density of 100 per cent. Each dot subtended $5'$ of arc. The homogeneous sub-matrix subtended either $1°$ or $2°$ on a side, and it was located in such a way as to have either $0'$ or $30'$ of crossed disparity. The three global densities were 15, 33, and 58 cells per $1°$

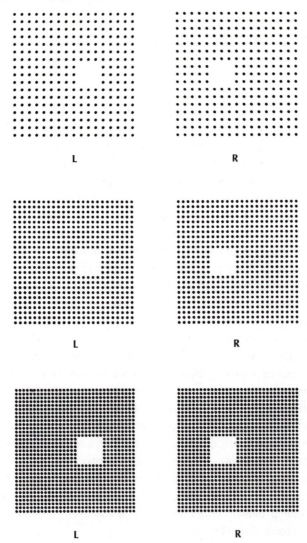

L   R

L   R

L   R

Fig. 5.3   Sample stereograms used to study the effects of global density on stereo-scopic contours. Under the conditions of viewing, global densities were 15 (top), 33 (middle), and 58 (bottom) matrix cells per 1° solid visual angle.

solid visual angle. In all, there were 12 stereograms: two sizes of sub-matrix seen against three global densities with and without form disparity ($2 \times 3 \times 2$). In Fig. 5.3 are shown samples of the three global densities for the 1° sub-matrix with 30' of crossed disparity. The generation of the stereograms in this experiment was not a simple matter because of the following two constraints: first, all matrices had to subtend the same visual angle; and, second, all sub-matrices, regardless of size, had to have the same disparity and their shift had to be across an integral number of cells.

Twelve observers who met our visual criteria for acuity, phoria, and stereopsis first developed a 5-point scale of contour sharpness according to the procedure previously described (1 = no contour, 5 = sharp contour). Each observer then viewed the 12 stereograms in random order three times. On each trial he reported both the amount of surface depth of the sub-matrix according to a previously practiced technique involving magnitude estimation and the sharpness of the contours of the sub-matrix through the assignment of a number from 1 to 5. As in our earlier experiment with contour scaling, the five-channel optical device on which an observer's contour scale was displayed remained available to him for reference.

The results of the experiment made clear that the contours of a homogeneous sub-matrix are sharpened in instances of surface depth. This general finding is illustrated in Fig. 5.4 where mean contour judgments are shown for the large and small sub-matrices with and without disparity as a function of global density. In no instance was surface depth of the sub-matrix reported in the absence of disparity. Accordingly, in these cases we may consider judgments of contour to have been dependent entirely upon the extent to which the surrounding dots defined an edge in a two-dimensional array. Results from a control condition showed the contours in the zero disparity stereograms to be no different than those obtained with monocular vision. Even with the highest density condition, the perception of sharp contours was not achieved in the absence of sub-matrix disparity.

When form disparity was present, the sub-matrix surface was shifted into depth and its contours were greatly enhanced, thus indicating that stereoscopic processes somehow sharpened contour. Again, contour sharpness was influenced by global density.

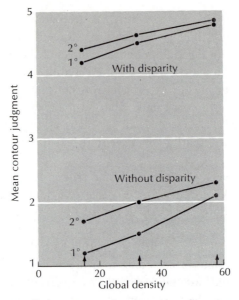

Fig. 5.4   Mean contour judgment on a 5-point scale, where 1 = no contour and 5 = sharp contour, as a function of global density for a 1° and a 2° form with and without disparity. Each data point is mean of 36 judgments (12 observers x 3).

In this experiment form disparity, global density, and sub-matrix size all had significant influences upon the sharpness of contour. From our earlier experiments with matrix targets and our observations of Julesz patterns, we fully expected that form disparity would be necessary to the perception of sharp contours, as indeed it proved to be. The quality of perceived contour was markedly different between the disparity and the no disparity conditions. What seemed a little surprising to us was the robustness of the stereoscopic contour in the disparity conditions even when global density was low.

With regard to the angular size of the sub-matrix, it should be noted that the sharpness of the stereoscopic contour (disparity conditions) always was better for the larger sub-matrix (2°) at each global density. This difference was significant, and it raises the question as to whether or not global density alone is an appropriate basis on which to predict the sharpness of stereoscopic contours. In Fig. 5.5 are shown sample monocular targets that contain the two sized sub-matrices. In these samples the surrounding matrices illustrate the lowest global density used in the experiment. Casual inspection of these targets suggests to us that there is apparently more structure to the larger than to the smaller inner square. Perhaps this is so because sub-matrix size interacts with density to provide more information along the boundaries of the homogeneous central region. Strictly, of course, no contours appear in either of these patterns when viewed freely, as reflected in the data presented in Fig. 5.4. On the other hand, if the form of the central square is somehow better defined when large, then this fact might account for the sharpening of stereoscopic contours as a function of sub-matrix size.

There are a number of ways in which one could attempt to quantify the amount of boundary information in these two patterns. One simple way is to express the summed angular diameters of the dots along a boundary as a ratio of the angular length of that boundary. A ratio of 1.0 would be achieved when the dots along a boundary just touch without overlapping each other. One could, of course, have an infinite number of dots that overlapped and, thereby, made a straight line with a width equal to dot diameter. However, to maintain the integrity of the matrix, the limit of spatial proximity excludes any overlap of adjacent dots.

In the patterns in Fig. 5.3, it is clear that a ratio of 1.0 was absent in the present experiment, because, even in the high density condition, space remained between adjacent dots. However, because dot diameter was constant, it is obvious that the boundary information ratio decreases as global density decreases.

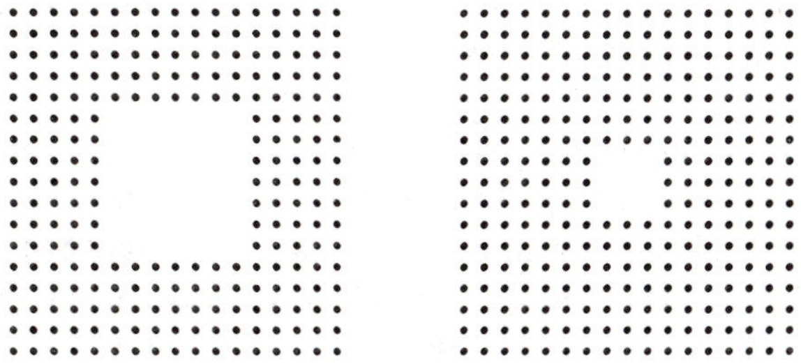

Large   Small

Fig. 5.5   A comparison of the 2° and 1° central form seen against the same low global density of 15 matrix cells per 1° solid visual angle. Data suggest there is more structure in the larger form. See text for explanation.

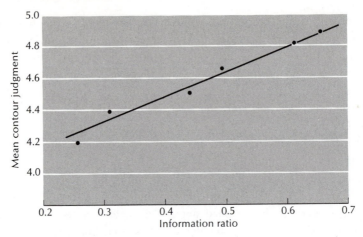

Fig. 5.6   Mean contour judgment as a function of the derived measure of contour information in the stereograms. Data from Fig. 5.4.

When the amount of boundary information is calculated in the manner described, it turns out to be different for the large and small sub-matrix in each density condition, with the larger one favored. Accordingly, the two sub-matrix sizes seen against the three global densities led to six different levels of boundary information. When mean judged contour is plotted against these six information ratios, as in Fig. 5.6, the relationship is approximately linear. These same six ratios could have been achieved with a constant sub-matrix size seen against six different global densities, but the effect on stereoscopic contour of this manipulation is unknown. What strikes us as important is that the size of the sub-matrix influences the sharpness of stereoscopic contour.

BINOCULAR CORRELATION

In the previous chapter we alluded to the effects of binocular correlation upon stereoscopic contour in connection with the discussion of the role of binocular correlation in the production of surface depth. Recall that when observers viewed random dot stereograms with global densities of 400 cells per 1° of solid visual angle and matrix densities of 50 per cent, the perception of surface depth in the disparate sub-matrix declined abruptly as binocular correlation fell from 100 to 70 per cent (see Fig. 4.3).

With targets identical to those used in the earlier experiment on binocular correlation, we had observers report on the sharpness of the contours of the sub-matrix according to the scaling method described earlier in this chapter. The results are shown in Fig. 5.7, where mean contour is given as a function of binocular correlation. The solid line represents mean judged contour for different levels of binocular correlation *whether or not the surface of the sub-matrix was perceived in depth.* However, we have already established that a disparate sub-matrix of the sort employed in this experiment gives rise to surface depth less and less frequently as binocular correlation is reduced. Accordingly, a more accurate representation of contour is gained when the data are plotted in such a way as to take into account the presence or absence of seen stereoscopic depth of the disparate sub-matrix.

In this experiment binocular correlations of 100 and 90 per cent always gave rise to surface depth whereas correlations of 60 and 50 per

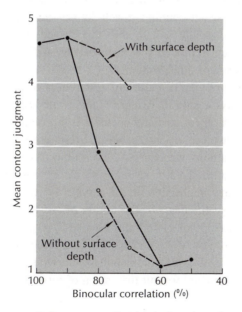

Fig. 5.7   Mean contour judgment on a 5-point scale, where 1 = no contour and 5 = sharp contour, as a function of the level of binocular correlation in random dot stereograms with global and matrix densities of 400 cells per 1° solid visual angle and 50 per cent, respectively. Each solid data point is the mean of 30 judgments (10 observers x 3). The open points have different *n*'s, as explained in the text.

cent never did. However, with intermediate levels (80 and 70 per cent) the reports of surface depth were mixed. The dashed lines in Fig. 5.7 show the mean contour judgments when the surface both was and was not seen in depth. Here, again, we see the strong enhancement of contour in those conditions that allowed the binocular system to abstract the disparate form so that it appeared in depth.

We conclude from these experiments on global and matrix densities and binocular correlation that sharp continuous contours can be produced with matrix targets provided that some aspect of the target carries disparity sufficient to define through binocular abstraction an unambiguous form that appears in depth as a surface. Factors of density and binocular correlation bear on the matter of stereoscopic contour insofar as they contribute to reduce ambiguity in binocular form abstraction.

INTERPOSITION AND FORM DISPARITY

The concept of form disparity needs to be examined further because a pair of half-images that contains a well-defined central region of homogeneity is not always sufficient to shift the surface of the form into stereoscopic depth even though the form carries a disparity. The reason centers on the issue of interposition.

When objects are viewed naturally, differences in their depths in the visual field always result in disparity and sometimes in interposition whenever a closer object partially occludes a more distant one. The importance and relevance of interposition to stereopsis was stated succinctly when Helmholtz wrote, ". . . such objects are always imagined as being present in the field of vision as would have to be there in order to produce the same impression on the nervous system . . . " (7, p. 4). This quotation is at the heart of the notion of *unbewusster Schluss* (unconscious inference) that Helmholtz used to explain stereopsis, among other phenomena. Today we can recognize that unconscious inference offers little by way of explanation, but the doctrine nevertheless represents a point of departure for our discussion of form disparity and stereoscopic contour.

Consider the half-images, shown in Fig. 5.8, that would obtain if one viewed the three-dimensional arrays depicted on the right. In the upper drawing the closer and smaller square of dots carries a crossed disparity relative to the larger and more distant square. While the disparity of the

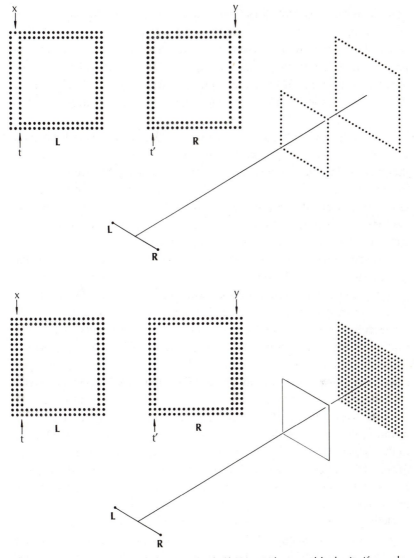

Fig. 5.8   Here are shown on the left the half-images that would obtain if an ob-server viewed the three-dimensional projections shown on the right. See text for explanation.

two squares of dots is obvious from inspection of the half-images, so also is the disparity of the central homogeneous square form. Nevertheless, when observers view this stereogram, only the inner square of dots appears in a closer depth plane. The surface of the enclosed form never appears in the plane of the closer square even though the form is clearly defined and carries a crossed disparity equal to that of the closer dots (*12*).

While it is true that the closer square of dots could have been *on* a surface, there was nothing in the display that *required* the presence of the surface in order to account for the differences between the half-images. In other words, even though form disparity was present, and could have resulted in the perception of surface depth with stereoscopic contours, the presence of such a surface was not necessary because there were no interposition cues present in the binocular view.

Consider now the bottom drawing of Fig. 5.8. Here are shown the half-images that would obtain if one viewed a dot matrix while an opaque square was present at the closer dashed plane, thereby selectively occluding some of the dots in the more distant matrix.

Stereoscopic viewing of these half-images always results in the perception of the central square form as a surface with sharp stereoscopic contours seen interposed between the observer and a matrix of dots located in a single more distant plane. Here, too, the monocular targets each contain a central form defined by its homogeneity, and relative to the surrounding matrix, the form carries a crossed disparity. But in this instance, in contrast to the upper drawing in Fig. 5.8, there is something in the display that requires the presence of a surface in order to account for the differences between the half-images. In terms of inference, according to Helmholtz, interposition of a surface accounts for the half-image differences.

Before accepting interposition and unconscious inference as anything more than a convenient rubric to describe a limited set of stereoscopic percepts, let us consider whether or not form disparity can be conceived in a way that comes closer to accounting for the fact that a disparate form is sometimes seen as a contoured surface of specific depth while at other times it is seen as a contourless surface of unspecified depth.

The upper and lower set of half-images shown in Fig. 5.8 differ only with respect to columns *x* and *y*. When these columns are vacant, as in the upper set, then each dot in the left half-image has an analogous dot in the right half-image, so that perfect binocular correlation is present. Under this condition the binocular combination of columns t and t', for example, is assured. On the other hand, when columns x and y are filled, as in the lower set, then ambiguity is added because either column x or t could combine with t'. In either instance one of the three vertical columns on the left in the left half-image has no analogous column in the right half-image with which to combine. Accordingly, perfect binocular correlation is absent. The same is true for the other side of the binocularly combined target.

Our results suggest that when perfect binocular correlation of the dots is absent, then the binocular system locks on the outer square which, in turn, determines the alignment of column x with column t'. The result is that two complete squares have perfect correlations and, relative to each other, they carry zero disparity. The extra lateral vertical columns in the right and left half-images are uncorrelated and represent monocular stimuli. However, it is their presence that provides the disparity of the enclosed central form. Monocular aspects of an otherwise binocularly locked display often show an instability in their depth localizations. The question may be raised as to why these monocular columns of dots were seen by our observers always in the same depth plane as the correlated and nondisparate dots.

Role of Perceptual Grouping. Our suggestion is that the uncorrelated columns of dots were organized as part of the surrounding matrix, thus placing all dots in a single plane, because by feature and spacing they matched the correlated dots. Here, of course, we bring to bear some of the principles of perceptual grouping. For these columns, specific depth localization based upon binocular correlation is absent, and this being so, perceptual grouping operated on the basis of feature similarity, continuity, and spacing.

There are, of course, many experiments that might be done to test the suggestion of perceptual grouping. We have done three which can be summarized briefly. First, we had observers report on the depth of the uncorrelated vertical columns of dots immediately adjacent to the lateral boundaries of the apparently interposed surface as a function of the size of the surrounding matrix. There were five stereograms used, and the extreme conditions are shown in Fig. 5.9, A and B. The disparity of the central form was constant relative to the surround, but its angular subtense decreased over the five stereograms as the number of correlated dots increased. The supposition was that the uncorrelated columns, as discussed in connection with Fig. 5.8, would be more likely to be grouped with the binocularly correlated dots of the matrix as their number grew larger.

In general, our supposition was confirmed. When our observers viewed the pattern shown as A in Fig. 5.9, two of the ten reported the location of the dots in the uncorrelated columns to be unstable in depth and to appear to float between the closer plane of the interposed surface and the more distant plane of the dot matrix. However, in all other instances the uncorrelated dots appeared co-planar with the matrix. We concluded that the appearance of all of the dots in a single depth plane meant that the uncorrelated ones had been grouped as a part of a uniform matrix.

The two exceptions noted are inconsistent with the results of an earlier experiment (12) in which observers who viewed identical targets reported that all the dots appeared in a single plane. The difference in the results for this particular stereogram can probably be attributed to the instructions we gave to the observers. In the present experiment on grouping, observers were explicitly instructed to attend to the depth of the uncorrelated lateral columns, whereas in our earlier experiment they were instructed to describe the interposed surface and the sharpness of its stereoscopic contours. Regardless, it appears that the grouping tendency of like-elements in a regular matrix with 100 per cent density is very strong because in four of the five conditions all observers reported that the dots appeared in a single plane.

In the next experiment on grouping, we systematically changed the density of the dots in the uncorrelated columns while leaving 100 per cent density in the remainder of the surrounding matrix. The effect of this manipulation was to alter the regularity of spacing in these columns and thereby alter continuity. Again, the observers were instructed to report on the depth of the dots in the uncorrelated columns. The effects were pronounced in that anything more than a slight perturbation of spacing resulted in the dots appearing to float, and when density fell below 50 per cent in these columns, they no longer served to define a dis-

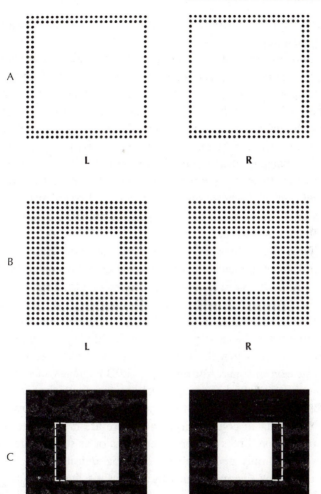

Fig. 5.9   In A and B are samples of stereograms used to study the grouping of binocularly uncorrelated dots. Stereogram C illustrates that uncorrelated aspects of half-images also are present in traditional patterns. See text for explanation.

parate form with the outcome that surface depth and stereoscopic contours disappeared.

In the third experiment the density in the uncorrelated columns was returned to 100 per cent, but the entries were changed from a dot to an x. Our supposition here was that the failure of feature identity would reduce the tendency for the x's to be grouped as part of the dot matrix. Here, too, the effects were pronounced. Even though the uncorrelated columns were adequate in maintaining form disparity, presumably by their regular spacing, the x's themselves were not grouped as part of the matrix. Instead, their depth position floated between that of the closer surface and that of the more distant dot matrix. Dissimilarity along the dimension of shape seems to have reduced the tendency to group all the matrix elements as a whole.

Based upon these three experiments, we conclude that numerosity, spacing, and shape influence the organization of the uncorrelated matrix elements. Furthermore, it is important to recognize that the issue of grouping is not unique to matrix targets even though it may appear to be. Traditional stereograms illustrate the same phenomenon, but the suppositions about the objects depicted make the idea of grouping less obvious. For example, when the global density of the matrix surrounding the disparate central square shown in Fig. 5.9B is greatly increased, then the surround essentially becomes a finely textured surface, as shown in Fig. 5.9C. Nevertheless, just as there are uncorrelated columns in B, so are there uncorrelated columns in C, but there are many more of them. Whether or not one thinks of them as columns or as surface areas would appear to depend only upon the level of global density in the surround. In either event, the regions defined by the dashed lines in C are uncorrelated: but because of similarity of texture (spacing) and brightness these regions are grouped with the correlated regions of the background and thus help to define the disparity of the central smaller square. As we stated in Chapter 4, the main difference between traditional and matrix stereograms of the kinds shown in Fig. 5.9 is one of texture. The central form in C is defined by one homogeneous texture and the surround by another of different luminance. Accordingly, the form may be said to be accompanied by continuous contours that result from abrupt gradients. In a way, it is the form disparity that makes the contours disparate. In B the form is defined by one homogeneous texture and the surround by another coarser one. The coarseness here eliminates the continuous contour, but the form remains and so does its disparity. The remarkable aspect of the binocular process is that the continuity and sharpness of the boundaries of the form can be restored as stereoscopic contours.

The essential similarity of all stereograms is important to bear in mind because not to do so is to fail to grasp the notion of form disparity. The danger is most evident if we reconsider Fig. 5.9A. Of this pattern Julesz wrote that the central area was somehow undetermined, thus missing altogether the idea of form and the fact of its binocular correlation in the stereogram. He stated that, ". . . perceiving undetermined areas in depth is not identical to stereopsis" (*10,* p. 261). His analysis focused upon the dots themselves without regard to the patterning that their absence can effect. We hold that these central areas are utilized as binocularly correlated forms and that their shift into depth *is* stereopsis and that no additional embellishments are required to account for them.

References

1. Gilinsky, Alberta S., and Cohen, H. H. Reaction time to change in visual orientation. *Percept. and Psychophysics,* 1972, *11,* 129-135.
2. Graham, Norma. Spatial frequency channels in the human visual system: effect of luminance and pattern drift rate. *Vision Res.,* 1972, *12,* 53-69.
3. Graham, Norma, and Nachmias, J. Detection of grating patterns containing two spatial frequencies: a comparison of single and multiple channel models. *Vision Res.,* 1971, *11,* 251-261.
4. Gulick, W. L. *Hearing: Physiology and Psychophysics.* New York: Oxford Univ. Press, 1971, Ch. 4.
5. Haber, R. N., and Hershenson, M. *The Psychology of Visual Perception.* New York: Holt, Rinehart and Winston, 1973, Ch. 3.
6. Hartline, H. K., and Ratliff, F. Inhibitory interaction of receptor units in the eye of *Limulus. J. Gen. Physiol.,* 1957, *40,* 357-376.
7. Helmholtz, H. von. *Helmholtz's Treatise on Physiological Optics,* Vol. 3, J. P. Southall (Ed.), New York: Optical Soc. Amer., 1925.
8. Hubel, D. H., and Wiesel, T. N. Receptive fields of single neurones in the cat's striate cortex. *J. Physiol.* (London), 1959, *148,* 574-591.
9. Hubel, D. H., and Wiesel, T. N. Receptive fields, binocular interaction, and functional architecture in the cat's visual cortex. *J. Physiol.* (London), 1962, *160,* 106-154.

10. Julesz, B. *Foundations of Cyclopean Perception.* Chicago: Univ. Chicago Press, 1971.
11. Kuffler, S. W. Discharge patterns and functional organization of mammalian retina. *J. Neurophysiol.,* 1953, *16,* 37-68.
12. Lawson, R. B., and Gulick, W. L. Stereopsis and anomalous contour. *Vision Res.,* 1967, *7,* 271-297.
13. Lettvin, J. Y., Maturana, H. R., McColloch, W. S., and Pitts, W. H. What the frog's eye tells the frog's brain. *Proc. Inst. Radio Engrs.,* 1959, *47,* 1940-1951.
14. Marshall, W. H., and Talbot, S. A. Recent evidence for neural mechanisms in vision leading to a general theory of sensory acuity. In H. Kluver (Ed.), *Visual Mechanisms, Biol. Sympos.,* 1942, *7,* 117-164. Lancaster, Penn.: Jacques Cattell.
15. Ratliff, F., and Hartline, H. K. The responses of *Limulus* optic nerve fibers to patterns of illumination on the retinal mosaic. *J. Gen. Physiol.,* 1959, *42,* 1241-1255.
16. Ratliff, F., Hartline, H. K., and Miller, W. H. Spatial and temporal aspects of retinal inhibitory interaction. *J. Opt. Soc. Amer.,* 1963, *53,* 110-120.
17. Riggs, L. A., and Ratliff, F. Visual acuity and the normal tremor of the eyes. *Science,* 1951, *114,* 17-18.
18. Riggs, L. A., Ratliff, F., Cornsweet, J. C., and Cornsweet, T. N. The disappearance of steadily fixated visual test objects. *J. Opt. Soc. Amer.,* 1953, *43,* 495-501.
19. Schumann, F. Einige Beobachtungen über die Zusammenfassung von Gesichtseindrucken zu Einheiten. *Psychol. Stud.,* 1904, *1,* 1-32.
20. Shapley, R. M., and Tolhurst, D. J. Edge detectors in human vision. *J. Physiol.* (London), 1973, *229,* 165-183.
21. Tolhurst, D. J. On the possible existence of edge detector neurones in the human visual system. *Vision Res.,* 1972, *12,* 797-804.
22. Weisstein, N. What the frog's eye tells the human brain: Single cell analyses in the human visual system. *Psychol. Rev.,* 1969, *72,* 157-176.

6
Experiments with Interposition

The stereoscopic contours with which we have dealt so far always have
had two limits: they have been *straight,* and they have been *adjacent* to a
row or column of dots. We begin this chapter by considering some experiments in which we examined these limits. Then we report a number
of experiments undertaken to learn how important matrix corners are
to stereoscopic contours. The chapter concludes with a discussion of the
perception of translucency. All of the experiments considered in this
chapter were conceived in the context of interposition.

STEREOSCOPIC CONTOURS IN HOMOGENEOUS SPACE
We know that when random dot stereograms, like those of Julesz, contain a shifted sub-matrix in the form of a square, then upon stereoscopic
presentation the square emerges as a surface with sharp contours. The
contours appear between those rows and columns of dots that show a
discontinuity of depth. That is, the rows and columns just *inside* the stereoscopic contours contain dots that appear in the plane of the contoured
surface, whereas the rows and columns just *outside* the contours contain
dots that appear in the more distant plane of the surrounding matrix.
There are, however, occasional exceptions (see Chapter 4, p. 112). It
should be noted here that the stereoscopic contour serves to separate the
depth planes of the closer and farther surfaces, but the contour belongs
to the *closer* surface.

The fact that with Julesz patterns the contour appeared between the rows and columns of dots led us, at first, to suspect that stereoscopic contours depended upon this kind of *depth discontinuity* in the parallel rows and columns that bounded the contour. However, we have established that *depth discontinuity in matrix elements is not necessary* to the appearance of sharp stereoscopic contours. The evidence comes directly from many of the experimental results previously discussed in connection with the role of form disparity in stereoscopic contour formation. Recall that in our targets the sub-matrices were defined by regions of homogeneity that carried a disparity, and under these circumstances the sharply contoured surface had no dots that paralleled the inside of the contour. Indeed, all of the dots were seen in a single plane, and yet sharp contours were reported.

Furthermore, we have also established that *depth discontinuity in parallel rows and columns is not sufficient* for the appearance of stereoscopic contours. Recall that neither surface depth nor contours appeared when observers viewed stereograms like the upper one shown in Fig. 5.8, where there is perfect binocular correlation for *all* dots and no requirement of interposition. The disparity of the inner square of dots led to its appearance in depth, thus producing a depth discontinuity; but no contours were reported.

As related earlier, it is possible with stereograms to simulate an interposed surface by presenting to the eyes the half-images that would obtain *if* such a surface were, in fact, interposed between an observer and a more distant two-dimensional matrix. It was in this context that we conceived experiments designed to study both curved and straight stereoscopic contours in homogeneous space. We felt that the case for stereoscopic contours as a class separate from those that occur with abrupt luminance gradients would be strengthened if it could be shown that they arose under more general circumstances than those we had previously observed.

Interposition and Contours. In our discussion of interposition and its relationship to binocular correlation in the previous chapter, we described our basic square pattern (Fig. 6.1A) as having good binocular correlation insofar as the central homogeneous square form was concerned. It is as though a white square chip had been placed upon a regular square matrix of black dots in such a way as to achieve a modest crossed disparity. In stereoscopic view the white square appeared as an opaque contoured interposed surface.

In Fig. 6.1A is shown a three-dimensional scheme of how an interposed *opaque* square could serve to reconcile the difference in the actual half-images used in our experiment, as shown on the left. It should be noted that the matrix behind the interposed surface need not be limited to a double frame of concentric squares. It could as well be a completed matrix.

In like manner, Fig. 6.1 includes three other stereograms with suggested interposed surfaces that account for the difference in the half-image pairs.

Although we had earlier used some patterns like these (*1*), our purpose in this experiment was to study the sharpness of the contours of all perceived surfaces according to the contour scaling technique described in the previous chapter.

Note that in the upper two stereograms (A and B), the main anticipated difference between them concerned the shape of the interposed surface, one with straight and one with curved contours; but in both stereograms the monocularly recognized central form, whether square or circle, is the *same* form as the one expected through binocular abstraction. Presumably, the selective occlusion of some of the dots would define a disparate form that would appear as a contoured surface. Of course, the structure of these two stereograms was such that the anticipated stereoscopic contours would lie just inside, but adjacent to, the surrounding dots.

This kind of contour adjacency with matrix elements is eliminated in the lower two patterns (C and D) because, although selective occlusion still requires an interposed surface to account for the half-image differences, the anticipated binocularly abstracted form is *no longer the same* form as the one available in monocular view.

These four stereograms, along with some control patterns to be mentioned later, constituted the displays for this experiment. Each of ten observers, naive to the purpose of the experiment with regard to interposition and shape, first established his 5-point contour scale (1 = no contour, 5 = sharp contour). Thereafter, he viewed in random order each of the experimental stereograms twice. On each trial our observers had two tasks: first, they were asked to describe what they saw, and

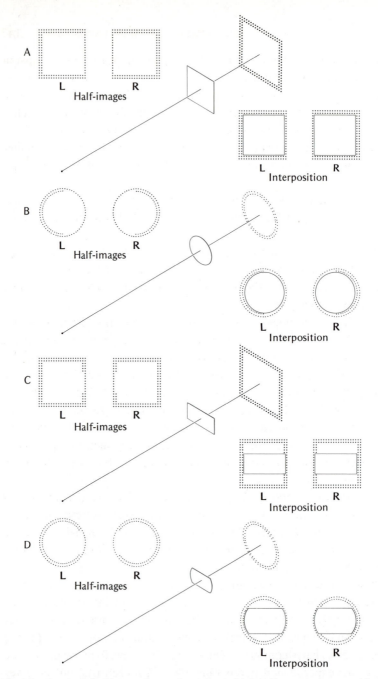

Fig. 6.1 On the left side are shown the right and left half-images that would obtain if an observer viewed a two-border square matrix behind an interposed square (A) and rectangle (C) and a two-border circular matrix behind an interposed circle (B) and bowed rectangle (D).

144

when the description included a surface in depth, they were required to draw its shape; and second, when a surface was reported, the observers were asked to assign a number to each of the contours defining the surface according to the method previously outlined.

The results of the experiment were striking. First, all observers reported interposed surfaces of the shapes predicted by interposition and shown in Fig. 6.1. Second, the contours of the surfaces were reported to be sharp, and there were no significant differences among the four sides. In the case of pattern B, the circle, four quadrants were identified: upper, lower, right, and left. Mean contour judgments for stereograms A through D were 4.76, 4.62, 4.70, and 4.58, respectively. Third, there were two kinds of control stereograms utilized in this experiment. The first consisted of an occasional trial on which identical half-images were used. They were selected at random. The second consisted of the experimental stereograms (Fig. 6.1) but with each half-image rotated 90° cw around its center in the frontoparallel plane so as to effect vertical rather than horizontal form disparity. In no instance of viewing either type of control stereogram did any observer ever report either surface depth or stereoscopic contours.

The results of this experiment demonstrate clearly that stereoscopic contours can occur in a homogeneous part of the visual field. In patterns C and D the two horizontal contours extended over an angular distance of 2° − 10′, and they were entirely unbounded by adjacent dots either inside or outside. Moreover, the sharpness of these unbounded stereoscopic contours was no less than the sharpness of the vertical contours which were bounded. It is also important to note that the shape of the binocularly abstracted form, which appears as a contoured interposed opaque surface, can differ from the shape of the monocular region of homogeneity when the difference in shape is consistent with the requirements of interposition.

Of special interest to us was the exclusive perception of the shape of the surface in pattern D by all our observers. While the curved contours in pattern B were expected on the basis of interposition, there were a number of possible shapes in pattern D, any of which would account for the half-image difference. For example, an ellipse with a horizontal major axis would do as well in accounting for the selective occlusion of the dots of the inner ring in the nasal quadrants. The fact that the two vertical sides showed themselves as bowed was expected, for only such bow-ing could account for the appearance to both eyes of the entire outer ring and the selective occlusion of the inner ring. However, we did not expect the two remaining contours to be straight.

While we demonstrated that stereoscopic contours could be curved or straight, we *failed to find evidence of curved contours in homogeneous space* even when the arrays of dots that gave rise to surface depth were arranged in curved patterns.

We concluded that, within the limits imposed by interposition in ac-counting for half-image differences, stereoscopic contours would always be straight. Curved contours would appear only when the interposed surface had to have curved boundaries to account for the differences in the half-images.

To test this conclusion, we executed two additional experiments in which we attempted to manipulate the amount of structured curvature in the half-images in an effort to see whether or not we could dem-onstrate curved stereoscopic contours under circumstances short of necessity.

Studies on Curvature. In the first of these experiments we employed ma-trix targets of triangular format, as shown in Fig. 6.2. The essence of the design of the experiment may be got through a comparison of the two stereograms shown in this figure. In the top stereogram the background matrix consisted of four concentric equilateral triangles of dots. The su-perimposed circle was absent in the displays seen by our observers, but it is included in the figure to illustrate that if such an opaque circle had been interposed between an observer and the matrix pattern, certain dots would be occluded. Note that the circle occupies a slightly different position in each half-image, thus showing itself to be disparate in the crossed direction. As a consequence, some of the dots in portions of the nasal sides of the triangles in each half-image would be occluded, as well as portions of the base in both half-images.

While no circle was present in the stereograms, the selective omission of these dots produced a partially structured curve. That is, the upper right portion of the hypothetical circle had structure in the *left* half-image while the upper left portion had structure in the *right* half-image. Both half-images lent structure at the bottom. Based on the combined half-images, shown in the insert labeled L + R, there remained three un-defined regions where the "circle" crossed the homogeneous regions of the background at each apex.

The experimental question was whether or not such partial struc-turing of the shape of an interposed surface would be sufficient to lead to the perception of a contoured circular surface interposed between the observer and the background matrix.

Four additional patterns were used, with each having added another inner triangle of dots. Accordingly, the borders contained 4, 5, 6, 7, and 8 parallel arrays of dots. Only the patterns with 4 (top) and 8 (bottom) are shown in Fig. 6.2. The purpose of increases in the width of the tri-angular frame was to reduce progressively the extent to which the apical regions lent ambiguity to the shape of the interposed surface. With the 8-border pattern, the circle was structured by the matrix about its entire circumference.

In all five experimental stereograms the sides of the outer triangle subtended $3° - 16'$, the circular area subtended $1° - 30'$, and the dots

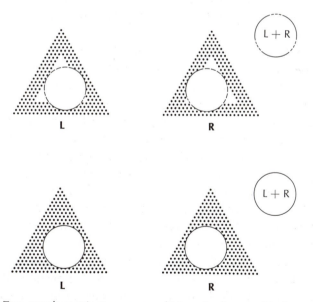

Fig. 6.2 Two sample matrix stereograms of triangular format with those dots selec-tively omitted as would have been occluded by an interposed circle with crossed disparity. See text for explanation.

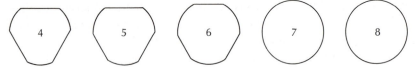

Fig. 6.3 Shapes reported and drawn by our observers when viewing triangular matrices like those shown in Fig. 6.2. The number within each shape refers to the width of the border of the triangle matrix.

subtended 4′ and were separated by 8′, center to center. Global density equaled 62 cells per 1° solid visual angle.

Ten observers who met our visual criteria viewed each stereogram twice in random order, including five control conditions in which identical half-images were used. On each trial the observer was asked to describe what he saw, and if his description included a surface in depth, he was asked to draw its shape on a protocol sheet on which a single line-drawn equilateral triangle appeared.

In terms of interposition, a perfectly circular surface could have accounted for the difference in the half-images in all five experimental stereograms, but only in the 8-border pattern did the matrix require a circle.

The results of the experiment confirmed our hypothesis based upon our earlier experiments in that, while all observers reported a sharply contoured interposed surface, the shape of the surface depended on the amount of structured curvature in the half-images.

In Fig. 6.3 may be seen the shapes reported by our observers in the five conditions. Recall that as the border width increased, the region of ambiguity at the apices declined, finally to be absent in the 8-border pattern. The only stereogram in which a single shape was not reported was the 7-border pattern. In this case the region of ambiguity at each apex was small, and observers could not easily discern whether the stereoscopic contour was straight or curved. In all other instances all observers drew the shapes shown in Fig. 6.3.

These results suggest that *straight* contours have a primacy. Despite suppositions among experimenters about Gestalt principles like "good form" and "closure," the binocular system would seem to prefer straight contours even though they make shape apparently more complex.

Our second experiment on curved stereoscopic contours will be treated briefly. The structure of the matrices in the first experiment suggested an interposed surface at least part of which was curved, but no curved continuous contours from luminance gradients were present in the half-images. Consequently, we considered the possibility that the curved structure provided by portions of the surrounding matrix might have been inadequate to effect perceptual closure. To test this notion we decided to provide additional structure by presenting disparate circles with continuous abrupt gradients except over a portion of their perimeters. Our thought was that sharply contoured partial circles available in monocular view might, upon binocular viewing, be adequate to cause the absent part of the boundary to be seen as curved.

The stereograms employed are described best by reference to Fig. 6.4, where at the top may be seen a sample pair of half-images. Note

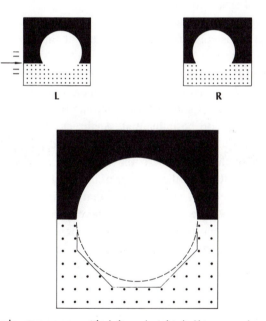

Fig. 6.4 Sample stereogram with left and right half-images showing a partially structured disparate circle. The solid shaded area in the upper half of each half-image ended at one of five locations, as indicated by the marks and arrow on the left half-image. Below is shown the result of our experiment. Whereas a completed circle (dashed line) could have accounted for the half-image differences, our observers reported the shape shown by the solid line.

that the partial circle carries a crossed disparity with reference to the solid surround. Near the bottom, the arc that would complete the circle is suggested by the selective omission of some of the dots in the matrix. The length of this arc changed as a function of the level at which the solid background ended, as shown by the marks and arrow in the left half-image. Beginning at the highest mark and moving downward, the length of the arc necessary to complete the circle was 180, 136, 100, 76, and 20°, respectively. For each of these five background conditions there were three global density levels (15, 33, and 58) in the matrix that bounded the arc.

The nature of the dilemma for the visual system is illustrated at the bottom of Fig. 6.4. In this schematic representation the arc to complete the circle is 180°, and it is shown as a dashed line against the intermediate level of global density. All those dots that would have been occluded by an interposed circle are absent.

The shape reported by our observers is shown by the solid line. The surface in depth was contoured as a 180° arc at the top and as half an octagon at the bottom.

The results of this experiment were entirely consistent with the earlier one in that *straight stereoscopic contours took precedence over curved ones,* and the presence of some curved contours based on luminance gradients did not appear to be influential. Again, curved stereoscopic contours seem limited to instances of highly structured matrix borders with fairly high global densities where the resolution of half-image differences requires curvatures in the contour of interposed surfaces.

Whereas we have been able to show that straight stereoscopic contours can cross homogeneous space, and thereby be free of any adjacent borders of dots, we have yet to find any evidence that curved stereoscopic contours can appear in homogeneous space. Their presence always is accompanied by immediately adjacent dots.

THE LOCATION OF STEREOSCOPIC CONTOURS

The treatment so far made suggests that the role of the elements (cell entries) in matrix targets is to define forms through binocular processing, forms which when disparate can lead to occurrences of stereoscopic contours. We need now to consider further whether or not the matrix elements lead to contour coding in a manner that is similar to that believed to operate with instances of abrupt luminance gradients.

If a matrix contained rows and columns of discrete elements too small in angular size and separation to be discerned individually, then there is no doubt that the perception of the edges of a central square sub-matrix would be characterized as having continuous contours. Furthermore, the perceived contours would be located so as to be spatially congruent with the luminance gradients upon which they depend.

On the other hand, when global density is degraded, so that the matrix elements become visible individually, then binocular processing can maintain sharp continuous stereoscopic contours even though a functionally continuous luminance gradient is absent. However, in such instances the location of the contour is no longer congruent with proximal matrix elements. Instead, it appears between rows and columns or in homogeneous portions of the field.

It would seem, therefore, that the role played by matrix elements in the production of contour differs in instances of high and low global density. When global density is very high, the elements produce an abrupt, continuous luminance gradient; whereas when density is low, the elements through patterning define a form the contours of which depend on stereopsis.

While the position of stereoscopic contours that arise from a particular matrix stereogram appear as spatially stable, there is nevertheless a range of positions that can satisfy the interposition requirement. For example, when global density is low so that the matrix appears coarse, as in Fig. 6.5, there is a rather marked loss of precision in contour localization.

At the top of Fig. 6.5 are shown the left and right half-images of a dot matrix with a central square of homogeneity displaced so as to achieve a modest crossed disparity. Below is a three-dimensional projection to illustrate how an interposed opaque square of specific size and location is adequate to produce the half-images at the top. For the sake of simplicity, only the right eye is treated by illustrating the solid angle of occlusion from the optical node (0′). What should be noted is the fact that the relative coarseness of the matrix texture lends ambiguity to the size and location of the interposed surface. To illustrate this ambiguity, consider the left vertical edge of the interposed surface.

The tolerable positions for this boundary lie between the lines denoted as *minimum* and *maximum* boundary, for only between these two limits can the left edge of the interposed surface produce the selective occlu-

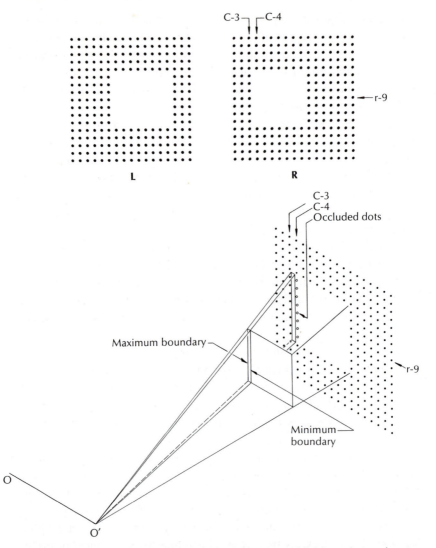

Fig. 6.5   An illustration of the ambiguity in the location of the boundaries of an interposed surface that can account for half-image differences. See text for an explanation.

sion required by the half-image. In like manner, similar limits apply for each of the other three sides of the interposed surface, and with each there is a triangular *wedge of ambiguity,* the width of which at the plane of the matrix is determined by the inter-dot space.

It follows, therefore, that as global density rises, with the texture becoming finer, the precision with which the interposed surface is defined also improves. In the extreme, when the texture is so fine as to be functionally homogeneous in brightness, then there is only a single solution to the interposition problem. If stereoscopic contours are present, they cannot be discerned because their locations are congruent with the contours arising from the abruptness of the gradient produced by the high global density of the matrix.

Size versus Disparity Solutions to Interposition. The regular appearance of sharp and stable stereoscopic contours with medium and low global density matrices with disparate forms raises several interesting questions regarding the manner in which the binocular system handles the interposition problem in the face of the wedge of ambiguity. Based upon our discussion of the wedges, we can now indicate briefly some of the likely solutions that meet the requirements of interposition.

Obviously, any quadrilateral whose sides fit within the wedges of ambiguity would satisfy the interposition requirement. To simplify this discussion, consider the ninth row (r-9) labeled in Fig. 6.5. This row, as seen by the right and left eye, is illustrated in Fig. 6.6. At the top of the figure (A) is shown the position of the lateral edges of an interposed surface as projected upon the matrix when the surface has *maximum* width. This arrangement may be contrasted with that shown below (B) where the position of the projected lateral edges corresponds to a surface of *minimum* width. In other words, in A the surface would be defined by a quadrilateral whose edges were congruent with the maximum boundaries of the wedges of ambiguity, whereas in B the surface would be defined by a quadrilateral whose edges were congruent with the minimum boundaries of the wedges of ambiguity. In both instances the disparity (η) of the lateral edges, shown by the arrows, is constant. Therefore, the perceptual difference between solutions of maximum and minimum size should not influence perceived depth of the interposed surface inasmuch as disparity remains constant. However, the position of the stereoscopic contours would be different. In A the contours should lie close to the bounding dots of the surrounding matrix, while in B the contours should appear displaced toward the center of the surface, with the displacement equal to the inter-dot space when projected back upon the matrix.

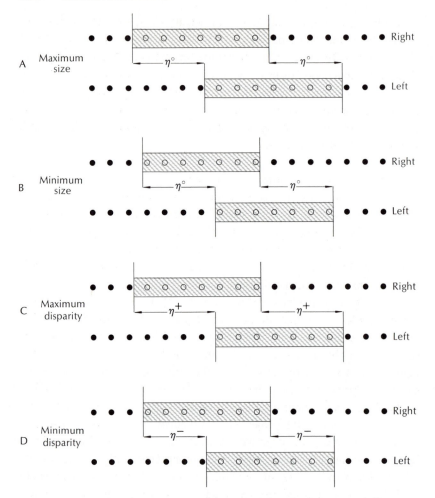

Fig. 6.6 An analysis of possible binocular solutions to ambiguity as applied to a single row (r-9, see Fig. 6.5). In A and B, disparity (η) is held constant, but the size of the interposed surface is changed; whereas in C and D size is constant, but disparity is changed. See text for explanation.

Figure 6.6 also illustrates another possible solution. In A and B the disparity (η) of the lateral edges remains constant while size changes. However, in C and D size remains constant while disparity changes. Consider the arrangement shown in C. For the right eye, the positions of the lateral edges of the interposed surface differ with respect to the wedges of ambiguity. The left edge corresponds to the maximum boundary, while the right edge corresponds to the minimum boundary. For the left eye the reverse applies. The consequence is that the size of the interposed surface is intermediate, but disparity is at a maximum. The arrangement shown in D does not change the size of the interposed surface, but disparity reaches a minimum.

The perceptual difference between solutions of maximum and minimum disparity would show itself as a difference in depth of the interposed surface relative to the more distant matrix. The location of the stereoscopic contours when projected back upon the matrix should be invariant in the arrangements illustrated in C and D. The *binocular* direction of the lateral contours should be such as to make them appear to bisect the inter-dot space.

We executed an experiment in order to determine whether the binocular system favored maximum-minimum size or maximum-minimum disparity. The stereograms consisted of square dot matrices $4° - 20'$ on a side in which each cell contained a dark dot ($5'$ of arc) except for a square central region of homogeneity $1°$ on a side. In the experimental stereograms the central region was displaced in the half-images to achieve a $30'$ crossed disparity. In all, three different global densities were used (58, 33, and 15 cells per $1°$ solid visual angle), and for simplicity we shall refer to them as *high, medium,* and *low* density. The right half-images of the three stereograms are shown in Fig. 6.7. Note that the largest square that would fill the homogeneous region without occluding any dots is the same size for all three global densities, and its location within each matrix also is the same. It is in this sense that all stereograms had disparities of the central homogeneous region equal to $30'$ of arc.

Ten observers who met our visual criteria viewed each of these stereograms five times in random order. On each trial the observer was asked to locate the vertical stereoscopic contours relative to the inter-dot space. In this way we could gain information regarding maximum *versus* minimum size as the preferred solution. In addition, on each trial observers were asked to judge the difference in depth between the planes of the contoured surface and the more distant matrix. The width of the matrix was used as a modulus of 10, and observers were asked to report the depth difference in scale units relative to this modulus. Depth judgments

Fig. 6.7   Three right half-images of a square dot matrix (2° solid angle) with a 1° central square of homogeneity that carried 30′ of crossed disparity. From top to bottom, global density was 58, 33, and 15 cells per 1° solid visual angle.

were obtained to gain information regarding maximum *versus* minimum disparity as the preferred solution. It is important to bear in mind that in the *high* density condition, the inter-dot space was so small that the difference between maximum and minimum disparity was negligible. On the other hand, the difference between the maximum and minimum disparity in the *low* density condition was enough to produce discriminably different depth planes for the contoured surface.

Our observers reported that the position of the stereoscopic contours appeared to bisect the inter-dot space, thus suggesting that neither maximum nor minimum size was preferred in structuring the interposed surface. Instead, size considerations gave way to the disparity dimension. As shown in Fig. 6.8, the depth difference between the plane of the contoured surface and the matrix increased as a function of increasing global density. Stated differently, the homogeneous region was coded as having *less* crossed disparity as matrix density was reduced despite the fact that the region of homogeneity occupied precisely the same locus in the half-images in all three density conditions.

These depth data indicate that when half-images of dot matrices require an interposed surface to account for their differences, the binocular system sets the lateral boundaries of the surface in such a way as to minimize disparity. In terms of Fig. 6.6, the preferred solution is D because no other one can account for the reduction in depth difference as a function of global density and the projected location of the stereoscopic contours.

Application of the logic illustrated in Fig. 6.6D to the particular patterns used in our experiment allowed us to calculate exactly the reduc-

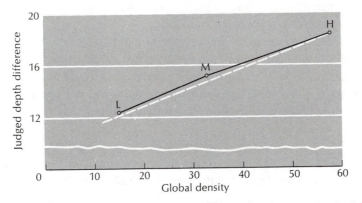

Fig. 6.8 Mean judged depth difference (solid line) with a constant level of form disparity as a function of global density. The dashed line represents theoretical calculation of depth. See text for basis of calculation.

tion in disparity across the three densities which would occur if the system minimized disparity. From other experiments directed toward establishing a functional relationship between disparity and perceived depth, we then determined the depth difference that should have obtained for the high, medium, and low density stereograms. This function is given as the dashed line in Fig. 6.8, and it may be seen that the mean depth differences based on our observer reports lie close to the calculated values. We conclude, then, that the binocular system is economical in that the surface which is structured to account for half-image differences never possesses more disparity than is just necessary to do the accounting.

STEREOSCOPICALLY CONTOURED CORNERS

The experiments undertaken to determine the conditions that give rise to stereoscopic contours have so far in our treatment avoided circumstances that would require a stereoscopically contoured corner to appear in the absence of a corner structured by the matrix. In the standard matrix patterns we have used in many experiments, the disparate and homogeneous central square form does produce stereoscopically contoured corners, as well as straight edges, but they are bounded on the outside by dots of the background matrix. Indeed, even in the patterns shown in Fig. 6.1C and D the structure of the matrix at the projected corners of the interposed surface may have played a critical role in the determination of the shape of the planar surface despite the fact that the straight stereoscopic contours appeared in a homogeneous field.

In order to examine the importance of matrix structure in the formation of stereoscopic corners, we executed two experiments with dot matrix patterns in which a square interposed surface could account for the half-image differences, but the matrix patterns did not contain dots in the regions of the matrix where the projected corner(s) of the interposed surface would appear.

In Fig. 6.9 are shown samples of the stereograms employed in the first experiment. The shaded area in A was absent in the stereograms viewed by our observers, but it is included to illustrate that a square with a modest crossed disparity could account for the half-image differences. The same applies to the stereograms shown in B and C. There are two things to note. First, the vertical right stereoscopic contour in A, B, and

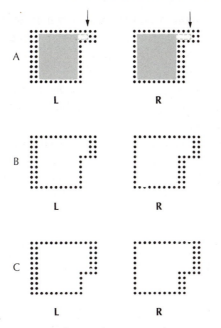

Fig. 6.9   Sample stereograms used to study stereoscopic contours at the upper right corner. The shaded area in A was absent in the displays actually employed, but it is included here to show that an interposed square could account for the half-image differences.

C must cross a homogeneous region of 6, 18, and 30′ of arc, respectively, in order to make the upper right corner of a square. Second, if the perceived surface took the shape of a key, that is, if it included the area shown by the dashed lines, then the surface could not appear in a single plane because the extreme right boundary (arrows) carried no disparity with reference to the matrix dots, whereas the remainder of the edges did carry a disparity.

The task for our observers was to describe and then draw the shape of any surface seen in depth. With the patterns A and B of Fig. 6.9, all ten observers always reported a square surface in depth, but in pattern C the shape was, for the most part, indeterminate. The left and bottom edges were well localized as in front of the matrix, but the top and right edges faded toward the critical upper right corner. Judgments on the distinctness of the upper right corner, as compared to the upper left, suggested no difference in patterns A and B but a very marked difference in C. In the latter instance the right vertical stereoscopic contour tended not to be seen as crossing the 30′ gap to form a corner with the top. Accordingly, we concluded that stereoscopically contoured corners could occur without full structure from the matrix provided that the angular distance over which the contours ran across homogeneous fields to form corners was 18′ of arc, or less.

In the second experiment on corners we employed different stereograms designed to remove matrix structure at all four corners of the interposed surface. Figure 6.10 illustrates the nature of these stereograms. In all, we used six stereograms, with the reduction in corner structure il-

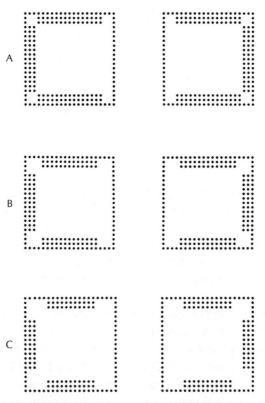

Fig. 6.10 Sample stereograms used to study stereoscopic contours at the four corners of an interposed surface.

lustrated in A, B, and C continued in E, F, and G (E, F, and G not shown in figure).

As before, the task for our observers was to describe and then draw the shape of any surface that appeared in depth. In addition, observers also judged both the clarity of the stereoscopic corners according to the contour scaling technique and the amount of depth that separated the plane of the surface and the plane of the matrix. The depth modulus of 10 was defined by the width of the matrix.

Ten naive observers trained in contour scaling viewed each of the six experimental stereograms three times in random order with the single restriction that the same stereogram could not repeat on consecutive trials.

With regard to the shape of the interposed surface, stereograms A and B always led to reports of a square in depth. However, the uniformity of the reports and stability of the percepts both declined with patterns C through G. For example, with C and D, some observers reported the "corners" as rounded while others reported them as straight but clipped at 45° off the vertical. No consistent percepts arose from patterns F and G.

Mean judgments of contour clarity at the corners and surface depth are shown in Fig. 6.11. Recall that a value of 5 on the contour scale signifies a sharp edge whereas 1 signifies no detectable edge. The clarity of the stereoscopic edges at the corners in patterns A and B was as good as any we have obtained, even with our standard patterns with corner dots present. Clearly, the patterns D through G were inadequate to any stable perceptual organization. While we expected that our observers would be unable to see corners in all six stereograms, we were surprised to discover that the depth between the surface and the matrix declined as it did, for even in pattern G there appeared to us to be ample disparity information along the central portions of the two vertical boundaries.

In this experiment, the stereoscopic contours remained sharp and formed corners only when they crossed a homogeneous region of the field not greater than 18′ of arc (pattern B). Furthermore, when the interposed surface was sharply contoured and stable, so also was its position in space stable and predictable from geometry. However, as the structure of the matrix in patterns C through G allowed more and more ambiguity to the shape of an appropriate surface that could account for

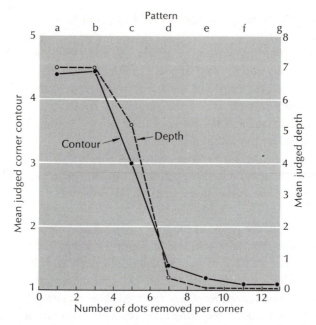

Fig. 6.11   Mean judged corner contour (solid line, read against left ordinate) where 1 = no contour and 5 = sharp contour, and mean judged depth (dashed line, read against right ordinate) as a function of the amount of matrix structure at the corners.

the half-image differences, the clarity of the stereoscopic contours declined quickly, and the definition of form was insufficient to allow disparity coding.

LUMINANCE AND TRANSLUCENCY

Our interest in establishing the determinants of form disparity and the generation of stereoscopic contours led us to the several tests of interposition that have been treated so far in this chapter. To explore further certain aspects of binocular organization related to form disparity, we executed additional experiments with targets in which contour disparities were absent but luminance disparities were present. One experiment utilized matrix targets, and the remainder utilized solid patterns. Both types were conceived in the context of interposition.

In preliminary work we learned that when observers viewed stereograms like the one shown in Fig. 6.12, they reported the appearance of a sharply contoured interposed surface that had the property of translucency rather than opacity. Note that both half-images contain three border squares of dots with perfect binocular correlation and no disparity due to dot location.

The appearance of a contoured translucent surface is explicable in terms of interposition, but there remain certain anomalies. Based upon our earlier studies, it seemed likely that the central square region of homogeneity would not appear in depth because it occupied the same locus in each half-image relative to the surrounding matrix. Indeed, in many of our control conditions in other experiments we had used patterns like the one shown in Fig. 6.12 except that all dots had a single luminance level. Under these circumstances our observers never reported depth or stereoscopic contours. Clearly, selective changes in luminance of some of the dots was sufficient to cause important changes in perceptual organization and in the binocular abstraction of form.

Inasmuch as the two inner vertical nasal columns in each half-image had a luminance greater than the remaining dots (but less than the background), if brightness disparity were sufficient to stereopsis then when the patterns were in binocular register the critical columns of dots should have been seen in depth. They were not seen in depth: instead, all dots appeared in a single plane although the critical columns appeared slightly brighter than other columns and rows, thus indicating binocular brightness averaging.

We assumed that if the luminance of the critical columns was reduced so as to match the remaining dots, thereby making the half-images iden-

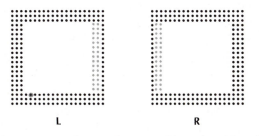

L   R

Fig. 6.12 Sample stereogram for translucency with perfect binocular correlation and no disparity based on dot location. The two pairs of inner nasal columns had a higher luminance level than the others, and when the matrix was in binocular register these columns resulted in a luminance dichopticity.

tical, then observers would report a two-dimensional target without either surface depth or stereoscopic contour. On the other hand, if the luminance of the critical columns was raised so as to match the background, then we assumed that observers would report a typical three-dimensional target that included an opaque interposed surface bounded by stereoscopic contours. This latter circumstance, of course, is no different than omitting some nasal columns.

Reports from our observers during preliminary work made it clear that they locked on the matrix patterns as a whole so that none of the dots carried any disparity based upon location. The nasal columns of like luminance in the half-images carried too much disparity to allow their binocular combination based on a luminance match. Had that happened, the remainder of the matrix would have been grandly misaligned in binocular view.

In terms of interposition, if one were to imagine viewing a three-border square of identical dots through a filmy surface of appropriate size and location, then it becomes plain that, while all dots would remain visible, those dots seen through the film would appear different in brightness. The direction of the change in brightness is influenced by the nature of the filmy interposed surface. For example, if the filmy surface acted like a neutral density filter, then the dots seen behind and through it would appear as dark, or probably darker, than other dots. However, if the filmy surface were illuminated, then the opposite could obtain. While there are a number of interesting observations to make about luminance differences in binocular organization, some of which we shall treat in a later chapter, we shall focus here upon the role of luminance differences in binocular form abstraction.

The left eye patterns shown in Fig. 6.13 serve to point out some relevant comparisons among stereograms with different levels of luminance in the critical nasal columns (see arrows). In pattern A the critical columns match the other dots, and when this pattern is combined stereoscopically with the right half-image, neither surface depth nor stereoscopic contours should be seen. In pattern C the critical columns match the background, and are therefore invisible, and when this pattern is combined stereoscopically with the right half-image, both surface depth and stereoscopic contours should be seen. The main difference between patterns A and C is that the homogeneous central region carries a dis-

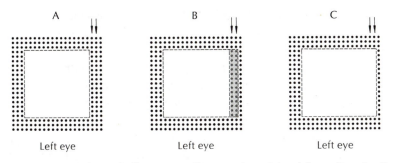

Fig. 6.13 Three left eye half-images to illustrate the origin of form disparity. See text for an explanation.

parity relative to the matrix only in C, and as we have shown in other experiments, this is both a necessary and sufficient condition for planar depth and sharp contours.

In pattern B the critical columns have a luminance level between the remaining dots and the background, and when this pattern is combined stereoscopically with the right half-image, observers reported a translucent contoured surface in depth. For depth to occur we must assume that the binocular system abstracted a disparate form. The fact that the critical dots in B were seen as co-planar with the others suggests that they were grouped perceptually as part of the matrix. Bear in mind that the geometrically corresponding columns in the right half-image did not have a higher luminance, so that the problem for the visual system might be phrased as follows: Why do the two inner columns of dots on the right side of the pattern appear lighter to the left eye and not to the right eye? A similar dichopticity occurs for the two inner columns on the left side of the pattern, but the luminance levels are reversed at the eyes. As mentioned, an interposed translucent surface could account for the half-image differences, but from the perspective of form disparity, the appearance of such a surface would require that the area defined by the critical columns (shaded portion in Fig. 6.13B) would have to be interpreted as belonging to the central homogeneous square. Had the surface area defined by the critical columns been interpreted as part of the surface upon which the matrix dots appeared, then there could have been no form disparity, and insofar as depth is concerned, the percept of B would have been like that of A rather than C.

Our hypothesis was that the introduction of luminance dichopticity might be sufficient to uncouple the organization of the critical dots from the surface upon which they were seen. That is, the dots of the nasal columns would be grouped as a part of the overall dot matrix while the background area of the same columns would be grouped as part of the central region of homogeneity rather than as part of the matrix background. Once organized in this way, an interposition interpretation leads to the prediction that the depth plane of the translucent surface (pattern B) would be identical to that of the opaque surface (pattern C) because form disparity would be the same in both instances. Moreover, variations in luminance level of the critical columns should not lead to any change in depth localization of the translucent surface because form disparity would be constant.

Matrix Targets. To test our hypothesis we prepared nine experimental stereograms with a three-border square format like the one shown in Fig. 6.12. Each half-image matrix was made by punching out holes in a very light gray paper with an especially machined template. Thereafter, the punched matrix was mounted on a dark gray paper and bound in glass for display in a prism stereoscope. Except for the dots in the critical nasal columns, the luminance of all the other dots and the background was 0.5 and 18 ft-L, respectively.

In a pilot experiment observers were asked to generate with neutral gray chips an equal brightness scale by the method of multiple bisection. The ends were anchored at 0.5 and 18 ft-L. In this way a nine-point scale was gained, and these grays were used beneath the critical columns in the experimental stereograms. Note that when the low anchor was used (stereogram E1), all dots had the same luminance, whereas when the high anchor was used (stereogram E9) the dots in the critical columns had a luminance equal to the background.

Ten observers trained in our contour scaling method and in depth magnitude judgments saw each of the nine stereograms in random order three times, and on each trial an observer had to assign a number to the contours of any surfaces seen in depth and to judge the depth difference between the surface and the matrix relative to a modulus of 10 defined as the width of the outer square matrix. Further, observers were asked to describe the quality of any surfaces seen in depth.

The results of the experiment were not entirely consistent with our expectations insofar as surface depth was concerned. While a surface with translucent properties was reported for slides E2 through E8, the depth difference of the surface relative to the plane of the matrix increased with the luminance of the critical columns. We expected no depth in slide E1 because the half-images were in every way identical. However, in all other stereograms we expected the surface to appear in the same depth plane. The results were otherwise, as shown in Fig. 6.14. The fact that the depth difference between the translucent surface and the matrix increased with the luminance of the critical columns suggests that the form-defining process must have interacted with disparity coding. At present we are unable to conceptualize how this could happen. The projected position on the half-image matrices of an interposed translucent surface able to account for the half-image differences would have been invariant for stereograms E2 through E8. Accordingly, its depth plane should also have been invariant. Indeed, our calculations of the nine levels of disparity that would have had to operate in order to give rise to the depth function of Fig. 6.14 indicate that the requirements of inter-

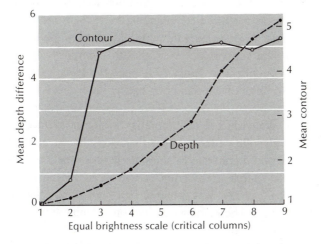

Fig. 6.14 Mean depth difference (dashed line, read against left ordinate) and mean contour (solid line, read against right ordinate) of a translucent surface as a function of the brightness of the critical nasal columns. On the equal brightness scale, 1 and 9 equaled 0.5 and 18.0 ft-L, respectively. The intermediate scale values were obtained through multiple bisection. See text.

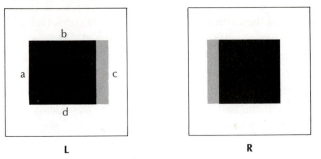

Fig. 6.15 Sample stereogram with homogeneous areas that leads to the appearance of an interposed translucent rectangle when viewed stereoscopically.

position could not have been met. That is, the only freedom for projected positions of the vertical boundaries of the interposed surface lie in the wedge of ambiguity, and the amount of disparity *change* between minimum and maximum locations was not sufficient to account for the obtained depth function. Perhaps the depth data can be interpreted as the effect of brightness disparity as it interacted with form disparity.

As for stereoscopic contours, our results were consistent with our expectation. Note in Fig. 6.14 that no contours were observed for stereogram E1, whereas for those stereograms that led to translucent (E3 – E8) and opaque (E9) surfaces in depth, the stereoscopic contours were sharp. These data support our view that the sharpness of stereoscopic contours is independent of depth (*1*), once the plane of the surface is discriminably different from that of its background.

Solid Targets. We wished to determine if translucent surfaces also could be obtained with solid patterns rather than dot patterns and if the depth of the surface would continue to show itself as a function of luminance dichopticity. A sample stereogram is shown in Fig. 6.15. The dark square (0.5 ft-L) always was centered in a light square field (18 ft-L) in each half-image. The nasal wings had one of nine luminance values, as previously described.

Each of ten observers trained in depth magnitude estimation saw each of the nine stereograms three times. On each trial the observer was asked to estimate the depth difference between the surface seen in depth and the plane of the field in relation to a modulus of 10 defined as the width of the field. The angular extent of the modulus in this experiment and in the matrix experiment was the same (2°). No reports of contour were sought inasmuch as those present were based on abrupt luminance gradients.

We assumed that when the wing luminance matched the central square (E1), thus forming a uniform rectangle with disparity, the percept would be of an opaque rectangle interposed between the observer and the lighter square field; and when the wing luminance matched the field (E9), we assumed that the percept would consist of a dark square seen in the plane of the field.

As with the matrix targets, the solid patterns E2 through E8 led to the perception of contoured surfaces described as translucent, with the amount of depth separation from the field related to the luminance of the wings. However, in the present experiment the function was negatively accelerated, a shown in Fig. 6.16 (Experiment 1). Note that the numbering of the abscissa in Fig. 6.16 is reversed when compared to Fig. 6.14. The numbers on the brightness scale refer to identical luminances in both figures, but in the matrix experiment the lowest level led

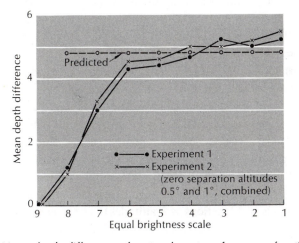

Fig. 6.16 Mean depth difference of a translucent surface as a function of the brightness of the nasal wings of stereograms like those shown in Fig. 6.15 (Experiment 1) and certain conditions with stereograms like those described by Fig. 6.17 (Experiment 2). On the equal brightness scale, 1 and 9 equaled 0.5 and 18.0 ft-L, respectively.

to identical half-images, whereas in the present experiment the highest level led to identical half-images.

In stereograms E2 through E8 the half-images can be accounted for if an interposed translucent surface is assumed. However, there is no reason to think that the location of the surface would change with the luminance of the wings because the contours that define the translucent surface are unaltered in location in all of these displays. Consider Fig. 6.15 anew. The contours labeled a, b, c, d represent the projected edges of the rectangular translucent surface, and while they carry a crossed disparity relative to the field, the amount of disparity is constant even as the luminance of the nasal wing is changed. Accordingly, if contour disparity were the only factor operating, stereograms E1 through E8 should have resulted in a constant depth difference shown in Fig. 6.16 as the dashed line. Stereogram E9 had no disparity and so no depth occurred.

Multiple correlated t-tests indicated that the mean depth differences for stereograms E1 through E6 were not significantly different one from the other. Stereograms E7 and E8 seem to represent a transition where the coding of disparity is compromised by the small luminance difference between the wings and the background. However, it should be pointed out that the boundaries of the wings in these two stereograms were easily discerned, thus leaving us somewhat uncertain as to why the shift of the surface into depth was attenuated.

As a further test of interposition, we executed a second experiment with solid targets. The conditions are best described by reference to Fig. 6.17. We utilized the same nine luminance levels for the wings, but, in addition, the wing was located in one of three positions and had one of three altitudes. The adjacent boundaries of the central dark square and the wing were congruent (zero separation) or separated by 5 or 10′ of arc, and for each of these three locations the altitude was 0.5, 1.0, and 1.5° visual angle. Thus there were 81 experimental stereograms (9 luminance levels × 3 locations × 3 altitudes). The nine stereograms with 0 separation and 1° altitude represented a replication of our first experiment with solid targets.

Our assumption was that interposition of a translucent surface could account for the half-image differences only in those stereograms in which the wing was contiguous to the central square *and* in which the

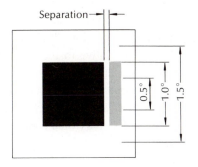

Fig. 6.17   Left eye half-image to illustrate manipulations in Experiment 2 with solid targets. Separation was 0, 5, and 10′ of arc and for each of these conditions the altitude of the wing was 0.5, 1.0, and 1.5° visual angle.

altitude of the wing was equal to or less than the altitude of the central square.

The same ten observers served in this experiment, and on each trial each was instructed to give an estimate of the depth difference between the interposed surface and the plane of the field, if any, according to the same modulus used in the first experiment. In addition, protocol was recorded on observer descriptions of what they saw.

In all stereograms in which the wings were separated from the central square, observers failed to report an interposed surface. Instead they reported that the wings themselves seemed to float off the plane of the field but their location in space was unstable and changing. This report is characteristic of monocular stimulation during binocular vision. The separation precluded any stable organization of the contours of the wings and the central square into a single disparate form.

With zero separation, surface depth was reported for wing altitudes of 0.5 and 1° visual angle but not for the 1.5° altitude condition. In the latter condition the wings were reported to float. Note that there is no surface of any shape which, if interposed, could account for the half-image differences in the 1.5° altitude stereograms. Accordingly, we concluded that boundary congruence between the wings and the central square *and* the requirements of interposition both are necessary conditions for the appearance of translucent surfaces.

The remaining two cells of the design (zero separation, altitudes of 0.5 and 1.0°) led to percepts of translucent surfaces, the depths of which were a function of the luminance level of the wings, as shown in Fig. 6.16 (Experiment 2). The depth function obtained in the 0.5° altitude condition was slightly depressed relative to the 1° condition, but insignificantly so. Consequently, they were combined.

In the 0.5° altitude stereograms with zero separation, observers reported stereoscopic contours that crossed the 1° central dark square. Here, then, is another instance of stereoscopic contours that cross homogeneous regions of a visual target.

Induced Brightness Change and Translucency. If one were to ignore for the moment the black vertical lines in the stereograms A and B of Fig. 6.18, then the dot patterns in both lead to the perception of an opaque

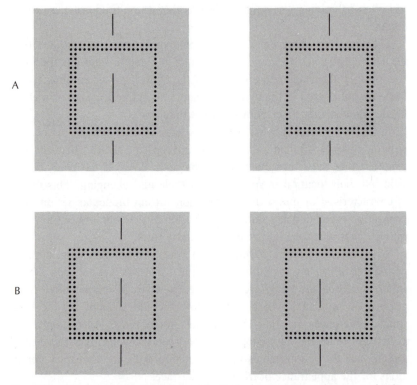

Fig. 6.18 Stereograms A and B have identical matrix patterns, but in A the line segments carry no disparity with reference to the outer square of dots, whereas in B they carry twice the disparity of the central homogeneous square.

interposed square with sharp stereoscopic contours because the central region of homogeneity carries a crossed disparity. However, when the black lines are added, the quality of the interposed surface in stereogram A changes to translucency. The reason seems to be due to the fact that the line within the matrix, having no disparity with reference to the outer square of dots, must be seen through the interposed surface. In terms of interposition, the surface must be at once *opaque* to account for the selective occlusion of the inner vertical nasal columns of dots and *transparent* (or translucent) to account for the appearance of the central line segment seen behind and through the surface. Observers reported translucency.

In stereogram B the line carries twice the disparity of the central form so that no conflict of interposition cues occurs. In this case, observers reported the three lines in a near plane behind which appeared a contoured opaque square with the dot matrix still more distant. Inasmuch as several observers noted that when viewing stereogram A the central line segment appeared different from the upper and lower lines not seen through the surface, we undertook an experiment to determine if the translucent surface produced by the paradox of interposition would result in a systematic change in the brightness of the central line segment.

Beside the stereograms A and B shown in Fig. 6.18, we added two more: C, which was in every way like A except that the missing nasal column of dots was added to each half-image, thus producing identical half-images; and D, in which the matrices were removed so that the three line segments appeared alone within the field.

When present, the matrix subtended 1° solid angle, and the luminance of the dots and the lines was 2.6 ft-L while the background field had a luminance of 7.0 ft-L. Each line segment had an altitude of 20' of arc and one of three widths (2, 4, and 5.9' of arc). In all there were 12 stereograms (4 patterns × 3 linewidths).

The targets were viewed in a prism stereoscope, and on each trial each of eight observers had to assign a number from 1 to 10 to the brightness of the central line segment, where 1 was defined as a gray equal to the field and 10 was defined as the blackness of the upper and lower referent lines.

The results of the experiment may be stated simply. In stereograms B, C, and D the mean blackness of the central line segment was 10, 9.8, and 9.9, respectively. Recall that in none of these patterns was there any reason to expect a change in the appearance of the central line segment, and none was found. Pattern B served as a control for the effects of the presence of the surrounding matrix when form disparity was present, and pattern C served the same function when form disparity was absent. Pattern D served as a control for any effects induced by the presence of a surrounding matrix.

To our surprise, stereogram A led to a systematic change in the brightness of the central line segment, as seen through the interposed surface. The mean blackness judgments of our eight observers are shown in Fig. 6.19, and each point is based on 24 observations (8 observers × 3 replications). Note that when the thickest line (5.9′) was viewed through the interposed surface, its appearance was no different than it was in the other conditions. However, as the line subtended less and less

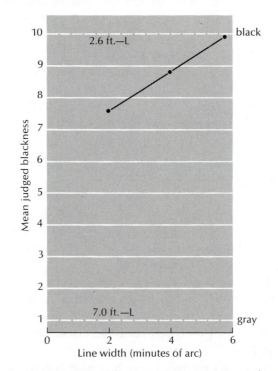

Fig. 6.19   Mean judged blackness of the central line segment seen through a stereo-scopically induced translucent surface as a function of the angular width of the line.

width, the interposed surface tended to wash out its blackness so that it appeared grayer. Of the 12 means (4 patterns × 3 line widths) only those for stereogram A with linewidths of 2 and 4' of arc were significantly different from each other and all others, as determined by t-test.

We concluded that surfaces brought into depth through binocular form disparity can be made to change from ones of opacity to ones of translucency when patterns contain conflicting interposition information, and that objects viewed through such surfaces can undergo perceptual changes in appearance at least insofar as brightness is concerned. Unfortunately, at the time this experiment was conducted we had not yet devised our contour scaling procedure, but there remains the possibility that the sharpness of the contours of the central line segment might also undergo change.

References

1. Lawson, R. B., and Gulick, W. L. Stereopsis and anomalous contour. *Vision Res.,* 1967, *7,* 271-297.

7

Stereoscopic Organizations

We begin this chapter with a caution regarding the use of dichoptic stimulation in stereoscopic vision. Thereafter, we report several experiments on perceptual organization in three-dimensional space. In particular, we consider, first, the applicability of the *adjacency principle* to stereopsis, with special attention given to simultaneous brightness contrast and the Ponzo illusion. This is followed by a brief treatment of three-dimensional figural aftereffects. The chapter concludes with a discussion of contour and surface location differences between crossed and uncrossed disparity.

DICHOPTICITY

Since the invention of the stereoscope by Wheatstone in 1838, the instrument has been utilized in hundreds of experiments aimed at discovering the principles that govern binocular vision. While investigations of depth perception have been central to its use, the stereoscope also has provided a convenient means to study many other binocular phenomena, such as fusion, suppression, rivalry, and color mixing.

One of the frequent questions that has been asked relates to the determination of the site within the visual system where a specific binocular process is believed to occur: That is, to what extent can a perceptual phenomenon be understood by retinal, as contrasted with central, processes?

In most instances where an answer to this question was sought, experimenters have used targets comprised of half-images that were dichoptic in the extreme. As examples, in studies of binocular suppression, a horizontal line might be presented to the left eye while a vertical one is presented to the right eye; and in studies of color mixing, a red target to one eye might have to be fused with a green one to the other eye. Surely, these two examples represent extreme levels of dichopticity, but such usage is by no means occasional.

There is, of course, some reason to suppose that dichoptic stimulation can assist an experimenter in his quest for the principles of binocular vision (see Chapter 9) and the site of the physiological processes responsible for a given phenomenon; yet when dichopticity is of the sort that deviates significantly from that which can occur naturally, then there arises in our minds some doubt as to the usefulness of the resulting observations, even though the visual system may achieve some sort of a perceptual solution to aberrant stimulation. We argue that the usefulness of information gained through studies with dichoptic stimulation declines as the contrived half-images depart more and more from patterns of stimulation that the visual system normally encounters, or could normally encounter.

The historical use of markedly different half-images may very well be the source of many of the conflicting results found in the literature with regard to the sites of origin, peripheral or central, that have been proposed to account for data. With this caution in mind, we turn now to consider the influence of stereoscopic depth upon perceptual organization.

Depth Adjacency

There is little doubt that the spatial relations among visual objects in a two-dimensional space influence their perceptual organization. This observation, described long ago by Gestalt psychologists as the *proximity principle,* recently has been the subject of study by Gogel and his associates. Whereas the proximity principle was applied primarily to phenomena of perceptual grouping, Gogel has attempted to extend the generality of proximity to include other aspects of perceptual organization; and in an effort to note his claim to greater generality, Gogel has introduced the phrase *adjacency principle* (7). According to him, the effectiveness of cues between two objects in determining their perceived characteristics and organization is inversely related to the separation of the objects in space. In his early formulation of this principle, separation was considered only in a two-dimensional space, with the consequence that measures of separation between objects could be expressed simply in terms of visual angle. Recently, however, Gogel has argued that the adjacency principle also operates in three-dimensional space. If so, then visual angle becomes an inappropriate metric for separation inasmuch as the directional separation of targets can be maintained, more or less, while depth adjacency undergoes change through the introduction of retinal disparity. Strictly, of course, the adjacency of imaged targets at the retina does change slightly with disparity, but these changes are quite small compared to those they produce in the stereoscopic location of the targets. We shall write more about this matter a little later in this chapter.

The relative independence of two-dimensional separation and depth separation invites inquiry as to how best to measure adjacency. It seems to us that the only single metric applicable to adjacency in three dimensions is a psychophysical measure of perceived space, and that is the metric we have employed.

ADJACENCY AND BRIGHTNESS CONTRAST

Simultaneous brightness contrast affords an opportunity to test whether or not the adjacency principle operates in the third dimension as it does in two-dimensional space. A gray square of constant luminance (test field) is known to appear darker in the presence of a second target of higher luminance (induction field) than it does when viewed alone, provided that the two fields lie in a common depth plane. In general, the contrast effect decreases as the two fields become ever more separated (25). Suppose, however, that the arrangement of the two fields is changed so that the centers of both fields lie along a single binocular line of sight, with the smaller test field surrounded by the induction field. Through disparity, the two fields can be separated in depth. If the level of simultaneous brightness contrast is independent of depth separation, then one would have to conclude that Gogel's adjacency principle failed to show its influence in the third dimension. Moreover, such a conclusion would suggest that the contrast effect is probably of retinal origin. On the other hand, if brightness contrast declined with depth separation, as it is known to do with horizontal and vertical separations, then Gogel's position would be sustained. Too, one would suspect that the contrast effect was, at least in part, of post-retinal origin.

The results of several experiments on brightness contrast as a function of depth adjacency have been reported, but the findings are contradictory. Whereas Gogel and Mershon (8, 24) found that simultaneous brightness contrast declined very nearly as a linear function of perceived depth separation, Lie (20, 21, 22) reported that contrast was independent of depth separation.

There were a number of procedural differences between the two sets of experiments, any one of which might account for the contradictory findings. Of these procedural differences, one strikes us as especially critical. Gogel and Mershon derived their measure of contrast from numerical judgments assigned by their observers according to a previously learned brightness scale. Lie, by contrast, used a traditional matching procedure rather than a memorial scale.

Apart from the particular differences between these studies, there are two additional factors that one encounters when a stereoscope serves as the apparatus in experiments on brightness contrast. First, the use of different levels of disparity between test and induction fields as a method to obtain changes in their depth separation means, as we mentioned earlier, that two-dimensional adjacency in the half-images of a stereogram cannot remain absolutely constant. Second, a target of constant angular size undergoes a change in perceived size as a function of disparity (see Chapter 10, p. 258). Because two-dimensional adjacency and relative field size both have been shown to influence simultaneous brightness contrast (25), it becomes important to take the two factors into account.

Aware of the confounding of disparity and two-dimensional adjacency, Mershon (23) has shown that the decline in brightness contrast which he obtained with depth separation cannot be attributed simply to the lateral displacement of his fields that accompanied his disparity manipulation. However, he did not consider the matter of changes in perceived size.

It was in the context of the treatment presented thus far in this chapter that we designed an experiment to determine the effect of depth adjacency on brightness contrast. The changes in two-dimensional adjacency between test and induction fields brought about in the half-images by

our disparity manipulation were relatively easy to assess by having observers see a number of control stereograms in which test field displacements of equal magnitude and direction occurred simultaneously in both
half-images so that disparity was absent.

With regard to the second factor, that of changes in perceived size as
a function of disparity, there is no way in which perceived size can remain constant without a concomitant change in two-dimensional adjacency. A target of constant subtense appears to grow smaller and smaller
as crossed disparity increases, and larger and larger as uncrossed disparity increases. Indeed, its relative perceived size at any given stereoscopic distance approximates that of the solid angle formed at the nodal
point of the eye by the target at the optical distance of the stereogram.
One could, of course, compensate for the change in perceived size with
perceived distance, but to do so would require changes in the angle of
subtense of the test field and, therefore, in the adjacency of the borders of
the test and induction fields.

In our experiment we chose the alternative of a constant angle of subtense for each field across disparity levels, but unlike other experimenters, we manipulated disparity in both the crossed and uncrossed directions. We reasoned that if depth separation showed itself as an effective
influence on brightness contrast, then a comparison of the effects obtained in the crossed and uncrossed directions would allow us to judge
the importance of changes in perceived size to simultaneous brightness
contrast. For example, if the same decline in contrast occurred with both
crossed and uncrossed disparity, then one could conclude that absolute
depth separation was the critical factor inasmuch as changes in perceived
size (smaller with crossed and larger with uncrossed disparity) had no
differential effect. On the other hand, if the effect were found to be asymmetrical, then perceived size could not be ruled out and additional experiments would be required.

Each of eight observers viewed experimental and control stereograms
of the form illustrated in Fig. 7.1. Each half-image consisted of a large
rectangular background (38.4 ft-L) upon which appeared two square
induction fields (3 × 3°), one above the other. The upper and lower
induction fields had luminances of 3.5 and 106.0 ft-L, respectively, and
within each was a small test field (1 × 1°) which carried in the experimental conditions one of five levels of disparity (+42', +21', 0', −21',

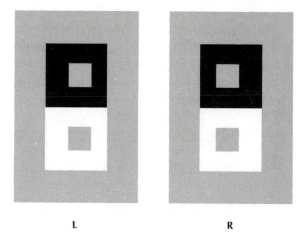

L   R

Fig. 7.1 A sample stereogram used to study the effects of depth adjacency on simultaneous brightness contrast. The small central squares were the test fields, shown here with a crossed disparity. The upper and lower test fields were seen upon a dark and light induction field.

and −42′ of arc) and had a luminance of 38.4 ft-L. In the control conditions the test fields always were at zero disparity, but they were displaced within the induction fields so as to match their displacements in the several disparity conditions. The experimental and control stereograms were placed in a single random order for each observer, and each stereogram was viewed three times.

Each observer was instructed to assign a number to each of the two test fields in each stereogram according to the following brightness modulus. The large rectangular background was said to possess a brightness value of 10 units, with the darker and lighter induction fields serving as anchors of 0 and 20, respectively. In addition, observers also were instructed to judge the altitude of the test field relative to that of the induction field and to judge the distance to the test field relative to the induction field.

While the disparity manipulation had predictable effects on the perceived size and depth location of the test field, we obtained no evidence to indicate that simultaneous brightness contrast changed with depth separation. Mean brightness is given in Fig. 7.2 for each test field as a function of disparity. Note that the test field appeared darker than the

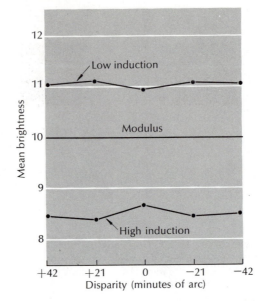

Fig. 7.2   Mean judged brightness of test fields relative to a modulus brightness of 10 as a function of depth separation brought about by test field disparity expressed in minutes of arc. The test fields were equal in luminance, but appeared to be different in brightness as a consequence of the luminance of the induction field. Depth separation had no significant effect on the level of contrast.

modulus when the induction field was of high luminance and lighter than the modulus when the induction field was of low luminance. Neither the level nor the direction of disparity had a significant effect on judged contrast. Accordingly, although brightness contrast occurred in this experiment, it was not influenced by depth adjacency or perceived size change in the test field. Furthermore, changes in two-dimensional adjacency that occurred in our control stereograms had no significant effect upon contrast. Perhaps depth adjacency influences some perceptual characteristics, but we think that brightness is not among them.

ADJACENCY AND THE PONZO ILLUSION
The classical Ponzo configuration is shown in Fig. 7.3. While the two vertical lines are equal in length, the apical line is usually perceived as longer. The Ponzo illusion has been of particular interest because it is prototypic of geometrical illusions that employ linear perspective as a

cue to depth. Some experimenters have interpreted the illusion in the context of size constancy in that the converging lines of the wedge falsely signal distance (*12, 19, 26, 27*). If, through perspective, the apical end of the wedge is made to appear farther away than the open end, and if both vertical lines are assumed to lie in the plane of the wedge, then the apical line would have to be longer physically in order to maintain an angular subtense equal to that of the other vertical line.

Despite the logic of the influence of linear perspective on perceived size, such an explanation of the Ponzo illusion cannot be noted for its parsimony or its amenability to experimental verification. By contrast, Fisher (*3, 4, 5*) has argued that the illusion is due to the mere presence of the enclosing lines and that linear perspective in the form of the wedge is not necessary to the illusion. Instead, he showed that the illusion depends upon the adjacency of the enclosing lines to the vertical ones, even when the former are parallel. Support for his interpretation also comes from line-frame studies which indicate that the area of a frame influences the perceived length of an enclosed line (*16*).

No matter which of these two accounts one happens to favor, it would seem that the perception of size is influenced by the proximity of other contours in two-dimensional space (*11, 13, 14, 27*), and as a consequence, many of the experimental data are consistent with Gogel's adjacency principle. Whether or not the Ponzo illusion declines in magnitude as the vertical lines which comprise the illusion become separated in depth from the wedge has yet to be established. However, based on one experiment (*6*), there is a suggestion that the illusion persists unaltered across different levels of depth adjacency; but the data provide only weak support inasmuch as the thrust of the experiment was directed at a

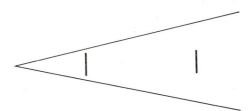

Fig. 7.3   The classical Ponzo configuration. While the two vertical lines are of equal length, the apical line usually appears as the longer one.

different issue that prompted the use of dichoptic half-images with the wedge and enclosed lines presented to different eyes.

Therefore, we set out to study the Ponzo illusion when the vertical lines were displaced in depth relative to the wedge under conditions wherein the full Ponzo configuration was present in both half-images (*10*). An example of one of the stereograms is given at the top of Fig. 7.4. Each of the three vertical lines (a, b, and c) had a vertical subtense of about 40′ of arc and the binocular lines of sight to lines a and b (and b and c) formed an angle of $2° - 40′$ at the midpoint of the inter-nodal axis. The wedge itself was of 40°. The disparity manipulation always was restricted to lines b and c, and in any given stereogram both of these lines carried identical disparities. Furthermore, disparity was introduced in such a way as to keep constant the visual directions of the lines when the half-images were in binocular register.

Line a never carried disparity with reference to the wedge, and it served as a reference against which observers made judgments of the height and distance of lines b and c. In the bottom part of Fig. 7.4 is shown the three-dimensional appearance of one stereogram with the lines b and c closer to the observer than was the wedge and line a. Observers were told to consider the height of line a as a modulus of 10 and to report the height of lines b and c with regard to this reference. Moreover, observers also were asked to use the distance to line a as a modulus of 100 in order to judge the relative depth of the other two lines.

We used five wedge stereograms which differed one from another only in the level and direction of disparity for lines b and c. Both crossed ($+38′$, $+19′$ of arc) and uncrossed ($-38′$, $-19′$ of arc) disparities were used, along with a zero disparity condition; and for each of these five wedge stereograms we also had a matched pattern of the three vertical lines but with the wedge absent.

Each of eight trained observers saw in random order each of the ten stereograms (five disparity levels, with and without the wedge) four times.

The results are clear cut. The mean judged depth of lines b and c was a linear function of their angular disparity, and the depth functions obtained for these lines were not significantly different from each other. Neither did the presence and absence of the wedge lead to significantly

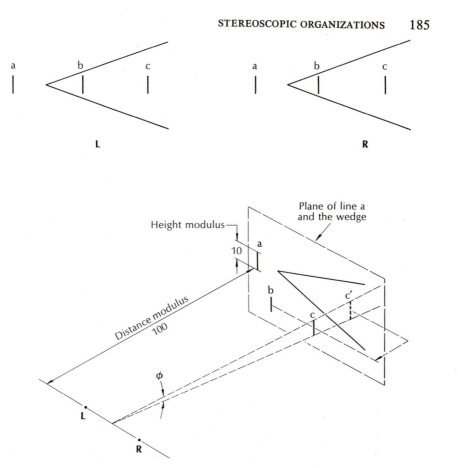

Fig. 7.4 A sample stereogram used to study the effects of depth separation on the Ponzo illusion. Below is illustrated the three-dimensional view of the stereogram, with lines b and c closer to the observer than line a and the 40° wedge. Line a served as a modulus for the height and depth of the other two lines. The angle ϕ illustrates that the height of lines must decline as crossed disparity increases if the projected size c' is to remain constant. See text for details.

different depth functions, although the slope of the function was slightly higher when the wedge was present. We believe this was due to the influence of directional separation, a topic treated in the next chapter.

With regard to the illusion, line b always was judged to have a larger vertical extent than line c as long as the wedge was present. Mean height

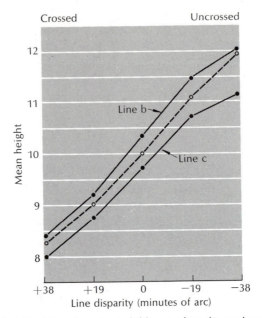

Fig. 7.5   Mean height of lines b and c (solid lines) when the wedge was present as a function of depth separation brought about through disparity expressed in minutes of arc. The dashed line is the mean height of both lines when the wedge was absent.

of lines b and c is shown in Fig. 7.5 as a function of their disparity. The solid lines represent height estimates in the presence of the wedge. When the wedge was absent (dashed line), the estimates of the heights of the two lines at each disparity were not significantly different, and the data therefore were combined.

Note that, both with and without the wedge, the lines underwent perceived size changes, being smaller as they approached the observer from the plane of the wedge and larger as they receded from the same reference plane. From the optical geometry and the judgments of line depth, we calculated the size lines b and c would have to assume in order to subtend a constant angle of 40′ of arc at the various depth positions they assumed at each disparity. Except for the extreme case of uncrossed disparity (−38′ of arc), the perceived size came close to the calculated value when the wedge was absent (dashed line). From Fig. 7.4 it may be seen that as line c carried more and more crossed disparity, and therefore came closer and closer to the observer, it would have to shrink in order to maintain a constant angle, ϕ, and a constant projected size, c'. So also would it have to lengthen when disparity is in the uncrossed direction.

The presence of the wedge seems at once to have augmented the perceived size of line b while it diminished the perceived size of line c. We calculated the magnitude of the Ponzo illusion at each disparity level by taking the difference in the mean height estimates for lines b and c, dividing this difference by the mean size of line b, and then multiplying by 100. These calculations represent the per cent of the illusion and the results are shown in Fig. 7.6. Clearly, the magnitude of the illusion is not a simple function of depth adjacency. With reference to the condition when the lines and the wedge were all in a single plane (zero disparity), the illusion decreased with depth separation in the crossed direction, but

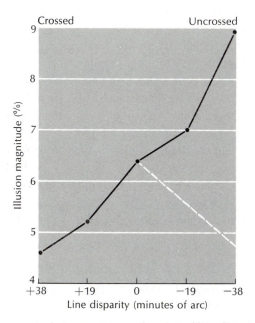

Fig. 7.6   Illusion magnitude in per cent as a function of line disparity in minutes of arc. See text for method of calculation.

it *increased* with depth separation in the uncrossed direction. Had depth separation been the critical determinant, then one would have expected the illusion also to decline with uncrossed disparity more or less in the fashion suggested by the dashed line in Fig. 7.6.

Our interpretation is that depth adjacency does not directly influence the magnitude of the Ponzo illusion. Instead, its magnitude is determined by the *apparent* adjacency of the vertical lines to the wedge. If an observer projected the lines to the plane of the wedge, as in the manner of line c′ shown in Fig. 7.4, then the apparent adjacency at the plane of the wedge would always be the same, no matter what the disparity level might be. If so, then the magnitude of the illusion should be constant. On the other hand, since the perceived height of the lines changes with disparity, it is possible that observers did not judge the apparent (projected) adjacency as constant. Rather, as disparity increased in the crossed direction, the reduction in perceived size of the lines reduced perceived contour adjacency and thus reduced the illusion. Conversely, as disparity increased in the uncrossed direction, the increase in perceived size of the lines brought them apparently closer to the wedge and thus increased the illusion.

Support for this possibility comes from an experiment by Greene (*9*). He asked his observers to judge the apparent vertical adjacency between the ends of the vertical lines and the enclosing lines, where the height of line a served as a modulus equal to 10. He found that the apparent adjacency changed along with disparity in a manner entirely consistent with our interpretation. His results are given in Fig. 7.7.

The magnitude of the Ponzo illusion seems to depend upon the apparent adjacency of the enclosed and enclosing contours rather than upon the level of depth adjacency. Accordingly, the case for depth adjacency as a factor of influence in perceptual organization is no stronger with the Ponzo illusion than it was with simultaneous brightness contrast.

Visual Aftereffects in Stereoscopic Space

One of the first documented visual aftereffects was reported in 1834 by Addams (*1*) after he had visited the Falls of Foyers in Scotland. His original account of the "waterfall" illusion is of interest because it contains the basic procedures employed in contemporary investigations of visual aftereffects. He wrote,

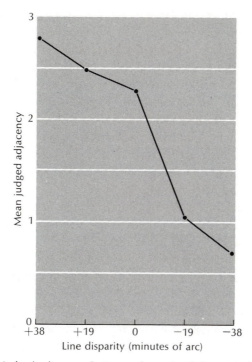

Fig. 7.7   Mean judged adjacency between the ends of the vertical line b and the wedge as a function of line disparity. Data from Greene (9).

> Having steadfastly looked for a few seconds at a particular part of the cascade, admiring the confluence and decussation of the currents forming the liquid drapery of waters, and then suddenly directed my eyes to the left, to observe the vertical face of the sombre age-worn rocks immediately contiguous to the water-fall, I saw the rocky surface as if in motion upwards, and with an apparent velocity equal to that of the descending water, which the moment before had prepared my eyes to behold this singular deception (1, p. 373).

Since Addams' original report, a variety of visual aftereffects have been observed, but most of them have been restricted to flat planar displays and targets that can be recognized monocularly. However, several notable exceptions have been reported. Köhler and Emery (15) demonstrated a three-dimensional aftereffect with line targets, as did Blakemore and Julesz (2) with matrix targets. In the Blakemore and Julesz study, observers fixed upon a marker near the center of the matrix.

While doing so two rectangular sub-matrices emerged in depth when the half-images were in binocular register. Relative to the surrounding matrix, both sub-matrices and the marker carried crossed disparities in amounts appropriate to place the upper rectangle a little closer than the fixation marker and the lower rectangle a little farther than the fixation marker. After a one minute inspection, observers then saw a test pattern where both rectangles had identical crossed disparities. The aftereffect consisted of the upper and lower rectangles' appearance behind and in front of the fixation marker, respectively. The effect was quite pronounced, with its duration related directly to the length of time the induction pattern had been viewed.

In order to determine the magnitude of the negative aftereffect of depth, Blakemore and Julesz employed test stereograms with very small disparities for the upper and lower rectangles and in the same direction as in the induction pattern. Stereoscopic viewing of an induction pattern with a disparity of ±2' of arc was just sufficient to flatten out a test pattern with a disparity of 0.5' of arc and thereby make the two rectangles appear momentarily aligned in the same stereoscopic depth plane. They concluded that the magnitude of the aftereffect is in the order of a change of 30" of arc in disparity, and that increasing the inspection time of the induction pattern beyond two minutes does not influence the magnitude of the aftereffect.

Recently, Walker and Kruger (28) employed random dot stereograms and reported stereoscopic contour displacements as an aftereffect. When in binocular register, the induction stereogram consisted of two vertical bars which were separated laterally and which appeared in a single plane closer to the observer than the background matrix. The depth in the vertical bars was achieved through form disparity, and each was defined by sharp stereoscopic contours. Between the bars were an upper and lower fixation target, both located closer to the *left* bar. Their test stereogram was the same except that the fixation targets were centered between the bars.

After viewing the induction stereogram, while alternately changing fixation between the upper and lower targets, their observers then viewed the test pattern and reported that the fixation targets appeared momentarily closer to the *right* vertical bar, thus suggesting that the location of the vertical stereoscopic contours had been displaced.

In all of these studies the possible influence of the *direction* of disparity has been ignored. Moreover, no attempts have been made to discover the interchangeability of stereoscopic contours with those arising from abrupt luminance gradients in the production of three-dimensional figural aftereffects.

With dot stereograms we have established that the direction of disparity carried by a sub-matrix defined by its homogeneity markedly influences perceptual organization beyond what would be expected on the basis of disparity alone *(17, 18)*. For example, when a homogeneous sub-matrix carries crossed disparity with reference to its surrounding dot matrix, the homogeneous region appears as an opaque surface interposed between an observer and the plane of the dots and it carries sharp stereoscopic contours. However, when the direction of the disparity is reversed, then the homogeneous region appears behind the plane of the surrounding dot matrix, but the stereoscopic contours remain as a part of the matrix to form a contoured window through which an observer sees the more distant surface. The left half-image of such a pattern is shown at the top of Fig. 7.8. With such a pattern the contours become uncoupled from the surface that defines the disparity.

In short, we have observed that when form disparity leads to surface depth and stereoscope contours, *the contours always are associated with the closer surface*. This finding is, of course, consistent with our conception of interposition, as treated in the previous chapter.

If the format of the stereogram is changed from one of dots to one of lines, as shown at the bottom of Fig. 7.8, then the direction of disparity no longer leads to an uncoupling of the contours from the disparate surface. In both the crossed and uncrossed directions the contours of the enclosed smaller line square are displaced out of the plane of the larger square because interposition is not required to account for the half-image differences. That is, cues of disparity and interposition do not conflict.

We were interested in determining if depth aftereffects would arise from line-drawn and matrix stereograms when the patterns carried crossed and uncrossed disparities. Furthermore, we wished to determine if depth aftereffects would arise when the induction stereogram con-

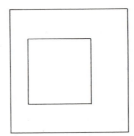

Fig. 7.8   A sample of a left half-image dot matrix with an uncrossed disparity in the homogeneous sub-matrix. Below is shown a comparable half-image comprised of lines.

tained disparate lines and the test stereogram contained comparable disparate forms in a dot-matrix, and vice versa. An illustration of one of our induction and test stereogram pairs is shown in Fig. 7.9. In this sample the induction pattern is of line-drawn rectangles while the test pattern contains two disparate rectangles of similar size and location. In both stereograms the observer is provided a fixation marker located midway between the upper and lower rectangles. With reference to the square field upon which the *induction* pattern of Fig. 7.9 was viewed, the upper rectangle, fixation marker, and lower rectangle carried uncrossed disparities of $4' - 42''$, $6' - 42''$, and $8' - 42''$ of arc, respectively. Therefore, when in binocular register, the fixation marker and both rectangles appeared farther away than the outer square frame, but the upper rectangle was a little closer than the fixation marker while the lower rectangle was a little farther away than the marker. In the paired test stereogram shown in the figure, the fixation marker and both rectangles had identical uncrossed disparities of 6′ − 42″.

The design of the experiment included induction-test pairs as follows: line-line, matrix-matrix, line-matrix, and matrix-line. These four combinations were tested under both crossed and uncrossed disparity levels at the values already specified. The aftereffect in the test stereogram showed itself as a temporary displacement of the two rectangles into different depth planes, with the direction of each opposite to that which obtained in the induction pattern.

Each of eight observers who met our visual criterion viewed each induction stereogram for two minutes and then reported the presence

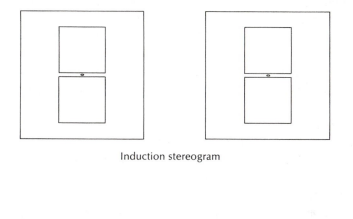

Induction stereogram

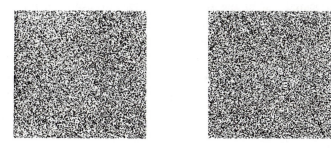

Test stereogram

Fig. 7.9   The upper stereogram of lines was used as an induction figure to determine if a depth aftereffect would occur in a matrix test pattern, shown below. Matrix pattern from Blakemore and Julesz (2).

Table VII-I   Mean duration in seconds of the depth aftereffect in line and matrix test targets following prior inspection of line and matrix induction targets. Each cell entry has an *n* of 24.

Induction format	Test format	Disparity	
		Crossed	Uncrossed
Line	Line	11.0	9.5
Line	Matrix	9.4	0.0
Matrix	Line	8.1	2.6
Matrix	Matrix	11.8	2.9

or absence of a depth aftereffect in the test pattern that followed each induction stereogram. When the aftereffect was present, observers operated a timing device through which its duration was measured in seconds. The experiment was repeated three times.

The results are presented in Table VII-I. Note that a depth aftereffect was obtained in all instances of crossed disparity and that it arose even when the visual system was adapted to one kind of contour process and then tested on another. However, when disparity was uncrossed, the strength of the aftereffect, as measured by its duration, was markedly reduced in all conditions except that one in which both the induction and test stereograms were comprised of lines.

These results suggest that depth aftereffects occur only when contours are shifted out of the reference plane in both the induction and the test patterns. This condition was met in every case of crossed disparity in that the central square, defined either by lines or stereoscopic contours, always appeared out of the reference plane. However, when a matrix target of uncrossed disparity was used as an induction or test pattern (or both), the stereoscopic contours remained in the reference plane, and the aftereffect was either absent or very weak. Whatever be the cause of the marked difference on aftereffects between crossed and uncrossed directions of disparity, it is clear that when disparity is crossed, then contours from abrupt luminance gradients and those produced stereoscopically are interchangeable.

Edge and Surface Organization

In the section just concluded we mentioned that the surface of a homogeneous sub-matrix with uncrossed disparity can be made to appear behind the plane of its surrounding dot matrix while the stereoscopic contours remain in the plane of the matrix to form a window. This perceptual organization uncouples the contours from the surface they enclose inasmuch as the contours and surface lie in distinctly different depth planes. However, as we know from the treatment in earlier chapters, this kind of uncoupling does not occur when the sub-matrix carries a crossed disparity, for in these cases the stereoscopic contours and the surface lie in a common plane interposed between an observer and the dot matrix.

We were interested in learning whether or not the phenomenon of uncoupling was unique to matrix stereograms, and so we ran a series of experiments with more traditional surface patterns where adjoining surfaces had edges defined by abrupt luminance gradients. Normally one thinks of edges as defining the surface they enclose, especially when two areas of homogeneous but different luminances comprise a target. For example, when one views a small dark square set upon a larger lighter square, the edges of the smaller square typically are perceived as contours belonging to the smaller square. If one makes half-images in such a way as to bring the smaller square toward the observer, then its surface and contours remain coupled just as they do with matrix targets. The question arises as to what happens if the smaller square carries an uncrossed disparity. Under such a circumstance the disparity cue would place the smaller square behind the larger one and thus conflict with the interposition cue. Our hypothesis was that the edges of the surrounding square would be organized as contours in the plane of the larger square while the surface of the surrounding square moved into a different plane. This hypothesis was based upon our work with analogous matrix targets.

In the first experiment we employed stereograms like those shown in Fig. 7.10. The half-images always consisted of three squares with angular subtenses of 6, 4, and 2° visual angle and luminances of 1, 8, and 0.1 ft-L, respectively. The surround upon which all were seen had a luminance of 20 ft-L. Disparity was introduced only in the smallest square, and it equaled 5, 10, 15, and 20′ of arc in both the crossed and uncrossed directions. In the control condition (A), the half-images were identical. Stereograms B and C in Fig. 7.10 illustrate the extreme crossed and uncrossed conditions.

Nine observers who met our visual criteria were instructed to report the depth of edges (e_2 and e_3) and surfaces (s_1, s_2, and s_3) relative to the

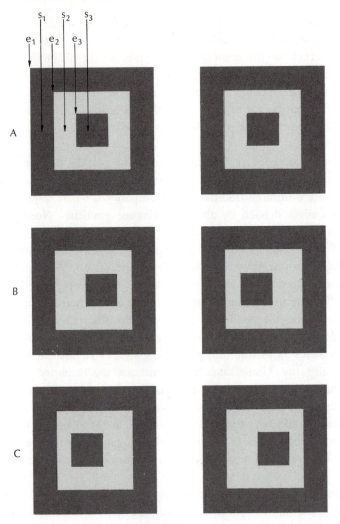

Fig. 7.10   Three stereograms where the inner square had zero (A), crossed (B), and uncrossed (C) disparity with reference to the other squares. At the top are identified the three edges (e) and surfaces (s) whose depth observers judged. See text for details.

depth of edge e_1, which constituted the reference modulus equal to 100. Each observer saw each of the nine stereograms in a random order on three occasions.

The results of the experiment confirmed our hypothesis. Regardless of the level or direction of disparity of the smallest square, the edge e_3

and surface s_3 remained coupled together in a single depth plane that approached or receded from the observer as a linear function of disparity. When disparity was crossed, all other edges and surfaces remained co-planar with the referent modulus. However, when disparity was uncrossed, the surface s_2 became uncoupled from its defining edge e_2. The edge of the middle sized square remained in the reference plane while its surface always had the same depth as the smallest square.

The mean depth estimates combined across observers and repetitions are given in Fig. 7.11 for the critical edges and surfaces. Note that the

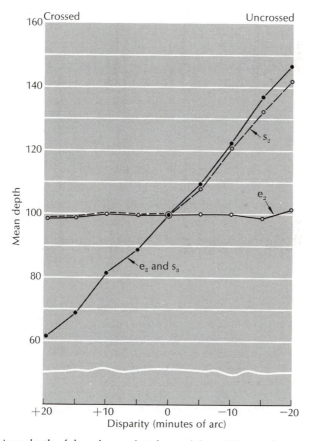

Fig. 7.11 Mean depth of the edges and surfaces of the middle sized square (e_2 and s_2) and the small square (e_3 and s_3) as a function of the disparity of the small square expressed in minutes of arc. Note that with uncrossed disparity the surface s_2 went into depth with the small square even though its edges never had any disparity.

uncrossed disparity of the smallest square was sufficient to bring the surface s_2 into depth even though its edge e_2 had no disparity and remained at a constant distance from the observer.

When disparity and interposition cues are consistent, it would appear that surfaces are associated with the edges that *enclose* them, and these edges are perceived as contours belonging to the enclosed surface. On the other hand, when disparity and interposition cues are in conflict, then these same edges are perceived as contours belonging to *the surface surrounding them*. When viewing stereogram C in Fig. 7.10, it is as if the largest square is the wall of a room with a square opening in it (e_2). Therefore, the edges e_1 and e_2 and the surface s_1 all are seen in a single plane. Through the opening one sees a darkened window (e_3 and s_3) in the exterior wall (s_2) of an adjacent building across an alley. While the size and depth of the darkened window are determined, only the depth of the adjacent exterior wall is known because it has no defining boundaries visible to the observer from his point of vantage. The remarkable ability of observers to judge the depth of such surfaces is considered further in Chapter 10.

Perhaps the major conclusion to be drawn from our results is that surfaces can derive a disparity from disparate contours *within* them even while they are enclosed by nondisparate edges. A second experiment in this series included simultaneous disparity manipulations of both the smallest and middle sized square, and our results simply confirmed what has been reported here for the simpler experiment.

References

1. Addams, R. An account of a peculiar optical phenomenon seen after looking at a moving body. *Phil. Mag.*, 1834, *5* (3rd Series), 373-374.
2. Blakemore, C., and Julesz, B. Stereoscopic depth after-effect produced without monocular cues. *Science*, 1971, *171*, 286-288.
3. Fisher, G. H. An experimental comparison of rectilinear and curvilinear illusions. *Brit. J. Psychol.*, 1968, *59*, 23-28.
4. Fisher, G. H. Gradients of distortion seen in the context of the Ponzo illusion and other contours. *Quart. J. Exper. Psychol.*, 1968, *20*, 212-217.
5. Fisher, G. H. Towards a new explanation for the geometrical illusions. I. The properties of contours which induce illusory distortion. *Brit. J. Psychol.*, 1969, *60*, 179-185.
6. Fisher, G., and Lucas, A. Geometrical illusions and figural after-effects.

The distorting and distorted components of illusions. *Vision Res.*, 1970, *10*, 393-404.

7. Gogel, W. C. Size cues and the adjacency principle. *J. Exper. Psychol.*, 1965, *70*, 289-293.

8. Gogel, W. C., and Mershon, D. H. Depth adjacency in simultaneous contrast. *Percept. and Psychophysics*, 1969, *5*, 13-17.

9. Greene, R. T. Ponzo illusion in stereoscopic space. Unpublished doctoral dissertation, Univ. of Vermont, Burlington, Vt., 1972.

10. Greene, R. T., Lawson, R. B., and Godek, Cynthia. The Ponzo illusion in stereoscopic space, *J. Exper. Psychol.*, 1972, *95*, 358-364.

11. Gregory, R. L. Distortion of visual space as inappropriate constancy scaling. *Nature*, 1963, *199*, 678-680.

12. Gregory, R. L. *Eye and Brain*. New York: McGraw-Hill, 1966.

13. Julesz, B. *Foundations of Cyclopean Perception*. Chicago: Univ. of Chicago Press, 1971.

14. Klix, F. *Elementaranalysen zur psychophysik der Raumwahrnehmung*. Berlin: Deutscher Verlag der Wissenschaften, VEB, 1962.

15. Köhler, W., and Emery, D. A. Figural after-effects in the third dimension of visual space. *Amer. J. Psychol.*, 1947, *40*, 159-201.

16. Kunnapäs, T. M. Influence of frame size on apparent length of a line. *J. Exper. Psychol.*, 1955, *50*, 168-170.

17. Lawson, R. B., and Gulick, W. L. Apparent size and distance in stereoscopic vision. In J. C. Baird (Ed.) Human Space Perception: Proceedings of the Dartmouth Conference. *Psychonomic Monog. Suppl.*, 1970, *3*, No. 13, 193-200.

18. Lawson, R. B., Gulick, W. L., and Park, M. Stereoscopic size-distance relationships from line-drawn and dot-matrix stereograms. *J. Exper. Psychol.*, 1972, *92*, 69-74.

19. Leibowitz, H. W., and Judisch, J. M. The relation between age and the magnitude of the Ponzo illusion. *Amer. J. Psychol.*, 1967, *80*, 105-109.

20. Lie, I. Psychophysical invariants of achromatic colour vision. III. Colour constancy and its relation to identification of illumination. *Scand. J. Psychol.*, 1969, *10*, 269-281.

21. Lie, I. Psychophysical invariants of achromatic colour vision. IV. Depth adjacency and simultaneous contrast. *Scand. J. Psychol.*, 1969, *10*, 282-286.

22. Lie, I. Depth adjacency and whiteness contrast. *Scand. J. Psychol.*, 1971, *12*, 303-304.

23. Mershon, D. Relative contributions of depth and directional adjacency to simultaneous whiteness contrast. *Vision Res.*, 1972, *12*, 969-979.

24. Mershon, D., and Gogel, W. C. Effect of stereoscopic cues on perceived whiteness. *Amer. J. Psychol.*, 1970, *83*, 55-67.

25. Stewart, E. C. The Gelb effect. *J. Exper. Psychol.*, 1959, *57*, 235-242.

26. Tausch, R. Optische Täuschungen als artifizielle Effekte der Gestaltungs-

prozesse von Grössen-und Formenkonstang in der naturlichen Raum-wahremung. *Psychol. Forsch.*, 1954, *24*, 299-348.

27. Thiery, A. Über geometrisch-optische Tauschungen. *Philosophische Studien*, 1896, *12*, 67-125.

28. Walker, J. T., and Kruger, M. W. Figural aftereffects in random-dot stereograms without monocular contours. Paper presented at *Psychonomic Society Meetings*, St. Louis, Mo., 1972.

8
Disparity and
Directional Separation

Most of the material presented in the foregoing chapters dealt with phenomena related to interposition in the context of complex matrix targets and stereoscopic contours. In this chapter we shall discuss several experiments in which geometrically simpler targets were used to determine additional principles of disparity coding. The experiments included here deal with several aspects of target geometry and its influence on the perception of depth.

DIRECTIONAL SEPARATION

Assume an observer has two small objects in binocular view. Directional separation (Θ) is the angle formed by imaginary straight lines drawn from the midpoint of the interocular axis to the centers of the objects. Such lines are often referred to as *binocular visual directions*. Use of the midpoint of the interocular axis as a reference against which to measure the angular separation of visual targets has a distinct advantage over other referents, such as the optical nodes, because it is singular and independent of binocular disparity. This independence is illustrated in Figs. 8.1 and 8.2.

At the top left of Fig. 8.1 is shown an observer viewing two black circles. The apparent positions of the more distant circle at a common plane (P) are shown for both eyes by the open circles. Stereoscopic half-images are shown in the center of the upper panel with the uncrossed disparity of the right circle denoted as η. To the right is shown the direc-

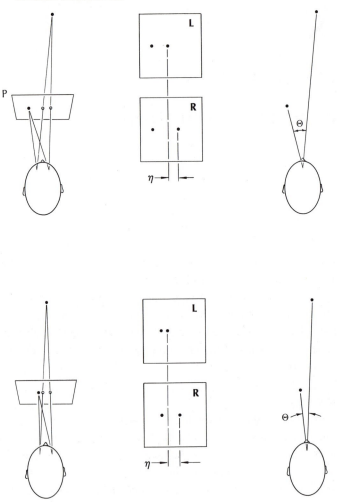

Fig. 8.1 A schematic illustration of how directional separation (Θ) can change while disparity (η) remains constant.

tional separation of the targets (Θ). The bottom panel of Fig. 8.1 illustrates that directional separation can vary while disparity remains constant. Disparity is not appreciably altered as long as the circles are moved laterally along straight lines perpendicular to the mid-saggital plane. Figure 8.2 is similar in format, and it illustrates how disparity can change while directional separation remains constant.

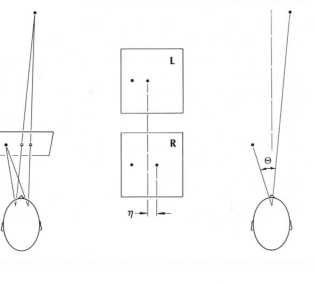

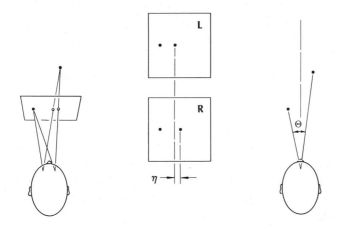

Fig. 8.2   A schematic illustration of how disparity (η) can change while directional separation (Θ) remains constant.

As illustrated in Fig. 8.1, the images of the circles on the retinas become more and more separated as directional separation increases. If one assumed that visual space was predictable from optical geometry, then the coding of disparity would have to be independent of the lateral separation of objects in space. The question arises as to how the visual system codes the disparity information. If the disparity detectors that have been found in the cortex of cats and monkeys also are present in man, it would seem reasonable to suggest that directional separation would not be a major factor of influence in disparity coding. While the size of receptive fields generally increases with retinal eccentricity, so that the precision of disparity coding might suffer, the disparity detector still would be driven by a pair of receptive fields that were misaligned relative to geometrical correspondence. Stated differently, for each level of misalignment, representing different amounts of disparity, there might be a disparity detector the behavior of which is determined solely by the location of a *single imaged target on each retina*. In a way, such a coding system is a simple and direct measure of geometrical misalignment of binocularly correlated images.

Suppose, however, that the coding of disparity in instances like those depicted in Figs. 8.1 and 8.2 depends on the abstraction of the *difference in retinal distances between the imaged circles on one retina relative to the other*. Under these circumstances one might expect directional separation to have an effect on disparity coding since the neural arrangement necessary to the establishment of disparity would have to be very complex, and it would have to be able to operate over relatively long neural distances.

Our interest in the possible effects of directional separation on perceived depth grew out of the literature on electrophysiological studies of disparity detectors. Of course, it was not possible to obtain single unit data on human observers; but, fortunately, the matter of the influence of directional separation on depth perception is answerable through psychophysical methods. While no direct tests of the two suggested alternative neural mechanisms could be undertaken, we felt that the perceptual data would be an important source of information to conceptions of disparity mechanisms.

SIMPLE DIRECTIONAL SEPARATION

Youngs (*1*), working in the Dartmouth laboratory, set out to determine the effects of directional separation on judged depth. Only a small portion of his work is treated here, that portion which bears directly on the matter at hand.

Six observers with normal uncorrected acuity, phoria, and stereopsis first were trained to make egocentric depth judgments to a test target relative to a standard target located at a constant distance of 1 m from the observer's interocular axis. This distance was defined as 100 arbitrary units. The distance to the standard target was the modulus against which the observer judged the distance to the test target. The standard and test targets were small black squares (4 mm on a side) mounted on transparent plexiglass sheets viewed through a rectangular aperture and seen against an illuminated background surface. On each of ten trials the observer was given the appropriate linear measure in terms of the modulus after he made his estimate. No specific criteria were invoked other than that each observer show understanding of the nature of egocentric depth estimation relative to a given modulus.

Following training, each observer made depth estimates to selected portions of stereoscopic targets in a mirror stereoscope in the same manner as earlier practiced on the training apparatus. The half-image targets consisted of small squares which subtended 16′ of arc on a side with a luminance of 3.0 ft-L seen against a homogeneous field of 85.3 ft-L. The total visual field was limited in height and width to 20 and 14° of visual angle, respectively.

The left square carried 0, 5, and 10′ of crossed disparity relative to the right square, and for each of these three disparity levels the squares carried directional separations of 0.5, 1.0, 2.0, 4.0, and 5.0° visual angle. In all, there were fifteen unique stereograms. The order of presentation was random, and each observer saw each stereogram five times.

On each trial observers gave egocentric depth estimates to the left square relative to the modulus of 100 arbitrary units, defined as the distance to the right square.

The results of the experiment, shown in Fig. 8.3, make clear that *judged depth is a function of directional separation as well as retinal disparity*. The three dashed lines (0, 5, and 10′) indicate predicted values based upon optical geometry, and if directional separation had no effect on disparity coding, then the obtained functions (solid lines) each would have been similar to the predicted values and had slopes equal to zero. Note that disparity gave rise to depth judgments that closely approximated optical geometry *only when the directional separation between the targets was small* (0.5° visual angle). However, with direc-

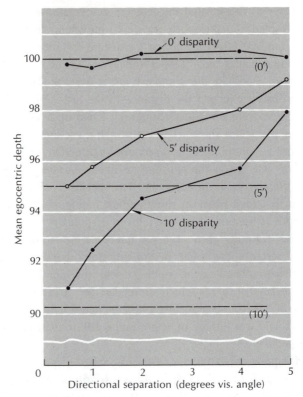

Fig. 8.3 Mean egocentric depth judgments relative to a modulus of 100 as a function of directional separation in degrees visual angle for targets of 0, 5, and 10′ of disparity. Dashed lines represent predicted values from optical geometry for each disparity level. Data from Youngs (1).

tional separations of 5°, the two squares appeared almost co-planar despite the fact that they carried 5 and 10′ of disparity.

The interaction between directional separation and disparity may be illustrated by *equal-depth contours,* as shown in Fig. 8.4. These contours represent the combination of directional separation and disparity that leave mean egocentric depth invariant. The contours are labeled as mean judged depth (95, 96, 97) relative to the distance to the standard square. For example, the perceived depth of the left square remained at 95 when it had a separation of 0.5° and a disparity of 5′ or a separation of 3.0° and a disparity of 10′ of arc.

With a slightly different psychophysical method, Youngs repeated this experiment (with the 10′ disparity level only) and verified the general finding that perceived depth is a function both of directional separation and disparity. The absolute depth values differed a little, but the shape of the function was the same. The results of the two experiments are compared in Fig. 8.5.

When one views the world normally, it is seldom comprised of two isolated objects seen against a homogeneous *Ganzfeld*. Instead, it is rich with texture and contours. Youngs' data suggest that *the relative depth planes of objects in normal viewing depend upon local disparity comparisons,* and that the visual system cannot code depth veridically when objects are widely separated unless the intervening space contains referent objects.

In this connection, we observed that two objects of 10′ disparity which appear *co-planar* when separated by 6° visual angle can be restored to appropriate depth planes when a hairline grid on glass is introduced into the viewing channels of our mirror stereoscope. We have not explored the effects of grids in any systematic way, but it is clear that vertical hairlines separated by 1° visual angle which form a pattern that extends over the 6° target separation works perfectly well.

If disparity coding is a local process, as we believe it to be, then it would be important to learn more about the effects of multiple referents

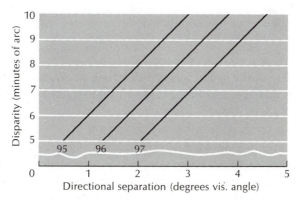

Fig. 8.4 Equal-depth contours based on data of previous figure. The combinations of directional separation and disparity represented by each function lead to constant depth perception.

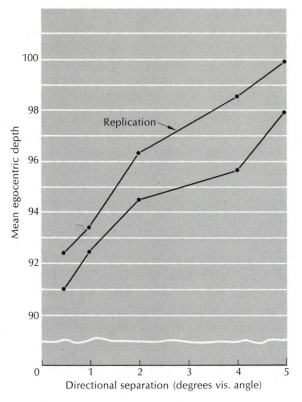

Fig. 8.5 Mean egocentric depth as a function of directional separation of two targets of 10′ disparity. The lower function is taken from Fig. 8.3, while the upper one
was obtained in a second experiment in which a different psychophysical method
was employed. Data from Youngs (1).

that intervene in the space between disparate targets and thereby have
their images on the retinas between those of the targets in question.

DIRECTIONAL SEPARATION WITH INTERVENTION
Surface Intervention. In our first experiment of this series we made stereograms where each half-image consisted of two vertical black lines 1°
in height and separated by 4°. The lines carried a disparity appropriate
to place them in a plane that intersected the frontoparallel plane at 45°,
with the right line farther away. Six observers trained in judging angles
had little difficulty in reporting that the lines appeared to lie in a plane

rotated out of the frontoparallel plane, but they seriously underestimated the rotation. The mean judged angle was 32.2° rather than the 45° predicted on the basis of optical geometry. We assumed that the loss in rotation was due primarily to the 4° directional separation and its effects on the coding of disparity. Once again, introduction of the grid restored appropriate depth (mean judged angle = 43.6°).

In the second condition of this experiment the half-images were changed to solid black rectangles (1 × 4°) with identical disparities of the vertical ends. Accordingly, the binocularly fused rectangle should have appeared rotated out of the frontoparallel plane at an angle of 45°. Observers reported a mean rotation of only 8.7°, with one observer unable to detect any rotation at all. The only difference between the stimuli in these first two conditions was that in the second one a surface connected the vertical lines so as to form a rectangle. However, insofar as rotation is concerned, the percepts were very different.

If one were to view a real rectangular surface of the size and orientation specified, then the horizontal edges would show a very slight perspective that was absent in our stereograms. To determine whether or not the loss in rotation of the rectangular surface, as compared to the plane of the vertical lines, was due to the absence of linear perspective, we ran a third condition which included perspective.

While perspective augmented rotation slightly, 10.2 rather than 8.7°, it did not have a statistically significant effect. On the other hand, the introduction of the grid immediately changed the orientation of the surface to one appropriate to the geometry (45° ± 2) for all stereograms, whether of lines or surfaces, with or without perspective.

We concluded that directional separation continued to be the dominant factor of influence in the coding of disparity, but we are unable to account for the dramatic reduction in rotation that accompanied the introduction of the surface in conditions two (without perspective) and three (with perspective). The attenuation of rotation clearly does not seem to be the result of the absence of linear perspective. However, it should be noted that the amount of perspective occurring in two short lines (the horizontal edges of the rectangle) is very slight when rotation is 45° *and* the lines are separated vertically only by 1° of visual angle. Perhaps the role of perspective would be stronger with patterns in which the vertical subtense separating the horizontal boundaries was much greater than 1°, for in such patterns the difference between the presence and absence of linear perspective would be more than marginally noticeable. We shall report later in this section an experiment that dealt with one aspect of perspective.

In the fourth and final condition of the present experiment we added two circular black dots of 10′ diameter to the stereograms containing the disparate rectangular surface. The dots were located lateral to the midpoint of the vertical edges of the surface at a distance of about 0.5°. They carried no disparity relative to each other or relative to the left edge of the surface. However, as before, the right edge of the rectangle carried a disparity appropriate to a 45° rotation. Based on the geometry of the patterns, the two dots and the left edge of the rectangle all should appear co-planar, with the rectangular surface rotated out of the frontoparallel plane at 45°.

We thought that the addition of the two dots, as adjacent nondisparate referents, would result in a greater rotation of the plane than that which occurred in the condition without the dots.

The results we obtained departed from what was expected on the basis of optical geometry, but they confirmed our view that disparity coding is a local process. Observers reported that the plane of the rectangle was only slightly rotated (7.3°) despite the presence of disparity appropriate to a 45° rotation. Moreover, the two dots that carried no disparity relative to each other, and therefore should have appeared in the same frontoparallel plane, were reported as rotated 33.8° in a direction opposite to that of the surface. Only a local disparity process can account for these observations. That is, the rotation of the rectangular surface was severely attenuated because the edges that carried the disparity information had a directional separation of 4°, and the rotation of the plane of the dots occurred because the system failed to code zero disparity over a directional separation of 5°. At the same time, the left edge of the rectangle and the left dot, separated by 0.5° visual angle, were correctly coded as having zero disparity inasmuch as they appeared equidistant from the observer. Likewise, the *relative* depth between the right edge and the right dot, also separated by 0.5° visual angle, was correctly coded as disparate inasmuch as they appeared in different depth planes. Failure to perceive the total pattern as consistent with geometry, therefore, was due to a failure of the system to code over long rather than short retinal distances.

A schematic summary of the results of the fourth condition of the experiment is given in Fig. 8.6. The upper panel depicts what would be predicted from geometry, while the lower one depicts what was actually observed. Note that the angle between the planes of the rectangle and the dots equaled 41.1° (33.8 + 7.3°), thus showing that *relative* depth between the right edge and dot was maintained reasonably well.

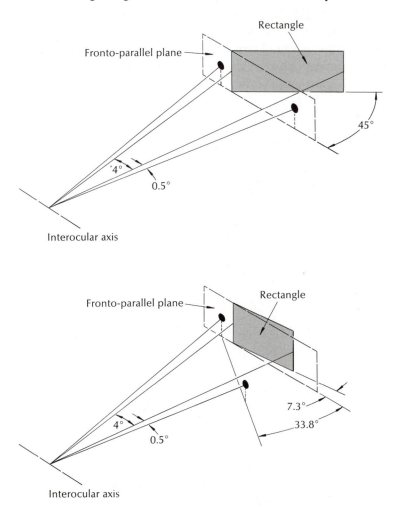

Fig. 8.6 The upper panel shows a display consisting of a dark rectangle rotated 45° out of the frontoparallel plane bordered by two dots. When appropriate half-images were viewed in a stereoscope, observers reported that the several aspects of the display were arranged as shown in the lower panel.

These data suggest that when multiple referents are available to the visual system, the binocular percept is the result of the *weighting* of disparity information. The weight varies inversely with directional separation, as shown by Youngs (*1*). A hypothetical weighting function is shown in Fig. 8.7 where the weight given to any level of disparity declines linearly from 1.0 to 0.0 at 5° of separation.

When these weights are applied to the visual display depicted in Fig. 8.6, then the weight matrix shown in Table VIII-I can be seen to account for the perception of our observers. Note that the matrix is symmetrical, so we need consider only the half of it above the diagonal. Only two cells have large weights, namely, the comparison of the left dot with the left

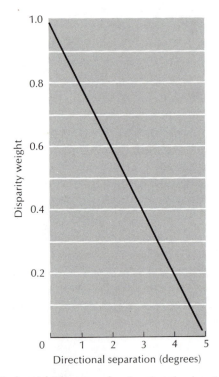

Fig. 8.7 Hypothetical weight function showing that the functional usefulness of a particular disparity declines as the directional separation between the contours which carry the disparity increases. Disparate contours separated by 5° or more in otherwise homogeneous visual space have no functional significance for stereopsis.

Table VIII-I. A disparity weighted matrix based upon the function given in Fig. 8.7 and applied to the visual display shown in Fig. 8.6. *ND* and *MD* refer to no disparity and maximum disparity, respectively.

	Left dot	Left edge	Right edge	Right dot
Left dot		0.9 ND	0.1 MD	0.0 ND
Left edge	0.9 ND		0.2 MD	0.1 ND
Right edge	0.1 MD	0.2 MD		0.9 MD
Right dot	0.0 ND	0.1 ND	0.9 MD	

edge of the rectangle and that of the right edge of the rectangle with the right dot. The former had no disparity (*ND*), while the latter had maximum disparity (*MD*). Given the close adjacency of the dots to their respective edges, and the resulting weights, we would expect that these aspects of the display would be more likely to result in appropriate relative depths than would any others, and of course that is what occurred. The weight operating between the left and right edges of the rectangle was low so that, even with maximum disparity present, the rotation of the rectangle was attenuated, as we would expect from the *equal depth contours* shown in Fig. 8.4. Finally, while the right and left dots carried no disparity relative to each other, their wide directional separation lent no weight to their coding. Accordingly, the dots were located appropriately relative to their adjacent edges rather than relative to each other.

Youngs repeated the condition of our experiment involving the rectangle and the dots, but instead of having observers judge angles, he had them reproduce the perceived spatial arrangement with a table top scale model which consisted of a movable black rectangle hinged on a pin at the left vertical edge and two dots movable along parallel tracks. The observer was free to move his head 90° from the headholder of the stereoscope to that of the model. From mean settings of the rectangle and dots, Youngs measured angles relative to the frontoparallel plane. His results confirmed earlier observations.

Perspective as Intervention. Our interest in the role of perspective arose during experimentation with rotated rectangular surfaces, as previously mentioned. When an artist employs linear perspective on a two-dimensional surface, the impression of depth occurs without disparity even when the scene is viewed binocularly. However, when a view is actually three dimensional, then binocular sight includes cues for stereoscopic depth. Perspective can occur, therefore, with and without accompanying disparity, and it was the latter case that took our attention.

A single horizontal line rotated out of the frontoparallel plane carries retinal disparity at its ends as a direct function of its rotation; but as long as it lies in the horizontal plane that includes the foveas (horizon), it is imaged on the horizontal meridian of each retina. However, if it is raised or lowered in the visual field, even though it remains objectively horizontal, its image becomes oblique relative to the same meridian. Stated differently, perspective does not occur at the horizon although foreshortening does. Above and below the horizon both perspective and foreshortening occur. While disparity is present in all instances of horizontal lines that lie in planes other than the frontoparallel one, a horizontal line may be considered to have perspective only when its image is oblique relative to horizontal retinal meridians.

This distinction is made plain in Fig. 8.8. Note that the two solid target lines are horizontal and parallel. They lie in a single vertical plane that intersects the frontoparallel plane at a 45° angle. The lower line (NP) also lies in the horizontal plane that includes the optical nodes and foveas of both eyes. When the line NP is projected onto the frontoparallel plane, as viewed by the right eye, it appears as NP'. While it is foreshortened, it remains horizontal and is imaged on the horizontal retinal meridian. The same thing occurs for line NP at the left eye, and the half-images that would obtain if an observer viewed such a line are shown at the bottom of the figure, where the disparity of the right end of the line is denoted as η.

The projected position of line P has an oblique orientation on the frontoparallel plane even though the line itself is horizontal. This is due to the fact that it lies above the horizon. Accordingly, it is imaged obliquely on the retinas, and thus it meets our definition of a perspective line.

The half-images for line P are also shown at the bottom of the figure. Both lines (NP and P) have identical end disparity, but only line P has perspective. Based upon optical geometry, one would expect that if one viewed these half-images in a stereoscope, then the lines would appear parallel and in a single vertical plane rotated to an angle of 45°.

We wondered whether or not the addition of perspective to disparity would change the perceived rotation of a line when disparity remained

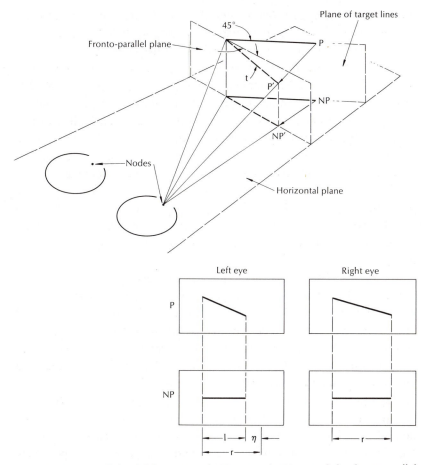

Fig. 8.8 Two parallel solid lines (*P* and *NP*) rotated 45° out of the frontoparallel plane project to the frontoparallel plane as converging line segments. The half-images at the bottom show that both lines have the same end disparity (η), but only *P* projects an image of oblique orientation on the retinas. See text for full explanation.

unchanged. Recall that the perceived rotation of rectangular surfaces reported earlier in this chapter was heavily attenuated compared to what was expected on the basis of disparity. The small vertical subtense of the rectangles (1°) means that, at best, the top and bottom edges were never more than 1° off the horizontal reference plane (horizon). This may account for the fact that the introduction of perspective had little effect on perceived rotation, the perspective being so slight.

With the aid of a computer, we calculated the metric values for stereoscopic half-images that would be appropriate to an objectively horizontal line at 45° to the frontoparallel plane and at 0, 5, 10, 15, and 20° elevation, as measured at the midpoint of the interocular axis. From these values we constructed five stereograms which were seen both with and without fixation. When a fixation point was used, it was located in the horizon plane at a distance equal to that of the left end of each line. In the 0° elevation condition it was congruent with the end of the line.

Eight observers who met our visual criteria were trained to judge the *plane* of rotation of lines. Thereafter, they viewed the experimental stereograms in random order six times. Half the observers had the fixation condition first, whereas the remainder had the no fixation condition first.

The results of the experiment indicate that depth perception is determined both by perspective and disparity. The latter was always constant and appropriate to a 45° rotation, but as the obliqueness of the imaged line increased as a consequence of line elevation, so too did judged rotation increase. Inasmuch as fixation had no significant effect on the results of the experiment, data were combined across replications and observers for conditions with and without fixation.

Mean judged rotation is plotted in Fig. 8.9, both as a function of line elevation (solid line) and the amount of obliqueness caused by elevation (dashed line). An example of the angle of obliqueness is given in Fig. 8.8 as angle t. In both instances, rotation appears as a positively accelerated function. The reduction in acceleration of the dashed line (read against the upper abscissa) is due to the fact that the angle of obliqueness of the line projected to the frontoparallel plane is itself a positively accelerated function of line elevation. The effect is to make the psychometric function more nearly linear.

Note that when perspective was absent, so that rotation depended upon disparity alone (0° elevation), mean rotation was slight and of approximately the same magnitude found with rectangular surfaces (9° *versus* 8.7°). The fact that constant fixation to the horizontal plane had no effect on judged rotation, as compared to free viewing, suggests that the primary influence of perspective rests upon image obliqueness rather than on the region of the retinas stimulated.

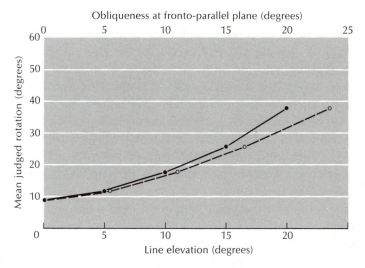

Fig. 8.9   Mean judged line rotation relative to the frontoparallel plane as a function of line elevation in degrees above the horizontal plane (solid line, lower abscissa) and projected line obliqueness at the frontoparallel plane in degrees relative to horizontal (dashed line, upper abscissa).

Inspection of the half-images for the perspective line (*P*) shown at the bottom of Fig. 8.8 makes clear that the degree of image obliqueness for a given line in visual space is actually different on the right and left retinas. Values of obliqueness in Fig. 8.9 (upper abscissa) are simple averages of the two separate calculations.

Our data indicate that the binocular visual system comes closer to veridical coding of line orientation when perspective (oblique images) is added to parallax (disparity images). At present we entertain the hypothesis that perspective achieves its influence because of the organization of paired receptive-fields that drive disparity detectors in such a way as to abstract disparity information from the "surface" of a line, a process which is impossible when perspective is absent.

The essential idea is illustrated in Fig. 8.10 where upon the left and right retinas are depicted oblique and disparate images that would occur if one viewed a rotated horizontal line out of the plane of the horizon. Retinal distance from the vertical foveal meridian is given in arbitrary units. The open circles, squares, and triangle are used as symbols of receptive fields. Our assumption is that the right and left retinas are coupled primarily by lateral connections to which we refer as *horizontal channels* in the figure. This organization is plausible in light of the horizontal separation of the eyes and the lack of capacity to code vertical disparities. We are not prepared to advance the view that there are no vertical organizations, for single unit studies on orientation and edge detection suggest that there are such couplings. However, disparity is uniquely a lateral affair in normal vision, there being no circumstance when vertical disparities of significance occur naturally; and so we propose that the portion of the visual nervous system which underlies stereopsis has within it disparity detectors that are driven by cells the distal origins or connections of which arise from the same horizontal retinal meridians of the eyes.

In Fig. 8.10 the left and right ends of the imaged line on both retinas lie along horizontal channels A and G, respectively, and each end triggers cells that could drive disparity detectors. The left end falls on geometrically corresponding places and would be coded as without disparity. The right end, however, falls on noncorresponding places and is therefore disparate. In terms of the retinal distance metric shown in the figure, the right end has a two-unit disparity $(8 - 6 = 2)$. The advantage of image obliqueness is that the horizontal channel organization of the binocular system allows it to code the disparity of portions of the line other than its ends. Channel D in the figure "finds" the midpoint of the line for both eyes (open squares) and establishes its disparity as half that of the right end $(4 - 3 = 1)$. Likewise, any horizontal channel between A and G can code disparity.

Were the images oriented horizontally on the retinas, say along chan-

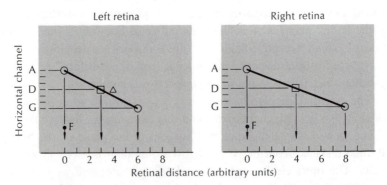

Fig. 8.10 An illustration of how oblique images on the left and right retinas can provide more disparity information than horizontal images. See text for explanation.

nel D, then the system could still code the disparity of the ends, but it would be unable to code any other disparities of the line. For example, with horizontal images, the receptive fields denoted by the squares and the triangle all would be activated. If the organization coupled square to square, then that portion of the "surface" of the line would be coded as having a disparity of one unit; but if the organization coupled the square of the right eye with the triangle of the left, then that portion of the line would be coded as having zero disparity. In short, with horizontal images there is ambiguity in the coding of disparity. On the other hand, with oblique images, the ambiguity is markedly reduced. The option of the square–triangle coupling is eliminated, and disparity coding of the central region of the line is assured.

Here, then, is the central idea of perspective as intervention. While the line itself is without texture, one can argue nevertheless that its "surface" can be coded as having a regularly changing level of disparity from one end to the other. The precision of the coding depends on linewidth, linelength, angle of obliqueness (amount of perspective), and the fineness of the mosaic of the horizontal channels in the retinal region stimulated. In a way, *it is the neural organization that abstracts a texture out of a textureless target,* but it can only do so under the conditions described. This effect, of course, is equivalent to a reduction in directional separation by the addition of multiple referents between the ends of the line.

Our finding that increased perspective (image obliqueness) leads to greater perceived line rotation seems to us to suggest that image obliqueness simply gives the binocular system more information about disparity, and thus leads to percepts that are more nearly veridical.

Perhaps it should be mentioned that image obliqueness is not sufficient for perceived rotation. For example, if one viewed binocularly an oblique line in the frontoparallel plane, then for each horizontal channel stimulated, the couplings would always result in zero disparity. This, in essence, is what occurs when the artist uses linear perspective on a two-dimensional surface. Impressions of depth are not based on stereopsis. However, when the line is out of the frontoparallel plane, then its image carries a different angle of obliqueness on each retina, and it is this *difference* that provides the binocular system the opportunity to abstract more disparity information from oblique than from horizontal images of lines.

Texture as Intervention. Consider again the case of a horizontal line at 0° elevation which has been rotated 45° out of the frontoparallel plane. We know that it is imaged horizontally on the retinas and that disparity information is limited to the ends of the line. We also know that the perceived rotation of such a line is much less than it should be relative to optical geometry, presumably because the directional separation between the ends of the line attenuates the influence of disparity. Unlike the perspective line, which allows the binocular system to add a "texture" even while the target itself is of homogeneous luminance, the line in question, having no perspective, requires its own texture if directional separation is to be reduced through intervening referents. Accordingly, we wished to compare the perceived orientation of linear target arrays with and without texture.

We expected that the influence of texture would show itself in perceptions of greater rotation, as compared to textureless targets. However, with finer and finer texture, we also expected that some level of fineness would be reached at and beyond which the binocular system no longer could utilize the texture to establish intervening referents. In such instances, rotation should be no different than it would be without texture, whether or not visual acuity remained sufficient to detect the presence of texture. Stated differently, an array could have a recognizable texture that was too fine to allow anything like a point-for-point comparison that would establish disparities through paired receptive fields and then lead to the stimulation of disparity detectors associated with them.

Stereograms in this study consisted of horizontal continuous and broken lines; and in every instance the binocular subtense of the array, that is, the directional separation between the ends, equaled 4°. The continuous line stereogram was without texture and served as a control, whereas the broken line stereograms had texture by reason of their interruption, with coarseness dependent upon the number of line segments in the array. The segments were always dark squares 8′ of arc on a side with a luminance of 3.0 ft-L seen against a homogeneous background of 32 ft-L. Perfect binocular correlation was maintained between half-images in all stereograms and the extreme left and right segments carried a disparity appropriate to a 45° rotation. The six textures employed are illustrated in Fig. 8.11 along with two controls (C1 and C2). A schematic drawing of the geometry and the resultant half-images for one

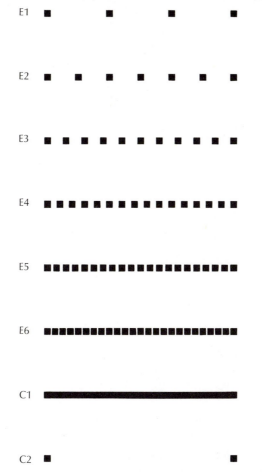

Fig. 8.11   Facsimiles of the six textures (E1-6) and two control stereograms (C1 and C2) used to determine the effect of texture on perceived rotation with end disparity held constant. Left half-images only.

target array both are shown in Fig. 8.12. When the line segments are projected to the frontoparallel plane from the vantage of each optical node, then the stereogram half-images that would obtain are shown at the bottom of the figure.

Six trained observers who met our visual criteria made judgments of angles of rotation for each of the eight stereograms (C1, C2, and E1-6) when displayed in a mirror stereoscope. Each observer saw each stereo-

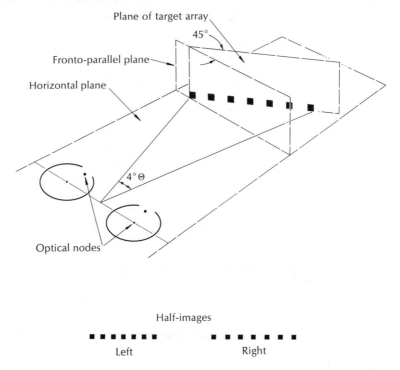

Fig. 8.12   An illustration of the geometrical arrangement for a given textured array and the resultant half-images.

gram five times in a random order with the restriction that no stereogram could be viewed a second time until each had been seen once, and so on through the five series of presentations. Observers were instructed to look directly at the display, but no specific point of fixation was established.

The magnitude of rotation of textured arrays always exceeded that obtained with the textureless line (C1). Mean angles of rotation are shown in Fig. 8.13 as a function of texture gradient, measured as the number of line segments in the array. The upper abscissa identifies the particular textures by code number, as presented in Fig. 8.11. Note that the middle textures led to perceived rotations that were very close to the predicted value of 45°. However, coarser and finer textures gave less perceived rotation.

In the case of maximum coarseness (E1), the segments comprising the array had directional separations of $1° - 20'$ of arc, and we suspect that the underestimation of rotation is attributable to the influence of directional separation. The next finer texture (E2) had directional separations of $0° - 40'$ of arc between the segments, and this value was sufficient to veridical perception. Between these two levels of directional separation ($1° - 20'$ and $0° - 40'$) lies a threshold value for texture where the distance between the intervening referents is just short enough to prohibit the influence of separation from interacting with disparity coding. Our estimate of the threshold is $1°$, a value consistent with our earlier observations with the hairline grids. The significance of our findings is that two isolated targets (C2) separated by $4°$ resulted in very little rotation even though disparity was present, whereas veridical perception occurred by introducing a texture (intervening referents) with identifiable contours as wide apart as $1°$. Additional referents did not increase perceived rotation. In the case of maximum fineness (E6), rotation was attenuated to the same extent as the uninterrupted line (C1).

Here, then, is a second limit. When intervening referents have identifiable contours separated by $0° - 1' - 40''$ of arc, or less, the binocular system cannot utilize the disparity information in the texture, and it apparently reverts to use of the end disparity alone. The acuity system can, of course, continue to detect the texture.

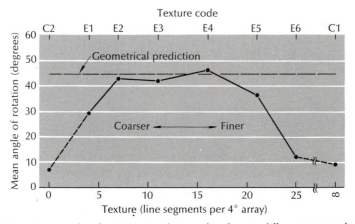

Fig. 8.13 Mean angle of rotation in degrees for the six different textured arrays (E1-6) and the two control conditions (C1 and C2). In every case end disparity was appropriate to a $45°$ rotation.

The textureless line (C1) was reported in this experiment to be rotated to approximately the same extent (9.2°) as were the rectangles (8.7°) in our earlier experiment. However, the second control stereogram which contained only the two end segments (C2) led to a mean rotation angle of 7.0°, a value much less than the 32.2° obtained with the vertical lines reported earlier (see p. 209). We cannot account for this difference, but it should be noted that, while disparity and directional separation were identical in both conditions, the square segments in the present experiment had a vertical subtense of 8′ of arc, whereas the lines of the earlier experiment had a vertical subtense of 1°. Perhaps the latter target, by virtue of its greater vertical subtense, allowed more horizontal channels to operate in the coding of the disparity.

References

1. Youngs, W. M. The coding of disparity as a function of directional separation and feature similarity. Unpublished doctoral dissertation, Dartmouth College, Hanover, New Hampshire, 1974.

9
Binocular Locking and Dichopticity

Both the stability and organization of the visual world depend upon the manner in which the respective images to the eyes are coded by the visual nervous system. With normal binocular sight, the information contained in the patterning of edges, textures, shapes, and brightnesses is sufficient to allow a remarkable synthesis of two interacting sensory channels into one visual world. Outside the laboratory, where controls cannot be exercised, visual arrays typically are rich in information for the mechanisms of coding; and so once a particular perceptual organization occurs, it is not apt to change. Accordingly, however the synthesis of analogous portions of the right- and left-eye images is achieved, the process is not easily opened to scrutiny.

In this chapter we shall consider several experiments in which simple patterns were viewed stereoscopically in order to determine some of the rules that govern binocular combination of monocular visual information. It seemed important to us to discover how the visual system establishes identities between the monocular images and what weight it gives to particular stimulus parameters when virtual identity is disallowed by the introduction of patterns in the right and left viewing channels of a stereoscope that contain different features (dichopticity).

The basic concept which lies at the center of our experiments we have referred to as *binocular locking* and *re-locking*. Given a specific attitude of the eyes, the visual system tends to *lock* the monocular images according to their analogous parts and so establishes a particular per-

225

ceptual organization. However, when the visual targets are of simple and redundant geometrical forms, then under certain circumstances, a slight change in fixation, especially one that involves convergence or divergence, can lead to a pronounced alteration in perceptual organization. As we shall explain, such an alteration involves binocular *re-locking;* that is, the images of certain objects in visual space which were fused previously now combine in a different way with the result that their retinal disparities and relative depth planes change. Simply conceived, *re-locking results when the visual system achieves a different cross correlation of identities in the monocular images.* Obviously, the ease with which re-locking occurs depends upon the extent to which the re-locked stimulus objects have features in common. Re-locking also can occur with constant fixation provided that target disparity is changed by some critical amount. This will become clear as the discussion proceeds.

We begin the treatment with a discussion of the details of binocular locking and re-locking when the channels of the stereoscope contain patterns with identical features (diopticity). Thereafter, we shall consider an experimental technique that we have employed to determine the hierarchy among several stimulus parameters that influence the probability of re-locking. The chapter concludes with a discussion of the effects of dichoptic stimulation on the perception of depth.

BINOCULAR LOCKING AND RE-LOCKING

Our discussion of binocular locking and re-locking will be facilitated if we introduce here the notion of a central cyclopean matrix. If one took the right retina and superimposed it upon the left one in such a way as to make the foveas and major axes congruent, then the resultant single map of the binocular input is all that we mean when we denote the map as a central matrix.

With reference to such a matrix, suppose a small circular target to be imaged on one retina at a locus between two identical targets imaged on the contralateral retina. In preliminary work we observed that the single target tended to fuse with which ever of the contralateral targets was spatially closer to it on the central matrix, provided that the arrangement of the targets on the retinas was such as to place them within Panum's fusional area. In circumstances wherein the laterally bounding targets were too widely separated, then the single target would fuse with neither of them and diplopia followed unless, of course, the attitude of the eyes changed appropriately through vergence movements.

We wished to explore this initial observation more systematically, and to do so we first constructed a special mirror stereoscope that had the property of allowing the experimenter to vary disparity in both the crossed and uncrossed directions without changing the locus of fixation. In these experiments a stationary fixation point (sometimes a line) always appeared centered within the binocular field of view at an optical distance of 83 cm, measured from the optical nodes of the eyes. Convergence, therefore, was symmetrical. The targets were mounted in the right and left channels on thin nonreflecting glass oriented in a plane perpendicular to the monocular lines of sight at the same optical distance as fixation. The mounts which held the glass were yoked and could be moved laterally relative to the line of sight to effect changes in disparity. A calibrated vernier was used to measure target disparity.

Inasmuch as the observer's fixation point remained invariant, yoked lateral movement of the half-image targets perpendicular to the line of sight produced a disparity between the targets and fixation so that the targets appeared displaced in depth along binocular lines of sight. The physical yoking of the target mounts was possible because target movement in both channels in a single direction had the effect of displacing the targets in opposite directions when seen through the stereoscope. It was the use of mirrors that afforded us this simple convenience. Accordingly, depending upon the direction of displacement of the yoked mounts, either crossed or uncrossed disparity was introduced simultaneously in identical amounts in both right- and left-eye channels. The introduction of disparity, in effect, displaced the images on the retinas and thereby afforded a means of changing the distance between the representations of analogous portions of the targets on the hypothetical central matrix.

Geometrical Analysis. Consider the left and right half-images shown at the top of Fig. 9.1. Each contains a fixation line and three circles which, for present purposes, have been coded by vertical and horizontal diameters to denote left and right, respectively. The position of the circles relative to the fixation line is identical in both half-images so that disparity is absent. If the two separate displays are superimposed so that

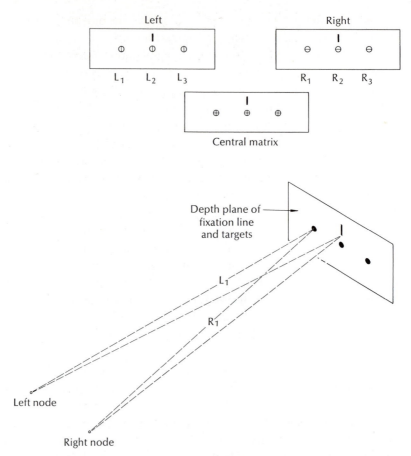

Fig. 9.1   Left and right half-images of a fixation line and three dots (top) shown superimposed on a central matrix. Below is a projection depicting the appearance of the display one would have if the half-images were viewed stereoscopically. The lines L_1 and R_2 are illustrative monocular lines of sight.

the fixation lines are congruent, as shown below on the *central matrix,* then analogous circles (L_1R_1, L_2R_2, and L_3R_3) also are congruent. At the bottom of the figure is shown a projected view of the binocularly combined half-images. With fixation to the line, the absence of disparity places the three circles and the fixation line all in a single plane. Note that the monocular lines of sight (dashed lines L_1 and R_1) intersect at the plane of fixation.

Suppose now the position of the circles in each half-image to be shifted relative to the same fixation line in such a way as to give them a slight crossed disparity, as illustrated at the top of Fig. 9.2. When the fixation lines again are superimposed, as shown on the central matrix, analogous circles are no longer congruent, but each pair carries an identical crossed disparity. Furthermore, as long as disparity is slight, analo-

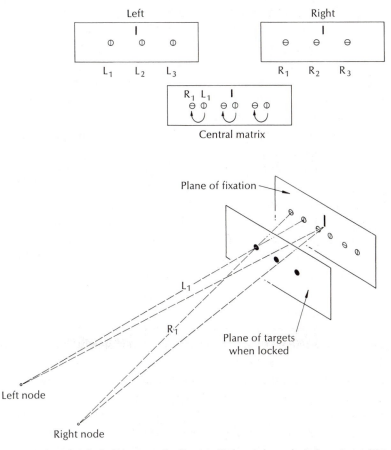

Fig. 9.2   Left and right half-images of a fixation line and three dots. Superimposition on a central matrix so that fixation is congruent leaves the dots disparate. Proximity of analogous dots (e.g., L_1 and R_1) leads to fusion in the direction of the arrows. Below is a projection depicting the appearance of the display one would have if the half-images were viewed stereoscopically. The lines L_1 and R_1 are illustrative monocular lines of sight that determine the depth plane of the fused (solid) dot.

gous circles remain closer together on the central matrix than do non-analogous ones. That is, L_1 is spatially closer to R_1 than it is to R_2, and so on. Our hypothesis was that in such cases, analogous dots not only would fuse, but they would, by their respective positions, define a particular level of crossed disparity.

The perceptual result would be the appearance of three circles in a common depth plane closer than the plane of fixation. The bottom portion of Fig 9.2 illustrates this organization. In binocular view, the depth of each dot is determined by the intersection of the monocular lines of sight to analogous circles, as shown by example for the leftmost circle (dashed lines L_1 and R_1).

As the circles are moved relative to fixation to achieve greater and greater crossed disparity, an amount of disparity is reached at which analogous circles are no longer closer than nonanalogous circles when the fixation lines of the half-images are superimposed on the central matrix. This fact is illustrated in Fig. 9.3. Note that L_1 now is closer to R_2 than it is to R_1. If analogous circles continued to be fused and to have their central matrix locations serve as the basis for disparity coding, then the binocular view would again contain three circles in a common plane closer than that of fixation (open circles). The only major difference between the percepts resulting from stereoscopic inspection of the half-images of Figs. 9.2 and 9.3 would be that the plane of the circles would be closer in the latter case because the level of crossed disparity is greater.

However, if nonanalogous circles fused, then two significant perceptual changes would be in evidence. First, if L_1 combined with R_2 and L_2 with R_3, then neither R_1 nor L_3 would have a circle with which to combine. Accordingly, the binocular percept would contain a total of four circles, with the central ones combined binocularly and the lateral ones uncombined, that is, monocular. Second, even though analogous circles carried a *crossed* disparity with regard to optical geometry, the visual system would code the binocularly combined circles as if they carried an *uncrossed* disparity. The perceptual effect would be that the circles would appear in a depth plane farther away than the fixation line (solid circles).

The lower part of Fig. 9.3 depicts the options. If analogous circles combine, then their depth plane is determined by the intersection of the

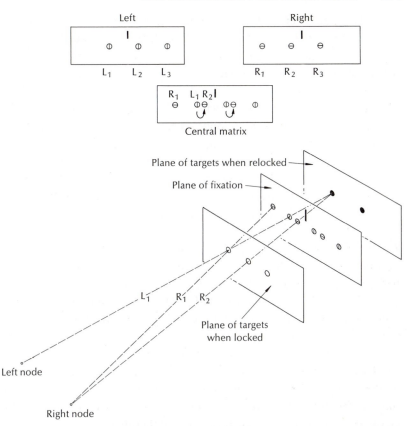

Fig. 9.3   Left and right half-images of a fixation line and three dots. Superimposition on a central matrix so that fixation is congruent leaves the dots disparate. Proximity of nonanalogous dots (e.g., L_1 and R_2) leads to fusion in the direction of the arrows. Accordingly, the depth plane of the fused dots is reversed relative to the fixation line. See text for explanation.

monocular lines of sight shown as dashed lines L_1 and R_1. Obviously, three circles appear in a plane closer than fixation. On the other hand, if nonanalogous circles combine, such as L_1 and R_2, then their depth plane would appear farther than fixation, as determined by the intersection of the monocular lines of sight shown as dashed lines L_1 and R_2.

We knew from our initial observations that when patterns similar to those shown in Figs. 9.2 and 9.3 were viewed stereoscopically, observers would sometimes report three circles closer than fixation while at other times they would report four circles farther than fixation. It seemed to us, as earlier mentioned, that the critical determinant was the relative proximity of analogous and nonanalogous circles on our hypothetical central matrix. For convenience, *we defined binocular locking as the combination of analogous circles and re-locking as the combination of nonanalogous circles.* By employing targets similar to those just described, there never was any doubt as to when an observer re-locked because its occurrence was accompanied by the perception of an additional circle and the depth plane of the circles relative to fixation was abruptly reversed. In the context of the discussion presented, the question to be answered was, where must L_1 be located between R_1 and R_2 on the central matrix to have an equal probability of fusion with each?

The Spatial Rule. To answer this question we executed an experiment in which six observers viewed a series of stereoscopic displays with disparity as the independent variable. Each half-image contained five solid black dots of 5′ diameter arranged horizontally with each separated center to center by 20′ of arc. A fixation line like that shown in Fig. 9.1 was used, and it appeared centered in the binocular field of view. By moving the glass target panels to predetermined positions noted on the vernier scale, the experimenter could vary the level of crossed disparity of the dots relative to the fixation line to one of eleven values that ranged from 0 to 20′ of arc in steps of 2′. Each observer saw each of the eleven disparity conditions six times in random order.

Observers were instructed to fixate the line and then report the number of dots they observed and the depth of the dots relative to fixation. The latter judgment was made relative to the distance to fixation which served as a modulus of 100 arbitrary units. Binocular locking would result in reports of five dots at depths of less than 100, whereas re-locking would result in reports of six dots at depths greater than 100. Recall that the effect of increasing the disparity between the dots and the fixation line was to shift progressively the positions of the dots on the central matrix from one in which analogous dots were superimposed (zero disparity) to one in which nonanalogous dots were superimposed (maximum disparity of 20′ of arc).

In Fig. 9.4 is plotted the percentage of re-locking as a function of disparity, where the data are combined across observers and repetitions.

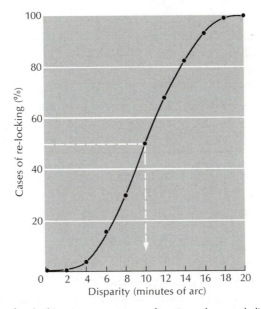

Fig. 9.4 Cases of re-locking in per cent as a function of crossed disparity in minutes of arc. The 50 per cent point (p = 0.5) is taken as the threshold for re-locking, and it corresponds to a disparity of 10′ of arc.

Note that re-locking had a p = 0.5 when the disparity equaled 10′ of arc. This disparity was such as to place the dots from the right- and left-eye patterns 180° out of phase on the central matrix. In terms of our earlier treatment of the geometry of locking and re-locking, the threshold for re-locking (p = 0.5) occurred when L_1 was situated on the central matrix exactly midway between R_1 and R_2. In the following treatment we shall limit our analysis to particular pairs of dots, but what is said of one pair applies to others.

The fact that the threshold corresponded to the 180° phase condition and that the psychometric function was symmetrical (Fig. 9.4) led us to conclude that *spatial proximity of geometrically identical target elements is the factor of influence that determines fusion and disparity coding*, no matter whether the proximate target elements are analogous or non-analogous. We refer to this as the *spatial proximity rule* of binocular organization.

The results pertaining to the depth of the dots were consistent with our expectation in that, as disparity increased, the plane of the dots became at first closer and closer to the observer up to that crossed disparity level at which re-locking occurred. With re-locking there was a sudden discontinuity in the depth plane of the dots in that they appeared farther away than the fixation line. As the crossed disparity continued to increase toward its maximum, the dots moved toward the plane of fixation, finally to appear co-planar with the line when the maximum disparity was reached. A summary of the depth magnitude judgments is given in Fig. 9.5.

There are two things to be noted with reference to Fig. 9.5. First, unlike the prior figure where each data point was based on an n of 36, the mean depth data points did not always have the same n. For example, when disparity equaled 10' of arc, of the 36 observations (6 0s × 6 repetitions) taken, half were of depth reports during locking and half during re-locking. Accordingly, the two data points of 10' of arc each had an n of 18. At 8' of disparity, of the 36 observations taken, 25 were of depth reports during locking and their mean is plotted in the figure.

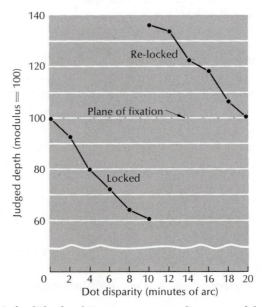

Fig. 9.5 Mean judged depth relative to a constant distance modulus of 100 as a function of crossed disparity in minutes of arc. See text for explanation.

Mean depth of the re-locked cases at 8′ of disparity is not shown. All data points plotted have n's between 18 and 36.

The second thing to note is that the functional coding of disparity changed from one of crossed to one of uncrossed direction as a consequence of re-locking. This matter is made plain if we reconsider the central matrix shown in Fig. 9.3. As circle L_1 moves from R_1 toward R_2, it may be considered at once to undergo an increasing crossed disparity with reference to R_1 *and* a decreasing uncrossed disparity with reference to R_2. The two cases are reciprocally related. What appears to happen is that as long as L_1 is closer to R_1 than it is to R_2, R_1 serves as a referent and the visual system codes the disparity as *crossed*. However, when L_1 is closer to R_2, then R_2 becomes the referent and the visual system codes the disparity as *uncrossed*. Furthermore, as shown by our depth data, once geometrical disparity is such as to align nonanalogous circles on the central matrix (20′ of arc in the experiment), then L_1 and R_2 occupy identical locations with reference to the fixation line and they are therefore coded as having zero disparity. Hence, at the maximum disparity we used, the binocularly combined nonanalogous dots appeared co-planar with the fixation line.

These findings have been replicated in additional experiments where dot size and inter-dot distance were slightly different. We have also determined that the spatial proximity rule can predict when re-locking will occur during the stereoscopic viewing of patterns that contain multiple horizontal rows of dots where the inter-dot distance in each row is different. A simple case is illustrated in Fig. 9.6.

Here may be seen the right and left half-images that contain two horizontal rows (A and B) of identical dots with different inter-dot distances. The disparity is crossed at a level which places analogous dots closer together on the central matrix in row A but nonanalogous dots closer in row B. The perceptual result is that the depth plane of the dots in row A is closer than fixation (monocular lines L_1 and R_1) while the depth plane of the dots in row B is farther than fixation (monocular lines L_2 and R_3).

DICHOPTICITY AND RE-LOCKING

In the half-images employed in our study of spatial proximity, all the target elements (dots) were identical. We wished to determine whether

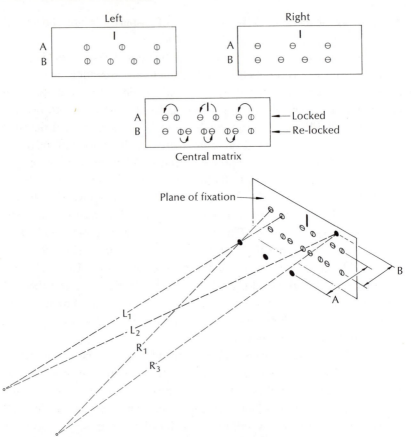

Fig. 9.6   A schematic illustration of how the spatial proximity rule predicts different depth planes for two horizontal rows of dots (A and B) with different center to center angular separations.

or not the threshold for re-locking would be shifted if the dots to be re-locked were made different along a particular dimension like luminance or size.

We chose to introduce the difference in the dots to be re-locked by utilizing a pattern of alternation in each half-image. For example, with regard to the five dots in the left half-image, counting from left to right, dots numbered 1, 3, and 5 would have one luminance level whereas dots numbered 2 and 4 would have another. The same pattern of alternation occurred in the right half-image, with the result that as long as analogous dots combined, the pairs in each combination always had identical luminances. On the other hand, when nonanalogous dots combined, as in re-locking, the pairs in each combination had different luminances. Re-locking, therefore, involved dichoptic combination whereas locking involved dioptic combination.

We expected that the threshold for re-locking ($p = 0.5$) would occur at greater levels of disparity when the re-locking involved dichoptic combinations than when re-locking involved dioptic combinations. In the context of our earlier discussion, this means that L_1 would have to be closer to R_2 than to R_1 when the probability of fusion to either was equal.

Luminance. Working in the Dartmouth laboratory, Bill (2) studied the effects of luminance differences on binocular re-locking. He used the five-dot format previously described except that the dots subtended about 10′ of arc and they were separated by 26′, center to center. Disparity relative to the fixation line ranged from 0 to 26′ of arc in eight equal steps (3.25′).

When the stereogram involved an alternating pattern of luminance, the odd-numbered dots in both half-images were always of higher luminance than the even numbered dots. Four odd–even patterns of luminance alternation were used, with ft-L values as follows: 33.0 and 2.1; 26.4 and 3.4; 19.4 and 6.7; 15.2 and 10.7. These four patterns comprised the experimental stereograms and produced dot luminance differences after re-locking of 30.9, 23.0, 12.7, and 4.5 ft-L, respectively.

To determine whether or not luminance level itself would influence the threshold for re-locking, Bill employed control stereograms identical in spatial properties to the experimental stereograms. However, in the case of the control patterns, all dots had a single luminance level within a single stereogram. Six different luminance values were used (33.0, 24.2, 15.2, 10.7, 5.1, and 2.0 ft-L).

Six observers followed a procedure similar to that earlier described. The order of presentation of the ten stereograms (four experimental, six control) was random for each observer, and for each stereogram the order of disparity level was also random. The entire sequence was repeated six times for each observer.

Data from the experiment confirmed the hypothesis that the threshold

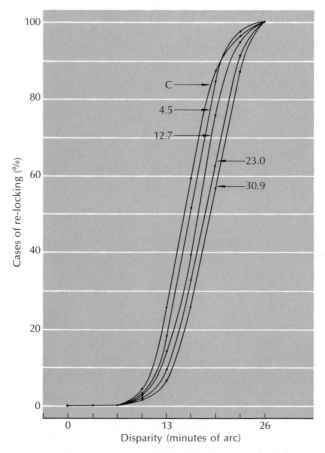

Fig. 9.7   Cases of re-locking in per cent as a function of crossed disparity in minutes of arc for the control condition (C) and four levels of luminance dichopticity.
Data from Bill (2).

for re-locking would show a systematic shift as the luminance levels of
the nonanalogous re-locked dots became ever more discrepant. Inasmuch as luminance level in the six control stereograms did not produce
any statistically significant effect on threshold, data for the control conditions are combined in Fig. 9.7 and appear as the function labeled C.
The other four functions represent the experimental stereograms. A disparity of 13′ of arc placed the dots on the central matrix from the left
and right channels exactly out of phase (180°). Note that the threshold

for re-locking in the control patterns occurred practically at this level of disparity; or stated differently, L_1 was located about midway between R_1 and R_2. However, as the luminance difference in the dots to be re-locked increased from 4.5 to 30.9 ft-L, then L_1 had to be progressively closer to R_2 in order to have an equal probability of fusion with R_1 and R_2.

The results of this experiment indicate that the spatial proximity rule is subject to modification when the locked binocular combination (L_1 to R_1) is dioptic and the re-locked combination (L_1 to R_2) is dichoptic. The effect of luminance dichopticity may be expressed as a transfer function like that shown in Fig. 9.8 where the disparity in minutes of arc at the threshold for re-locking is plotted as a function of dichopticity level, measured as the dot luminance difference in the alternating patterns. With zero dichopticity (diopticity), threshold equaled $13' - 30''$ of arc, a level that placed L_1 about midway between R_1 and R_2, as shown by the right ordinate. If luminance difference had no effect upon re-locking, then the threshold would have remained constant at $13'$. The relative

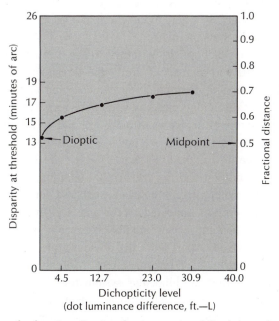

Fig. 9.8   A transfer function showing the progressive shift of the re-locking threshold as a function of luminance dichopticity.

locus of L_1 between R_1 and R_2 on the central matrix may be obtained by projecting the data points to the right ordinate.

Size. Under similar procedures we conducted an experiment to determine the effect of dot size on the threshold for re-locking when the five dots in each half-image alternated in size. As before, the dots were separated by 26′ of arc, center to center, but in this experiment they all had a single luminance level. The odd numbered dots in each half-image always subtended 10′ of arc with the even numbered ones sometimes larger in diameter (13, 16, and 20′) and sometimes smaller (7, 6.25, and 5′). These particular diameters were selected to give us three dichoptic size ratios; namely, 1.3 (10:13 and 7.7:10), 1.6 (10:16 and 6.25:10), and 2.0 (10:20 and 5:10). To determine whether size alone would influence the threshold for re-locking we used three control stereograms in which all the dots had a single diameter of 5, 10, or 20′ of arc.

Just as in Bill's experiment, the locked binocular combination (analogous dots L_1 and R_1) is dioptic whereas the re-locked combination (non-analogous dots L_1 and R_2) is dichoptic, except in the case of each of the control stereograms where both combinations are dioptic because all the dots had the same diameter.

The effect of size dichopticity is shown in Fig. 9.9 as a transfer function where disparity in minutes of arc at the threshold for re-locking is plotted as a function of dichopticity level, measured as the ratio of dot diameters in the alternating patterns. Our observers were unable to relock dots as discrepant in size as 10 and 20′, and so the data obtained from this particular stereogram are not included in the mean for the ratio 2. That is, the mean threshold shown for the size ratio of 2 includes only the 5:10 condition and not the 10:20 condition. All other thresholds include conditions wherein the even-numbered dots were both larger and smaller, in the ratios indicated on the abscissa. In the 10:20 condition, no stable re-locking seemed possible because no satisfactory fusion of these dots occurred. Apart from the obvious conclusion to be drawn with regard to the limits of fusion, failure to obtain re-locking in this condition suggests that the binocular system may more readily accept size discrepant targets of a given ratio as "identical" when the angular subtense of both of them is small as compared to when it is large.

To keep the probability of fusion to R_1 and R_2 equal, it was neces-

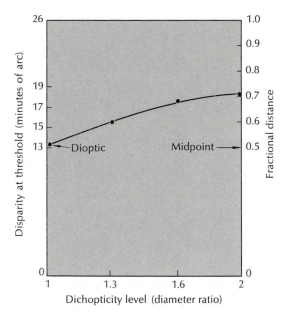

Fig. 9.9   A transfer function showing the progressive shift of the re-locking threshold as a function of size dichopticity.

sary to locate L_1 progressively closer to R_2 as the size of R_2 became more and more discrepant from L_1. Here again we note that the spatial proximity rule is subject to modification when the targets to be re-locked differ in size. The threshold position of L_1 between R_1 and R_2 may be obtained by projecting the data points to the right ordinate.

FUNCTIONAL HIERARCHY

The re-locking paradigm we have used to establish the spatial proximity rule and its modification by the introduction of luminance and size differences also can be used to assess the relative weights of these dimensions in their binocular processing.

When acting separately, we know that luminance and size differences both have the effect of shifting the threshold position on the central matrix from the midpoint toward the locus of R_2. Based upon the transfer functions given in Figs. 9.8 and 9.9, we can select levels of dichopticity for luminance and size that have identical threshold shifts. For example, a luminance difference of 4.5 ft-L and a size difference in the ratio 1.3 both resulted in the same threshold for re-locking; namely, equal probability for fusion to R_1 and R_2 occurred when L_1 had a disparity of 15.5' of arc and a central matrix location of 0.6 of the distance from R_1 to R_2.

The fact that the levels of dichopticity specified for luminance and size differences had identical effects on re-locking does not mean that the binocular system necessarily would give equal weight to them when one perceptual organization (re-locking) favored a match of luminance at the expense of size while a second perceptual organization (locking) favored a match of size at the expense of luminance. All that is known is that when these luminance and size differences operated alone, they had identical effects. Here it should be recalled that, in the two experiments on dichopticity so far reported, the locking of analogous dots always involved the binocular combination of dioptic pairs. Only with re-locking of nonanalogous dots were the combined pairs dichoptic.

The question we asked was this: Where would L_1 have to be located between R_1 and R_2 to effect an equal probability of fusion to each when R_1 matched L_1 in size while R_2 matched L_1 in luminance? Under this experimental arrangement either binocular combination would involve dichoptic pairs.

Our thesis was that the locus of L_1 at threshold would indicate the relative weights of these two stimulus dimensions. Consider the schematic diagram of a portion of the central matrix shown in Fig. 9.10. The dots R_1 and R_2 are separated center to center by 26' of arc. At the top is shown the threshold position of L_1 in our control conditions where all dots have the same features. It lies at the midpoint between R_1 and R_2 at a fractional distance of 0.5. Directly below are shown, in turn, the displacement (Δ) of L_1 at threshold brought about by a luminance difference of 4.5 ft-L and a size difference in the ratio of 1.3. At the bottom may be seen the two kinds of dichopticity operating simultaneously, with the luminance condition reversed left to right to place them in opposition.

If either luminance or size difference had the same effect on threshold when in opposition as when operating singly, then the position of L_1 at threshold would be at the fractional distance of 0.4 or 0.6, depending only upon which stimulus dimension the system utilized to the exclusion of the other. However, if both luminance and size affected the threshold

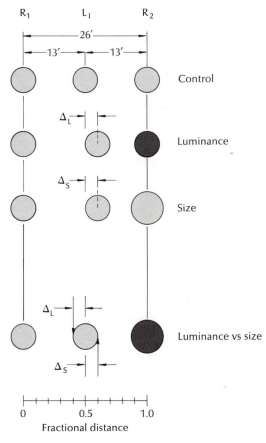

Fig. 9.10   A schematic illustration of how two different kinds of dichopticity can be placed in opposition.

for binocular combination, then the position of L_1 would be somewhere between 0.4 and 0.6. Clearly, L_1 should be closer to R_1 than R_2 to compensate for the luminance difference between them; but just as clearly, L_1 should be closer to R_2 than to R_1 to compensate for the size difference between them. Inasmuch as L_1 cannot at once be closer both to R_1 and to R_2, we reasoned that its threshold position would signify the hierarchy of these two stimulus dimensions. Only if the opposition of these effects was such as to place L_1 at the midpoint could we then conclude that they were equally salient to binocular organization.

Dichopticity in Opposition. Six observers viewed five-dot arrays like those earlier mentioned, but in this case there were two patterns of alternation in each half-image, one of size and one of luminance, and both alternated according to the values specified in the discussion just concluded. To effect the opposition we sought, the alternation of size across the five dots was in phase in both half-images whereas the alternation of luminance was out of phase.

The difference we used in luminance and size were sufficiently small to allow our observers ease of fusion, and on each trial an observer reported both the number of dots seen and their depth plane relative to fixation. The same levels of disparity as previously mentioned were used, and as before, the order of disparity level was random.

Based on reports for all observers across the five repetitions, we first plotted the percentage of cases of re-locking (L_1 to R_2) for each disparity level and then determined the disparity of the threshold location of L_1 in the same manner as we had done before.

In this experiment the position of L_1 which produced equal probabilities of fusion to R_1 and R_2 corresponded to a disparity of $12' - 4''$ of arc so that on the central matrix L_1 was located closer to R_1 than to R_2 (fractional distance = 0.42). We concluded from this experiment that luminance is more important than size as a determinant of binocular organization.

If the locus of L_1 at threshold had been at a fractional distance of 0.4, the locus predicted on the basis of luminance difference alone, then we would have concluded that the size difference had no effect at all. Stated differently, luminance had a maximum weight while size had a zero weight. On the other hand, had the locus of L_1 at threshold been at a fractional distance of 0.6, the locus predicted on the basis of size difference alone, then we would have concluded that the weights were reversed. Finally, if L_1 had been at the fractional distance of 0.5, then luminance and size would be weighted equally.

Figure 9.11 shows hypothetical linear weight functions for luminance and size. The arrow indicates the obtained threshold locus for L_1 and from the functions given the weights for luminance and size are 0.9 and 0.1, respectively.

We believe that the re-locking paradigm is suitable to studies of the principles that describe the probabilities of alternate binocular organiza-

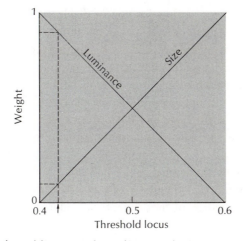

Fig. 9.11   Hypothetical linear weighting functions for luminance and size. See text for explanation.

tions. Furthermore, we feel that the method allows an experimenter a psychophysical alternative to single unit recording from cortical cells.

DEPTH AND DICHOPTICITY

In several of our experiments on re-locking we had observers make depth magnitude estimations to the plane of the re-locked dots relative to the distance to the fixation line. While the observations showed that depth was a function of the disparity of the dots, they also suggested that, for any given level of disparity, perceived depth was usually attenuated when the binocularly combined targets were dichoptic as compared to when the combined targets were dioptic.

We wished, therefore, to pursue this possibility in a systematic study that involved the simplest task possible. Accordingly, Galla (3) executed an experiment in the Dartmouth laboratory in which observers judged the stereoscopic depth of single circles relative to a fixation line under conditions in which the half-image circles were both dioptic and dichoptic.

The stimulus configuration consisted of a fixation line centered in the binocular field of view at an optical distance of 83 cm. The black circular target (3 ft-L), seen against a homogeneous background (76.5

ft-L), appeared directly below fixation or displaced 2 or 4° to the right of fixation. These three retinal positions afforded the opportunity to study the effects of retinal eccentricity on the perception of depth. Our interest in eccentricity and dichopticity will become plain later.

Of the six stereograms used, three were dichoptic and three were dioptic in size. In the dichoptic conditions the diameter of the circles in the half-images differed by 2, 4, and 6′ of arc with the restriction that the mean subtense be 13′; and with these dichoptic targets the presentation of target size to each eye was completely counterbalanced. In the three dioptic stereograms the circles in the half-images were identical within each stereogram at 10, 13, and 16′ of arc. These three conditions were used to learn whether or not target size alone would alter depth perception.

For each of the six stereograms viewed, there were nine levels of disparity that ranged from +12′ (crossed) to −12′ (uncrossed) in steps of 3′ of arc, including zero disparity, all measured center to center. There were 162 unique viewing conditions (6 stereograms × 9 levels of disparity × 3 retinal positions).

Each of seven observers who met our visual criteria first was trained to make depth magnitude estimations to visual targets relative to a fixation line which served as a constant distance modulus of 100 arbitrary units. Training occurred on a special apparatus and during each of 10 training trials an observer was told the appropriate distance to the test target immediately after he provided his estimate. No criterion of accuracy was invoked.

The order of presentation of the stereograms was random for each observer, but all nine disparity levels were presented randomly for a given stereogram before a second was seen. The entire experiment was repeated four times.

Observers were instructed to fixate the line at all times and to give an estimate of the depth of the circle relative to the constant modulus of 100.

Galla found that judged depth always was a linear function of binocular disparity, but the slope of the psychometric functions was influenced both by dichopticity and retinal eccentricity. An analysis of variance indicated that these two parameters and their interaction all were significant sources of variance.

The influence of size dichopticity on depth is shown in Fig. 9.12, where mean depth is plotted as a function of disparity for the 2, 4, and 6′ half-image size differences. These three functions also may be compared to the control condition (0′, dioptic). Data are combined across retinal locations of 0, 2, and 4° eccentricity. Note that slope decreases as dichopticity increases so that, for any given level of disparity, the shift in the depth plane of the circle relative to fixation (100) is attenuated more or less in proportion to dichopticity level. Nevertheless, each depth function remained linear.

Figure 9.13 illustrates the influence of retinal eccentricity on depth perception. Mean depth is plotted as a function of disparity level for each of the three retinal locations, and data are combined across dichopticity levels.

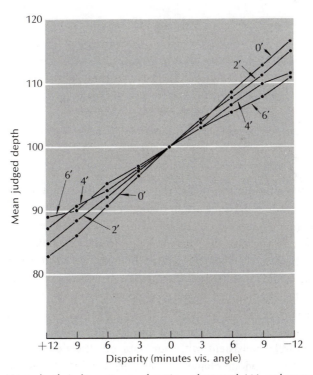

Fig. 9.12 Mean depth judgments as a function of crossed (+) and uncrossed (−) disparity for three levels of size dichopticity (2, 4, and 6′) and the dioptic control conditions (0′). Data from Galla (3).

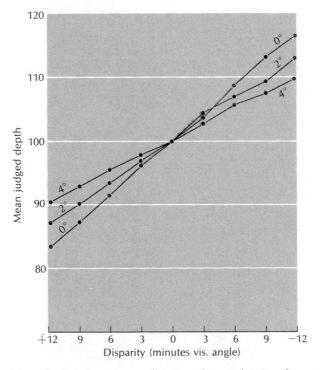

Fig. 9.13   Mean depth judgments as a function of crossed (+) and uncrossed (−) disparity for three levels of retinal eccentricity. Data from Galla (3).

While the absolute size of the targets in the three dioptic control conditions (10, 13, and 16′ of arc in diameter) did not selectively influence depth judgments, dioptic targets imaged on the foveal meridian (0° eccentricity) always gave the greatest slope to the psychometric function. Slopes of the best fit linear regression lines are given in Table IX-I for conditions of dichopticity and eccentricity. It appears that dichoptic size has a greater attenuating influence on depth perception when the targets are imaged close to the fovea than it does when they are imaged extra-foveally. The fact that eccentricity led to attenuations of depth is, of course, entirely consistent with our data on directional separation reported in the previous chapter. However, the interaction between dichopticity and eccentricity is not explicable in terms of directional separation.

Table IX-I.   Slopes of the best fit linear regression lines for the depth functions obtained under conditions of size dichopticity and retinal eccentricity. Data from Galla (3).

	Level of dichopticity			
	0′ (Dioptic)	2′	4′	6′
0°	1.38	1.35	1.28	1.12
2°	1.25	1.15	1.05	1.02
4°	1.00	1.03	0.90	0.81

Our interpretation is that the receptive fields in and near the fovea are capable of a level of feature abstraction that is more precise than that which is possible with receptive fields that lie extrafoveally (1). Accordingly, the binocular system may have a narrower filter band through which it compares foveal targets for "identity." In other words, the progressive loss of precision in the feature abstraction process which occurs as the receptive fields lie ever more peripherally may mean that the range of stimulus variation that is tolerable for disparity coding is extended. The consequence would be that dichopticity would show itself of smaller influence at the 4° location than it would at the fovea, even while eccentricity itself wielded its own influence.

References

1. Barlow, H. B., Blakemore, C., and Pettigrew, J. D. The neural mechanism of binocular depth discrimination. *J. Physiol.,* 1967, *193,* 327-342.
2. Bill, J. C. The role of dichoptic brightness in binocular vision. Unpublished doctoral dissertation, Dartmouth College, Hanover, N.H., 1973.
3. Galla, J. P. The effects of size dichopticity on the perception of depth. Unpublished doctoral dissertation, Dartmouth College, Hanover, N.H., 1974.

10
Stereoscopic Size-Distance Relationships

The psychophysical problem of relating physical size and distance to perceived size and distance has occupied a central role in experimental psychology. Our purpose in this chapter is to report stereoscopic size-distance relationships which we have determined from experiments with targets defined by stereoscopic contours and by contours arising from abrupt luminance gradients. Inasmuch as the angular size of a disparate target in a stereogram remains constant while perceived size and distance vary with its disparity, the stereoscopic size-distance findings can be used to determine the nature of this relationship. Before we treat in detail the effects of binocular disparity upon size-distance relationships, we shall review briefly the effects of convergence and accommodation upon judgments of visual extents. We wish to state as clearly as the present evidence allows the individual effects of oculomotor adjustments and disparity on judgments of size and distance.

CONVERGENCE AND ACCOMMODATION

As the distance of a fixated object changes, so does the angle formed at the object by the foveal lines of sight. Vergence movements of the eyes allow foveal vision of a binocularly viewed target regardless of its distance from an observer. The eyes are mobilized through the coordinated action of the rectus muscles, an action which is modulated by feedback from the sensory influx. The angle of convergence (γ) is calculated by the following formula:

$$\gamma \text{ (in degrees)} = 57.3 \left(\frac{0.065}{D}\right),$$

where D is the distance to fixation in meters. The values of 57.3 and 0.065 represent a trigonometrical constant and the average inter-pupillary distance, respectively. The relationship between distance and convergence angle is given in Fig. 10.1. Note that convergence angle undergoes rapid change for distances within 1 m from an observer, but only small changes for distances beyond 2 m.

Changes in fixation distance that lead to vergence movements of the eyes also lead to lenticular accommodation, especially for objects within 2 m of an observer. The change in the shape of the lens is required in order to adjust the refractive power of the optical system so as to allow a sharp focus of the image in the plane of the retinal mosaic. Inasmuch as the greatest refraction occurs at the air-cornea interface, the lenticular accommodation mechanism may be considered as serving the purpose of a fine tuner which is invoked only for close vision. As objects approach an observer from a distance of about 2 m, the increasing tension in the ciliary muscles *reduces* the tension in the suspensory system for the lens and thereby allows the lens to assume passively a more con-

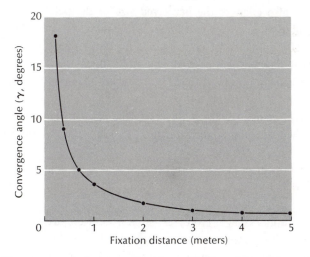

Fig. 10.1 Convergence angle (γ) as a function of fixation distance, in meters. Function shown assumes interpupillary distance of 65 mm.

vex shape. The intra-ocular muscles responsible for accommodation, like the extra-ocular muscles for convergence, are modulated by feedback from sensory influx.

As indicated in the chapter on the history of stereoscopic vision, the oculomotor mechanisms of vergence and accommodation both have been considered, from time to time, as important factors in the perception of size and distance. The first important statement of their role came from George Berkeley (*10*), and subsequent discoveries regarding the details of these mechanisms have provided impetus to his position.

The "wallpaper" phenomenon represents an early example of a case where changes in convergence produce concomitant changes in perceived size and distance (*24*). We have already treated certain of the distance effects in the previous chapter on binocular locking, although our method was somewhat different than the one usually employed. Nevertheless, it should be plain that re-locking can be brought about through a change in the angle of convergence. For example, if one has an inappropriate fixation distance, that is, the angle of convergence is too large or too small, then nonanalogous targets fuse and the perceived distance to them is altered because their disparity is miscoded. Furthermore, inappropriate convergence on a target that contains a repeating pattern, such as a wallpaper, not only changes the perceived distance to the wall, it also changes the perceived size of the pattern so that it appears smaller when closer and larger when more distant (*22, 30*).

Beside the influence of convergence on the perceived size of objects of constant angular subtense stands the influence of accommodation. Long ago Hering observed that, ". . . when changing from a monocular fixation of a distant object to viewing one close by, the distant object appears to diminish in size. Conversely the size of the nearer object increases when accommodating farther" (*18,* p. 172). Von Kries (*29*) reported a similar observation.

A reduction in perceived size brought about by convergence and accommodation has been called micropsia, and some researchers have assumed that it is due to the effects of these oculomotor processes on the size of the retinal image. However, some recent empirical evidence does not support this assumption. For example, on the basis of ray tracing models that take the refractive properties of the eye into account, Pascal (*26*) has concluded that neither convergence nor accommodation influence image size. Furthermore, photographs of the retinal image taken under different levels of accommodation and different angles of convergence do not reveal any significant changes in image size (*16*). Finally, Biersdorf and Baird (*3*) have shown that large differences in accommodation between the eyes of a single observer did not lead to differences in psychophysical matches of retinal size. In their experiment the level of accommodation in one eye was allowed to undergo wide change while the accommodative mechanism in the other eye was made inoperative through a paralysis induced with a cycloplegic drug. The results of these studies suggest that micropsia occurs despite the fact that the size of the retinal image remains unaltered by convergence and lenticular accommodation.

MATRIX TARGETS

Random Dot Stereograms. Charles Wheatstone (*30*) was the first to report the change in the apparent size of a single disparate target when it was put into binocular register. He noticed that with crossed disparity the target grew smaller, whereas with uncrossed disparity the target appeared larger in the stereoscopic field. Subsequent scientific interest focused *only* upon the role of convergence for the stereoscopic size changes without much regard for concomitant changes in apparent distance (*1, 19, 22*). Bleything (*7*) was perhaps the first to present stereoscopically disparate ringed targets and to obtain systematic size and distance judgments of the fused rings. He reported that, "stereoscopic size increases with stereoscopic localization distance and at a rate slightly greater than the rate obtained if the size is predicted from the visual angle subtended at each particular distance measured" (*7*, p. 429). Roelofs and Zeeman (*28*) also found with contour disparate ring targets that the apparent size of the fused rings varied directly with the magnitude of disparity. Unfortunately, observers reported only the relative size and distance of simultaneously presented targets rather than the distance between themselves and the fused ring (egocentric distance).

Although early interest in size-distance relationships in stereoscopic vision focused upon the role of convergence, we wished to determine whether or not the influence of disparity on size would show itself with dot-matrix stereograms. One of the unique features of dot-matrix stereograms is that they give rise to stereoscopic contours that are, under certain conditions, perceptually indistinguishable from contours arising from abrupt luminance gradients. Consequently, matrix targets afford an excellent opportunity to study stereoscopic size-distance relationships because *both contour perception and stereoscopic depth arise directly from disparity.*

It was evident to us from the outset that the Julesz random dot patterns would not be suitable to our purpose because the method by which disparity is introduced into the sub-matrix confounds its angular subtense. Recall from our earlier treatment (see Chapter 4, p. 112) that ambiguity is present at the lateral boundaries of the sub-matrix with the result that the width of the sub-matrix over which perfect binocular correlation occurs actually decreases as disparity increases. Therefore, as the stereoscopically contoured sub-matrix is seen to appear closer and closer to the observer on account of increasing crossed disparity, any reduction in its perceived size would have to be attributed to the fact that the sub-matrix actually subtends a smaller and smaller angle. Bridgman (*8*) treats this matter fully in a brief but important note.

In Fig. 10.2 may be seen a schematic illustration of the size reduction effect due to the method by which disparity is introduced. In the upper portion is shown a stereogram in which the random pattern is shown only for the central square sub-matrix. The columns are denoted by different symbols for purposes of illustration. Note in the upper stereogram that the sub-matrix has a width of six columns, no disparity, and perfect binocular correlation throughout. In the lower stereogram the left half-image remains the same, but the columns in the right half-image have been shifted leftward by one in order to give the sub-matrix a crossed disparity. According to the Julesz method, the vacant sixth column, counting from left to right, is filled with what had been the first column (*x*'s). This manipulation effectively reduces the width of the sub-matrix from six to five columns because only in five columns is disparity *and* binocular correlation preserved. The lateral columns of *x*'s in both half-images have no comparable columns with which to fuse. Thus, the size of the sub-matrix is reduced inadvertently. Accordingly, reports that the size of a stereoscopically contoured surface (sub-matrix) grows smaller as crossed disparity increases ought not to be attributed to stereoscopic distance judgments when stereograms are comprised of random dot or letter matrices (*9*).

Homogeneous Sub-Matrices. The size reduction effect due to the disparity manipulation just described is eliminated when the central sub-matrix

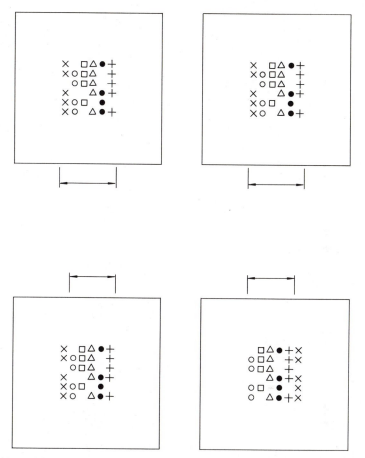

Fig. 10.2   The upper stereogram shows a 6 x 6 sub-matrix with perfect binocular correlation across all cells. The lower stereogram illustrates how the introduction of disparity reduces the width of the correlated sub-matrix. See text for explanation.

is defined by the omission of dots while the surrounding matrix has a density of 100 per cent. With such targets the angular subtense of the sub-matrix remains constant even as its disparity changes.

CLASSICAL AND MATRIX TARGETS COMPARED

We conducted three experiments to compare size-distance relationships during stereoscopic vision. Taken as a whole, our general purpose was to compare matrix targets with analogous line-drawn and solid patterned

Fig. 10.3 An illustration of the stereograms employed to compare size-distance dependency in line-drawn and matrix targets.

targets over a range of disparities in both the crossed and uncrossed direction.

Experiment One. In this experiment we employed matrix and line-drawn targets, as illustrated in Fig. 10.3. The central square in each type of stereogram carried one of five levels of crossed disparity (from 0 to 22′

of arc, in steps of 5′ − 30″) and subtended a solid visual angle of 1° of arc. The outer square subtended 2° − 12′ of arc.

Each of 10 observers who met our visual criteria viewed each stereogram in a prism stereoscope. The order of presentation was random. On each trial, observers judged the depth separation between the planes of the outer square (line or matrix) and the inner square (line or stereoscopically contoured surface) relative to the width of the base of the outer square which served as a reference modulus equal to 10. After the depth difference had been judged, observers used the same reference modulus to estimate the height and width of the centered square, which was referred to as an "object" in our instructions to them.

The results on judgments of depth differences indicate clearly that stereoscopic distance varied directly with disparity magnitude for both matrix and line-drawn stereograms. As Fig. 10.4 illustrates, the stereoscopic position of the inner square for both types of target was a linear function of disparity. Increasing the disparity carried by the inner squares made them appear progressively closer to the observers, regardless of the type of contours bounding the squares in the stereoscopic field. These

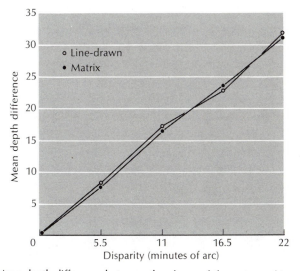

Fig. 10.4   Mean depth difference between the planes of the outer and inner squares as a function of disparity in minutes of arc. Depth difference was not influenced by the type of pattern (line-drawn and matrix) observed.

findings demonstrate that the disparity-detecting mechanism is sensitive to laterally displaced targets regardless of the level within the visual system at which the contours arise.

With regard to judgments of the size of the disparate central square, our observers saw both height and width as growing smaller as disparity increased. Mean height for both types of target is plotted in Fig. 10.5 as a function of disparity. Height-width ratio equaled 1.0 ± 0.1, thereby indicating that the *shape* of the "square" did not change with disparity. Width estimates were insignificantly different from those for height, and the change in size was essentially the same for line-drawn and matrix formats.

In effect, then, targets of constant angular size that carry a crossed disparity are seen in different stereoscopic depth planes as a function of the magnitude of the disparity, with the perceived size of the targets varying concomitantly with changes in stereoscopic localization. The fact that the stereoscopic size changes were the same for both types of target suggests that the size scaling mechanism is probably located beyond the neural level at which stereoscopic contours are formed.

Presently, two neural sites have been suggested as the location of

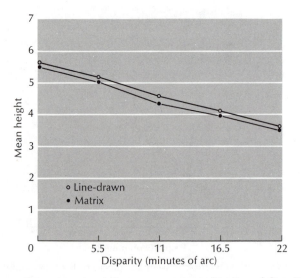

Fig. 10.5   Mean judged height of the inner square as a function of disparity in minutes of arc. Height estimates were not influenced by the type of pattern (line-drawn and matrix) observed.

the perceptual size scaling mechanism. Richards (27) has argued for the lateral geniculate nucleus as a consequence of his observation that the minimum angular dimensions for two uncorrelated random dot-matrix patterns to undergo retinal rivalry varied slightly with the distance at which they were viewed. Accordingly, he concluded that some sort of size re-scaling arose before the binocular combination of the signals from the two eyes. On the other hand, Blakemore, Garner, and Sweet (6) have suggested that the size scaling mechanism probably is located in the inferotemporal cortex because of recent findings concerning an orientation aftereffect (4, 5, 11). If an observer adapts to a high-contrast grating of black and white bars, then a subsequent low-contrast grating of the same orientation is difficult to detect while the visibility of stripes orthogonal to the adapting pattern is not reduced significantly. However, the elevation of the threshold is limited to test gratings with bars whose width is similar to those of the adapting pattern. Inasmuch as this effect still persists when the adapting grating is presented to one eye and the test grating to the other eye, the underlying neural units must be tuned binocularly (4, 5). Interestingly enough, Blakemore and his colleagues found that, with an adapting grating at three times the distance of a test grating, the maximum elevation of threshold was restricted to exactly the same *angular* spatial frequency as that of the adapting pattern. Accordingly, the maximum aftereffect occurred when the adapting and test patterns appeared to be totally different in bar width. There is little doubt that this aftereffect depends upon central processes, and this suggests that size scaling occurs farther along in the visual system, perhaps in the inferotemporal cortex. This notion is supported by the fact that the size of human receptive fields, measured at the cortex, varies with the distance of visual targets (25), and by the fact that lesions in the inferotemporal cortex abolished the ability of monkeys to make discriminations of the actual sizes of objects regardless of their distance from the animal (21). The present findings that stereoscopic size and distance varied directly with the magnitude of disparity for both line-drawn and matrix targets supports further the suggestion that the size scaling mechanism probably has a cortical, rather than a geniculate, locus.

Experiment Two. The purpose of the second experiment was to determine the effects of the *direction and magnitude* of disparity upon stereo-

Fig. 10.6 Samples of square and rectangular patterns used to determine the effects of the direction and magnitude of disparity on size and distance during stereopsis.

scopic size and distance with targets like those shown in Fig. 10.6. The outer square subtended 2° on a side in both the square and rectangular patterns. The black square (53 × 53′) and rectangle (53 × 67′) carried one of seven levels of disparity from +15 to −15′ of arc, in steps of 5′.

The procedure employed for the estimation of the size of the centered figure was the same as that used in the first experiment except that the base of the outer line-drawn square defined a reference modulus equal to 20 rather than 10. However, the depth of the disparate figure (solid square or rectangle) was judged egocentrically relative to the location of the outer line-dawn square which was said to be at a distance of 100.

As usual, the depth of the disparate figure was found to be a linear function of its disparity and stereoscopic location was not influenced by the shape of the central figure. The effect of the magnitude and direction of disparity upon the perceived size of the square is shown in Fig.

10.7, where mean height is plotted against disparity. As in the first experiment, the height-width ratio remained at 1 ± 0.12, and the change in size is approximately a linear function of disparity. Thus, the results of the second experiment with solid square targets confirm our earlier work and show that perceived size changes are not limited to crossed disparities.

The size effect found with the square pattern also occurred with the rectangle, except that an irregularity was observed for the extreme level of uncrossed disparity. Mean height and width judgments of the rectangle are given in Fig. 10.8. The ratio of height to width remained constant at 1.38 ± 0.08 (the objective ratio equaled 1.3), but our observers reported difficulty in keeping the half-images in binocular register when the rectangles carried an uncrossed disparity of 15′ of arc. We suspect that failure of stable fusion in this condition is the reason why perceived size does not continue its linear trend, although there are two difficulties with such an interpretation. First, if fusion were unstable, then it seems

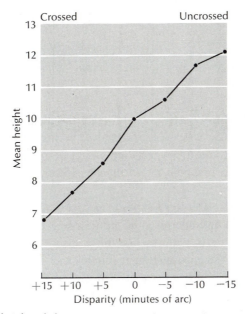

Fig. 10.7   Mean height of the square pattern shown in the previous figure as a function of disparity in minutes of arc.

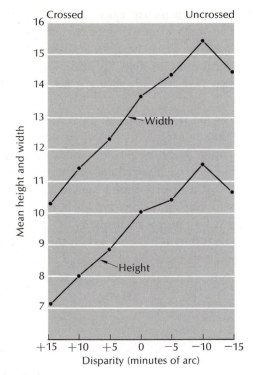

Fig. 10.8   Mean height and width of the rectangular pattern shown in Fig. 10.6 as a function of disparity in minutes of arc.

remarkable that our observers could judge the depth so well; and, second, unstable fusion would be expected to influence estimates of width but not of height, and the expectation would be for a rectangle that appeared wider than it should rather than narrower, as observed.

Experiment Three. The third experiment was similar to the first except that both crossed and uncrossed disparities were used. The targets were line-drawn and matrix patterns like those shown in Fig. 10.3. The angular subtense of the inner and outer squares was 50′ and 1° − 48′ of arc on a side, and the inner square carried one of nine levels of disparity from +32 to −32′ of arc, in steps of 8′. As before, estimates of the height and width of the central figure were made relative to the width of the outer square (line-drawn or matrix) which served as a reference modulus equal to 10. Egocentric depth estimates were made in the same way as in the second experiment. Eight observers who met our visual criteria and who were trained in magnitude estimation saw the 18 stereograms in random order twice.

The results of this experiment are quite interesting because they provide some unique information about the operation of the human binocular visual system. As shown in Fig. 10.9, the inner square of both types of target was seen progressively closer to the observers (depth estimates less than 100 units) as crossed disparity increased; and contrariwise, it

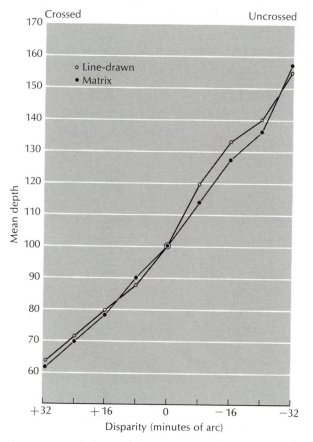

Fig. 10.9 Mean egocentric depth of the inner square for two types of pattern as a function of disparity in minutes of arc.

was seen progressively farther away from the observers (depth estimates greater than 100 units) as uncrossed disparity increased. However, although the stereoscopic size of matrix and line-drawn squares was approximately the same with crossed disparity, it was markedly different with uncrossed disparity, as shown in Fig. 10.10. Whereas the size of the inner line-drawn square increased with uncrossed disparity, the size of the inner square in the matrix pattern remained constant. According to our observers, the perceptual organization of the matrix targets with uncrossed disparity was to have the inner square appear behind a stereoscopically contoured window in the plane of the matrix, and apparently the observers judged the size of the window rather than the more distant surface.

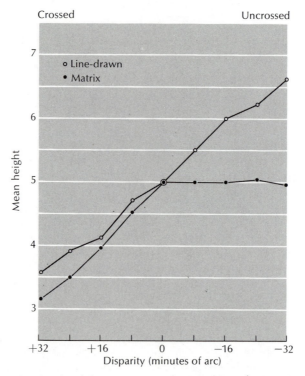

Fig. 10.10 Mean height of the inner square for two types of patterns as a function of disparity in minutes of arc. Line-drawn and matrix targets were seen as similar in size for conditions of crossed disparity (+) but different when disparity was uncrossed (−).

As we mentioned in Chapter 7 in connection with our discussion of the uncoupling of surfaces and edges, it is difficult to understand the basis upon which observers were able to judge the depth of a homogeneous, but contourless, surface. Given the fact that the stereoscopic contours appeared in the plane of the matrix, failure to find any effect on perceived size during uncrossed disparity is not surprising. At first we concluded that the depth of the surface of the inner square in the matrix targets with uncrossed disparity was due to the presence of a very fine texture; and yet when, in a subsequent experiment, special pains were taken to insure that no texture was present, observers still located the surface at a depth appropriate to the disparity of the inner square.

Stereoscopic contours can be used to define surfaces in stereoscopic space, and the size of these surfaces can be judged as readily with stereoscopic contours as with contours from abrupt luminance gradients *provided that disparity is crossed*. With uncrossed disparity, visual objects and their sizes are defined and localized very differently, depending upon the type of contour involved. With line-drawn patterns, both the outer square and the more distant inner square can carry a contour on the basis of which their size can be judged. However, the present results indicate that, with matrix patterns, the uncoupling of the contour from the more distant surface during uncrossed disparity conditions precluded size judgments of the surface.

For purposes of simplicity, we used the outer frame in each of the two types of stereograms as the reference against which disparity was measured. When conceptualized in this way, the matrix-defined form does carry an uncrossed disparity. If, however, one thinks of the enclosed form as the frame of reference, then the surrounding matrix carries a crossed disparity relative to this referent, and it appears interposed between the observer and the enclosed form, and it has stereoscopic contours (the window effect). Here, the interposed matrix serves to occlude portions of the more remote surface. It is important to realize that the location of stereoscopic contours is no different from the location of contours from abrupt luminance gradients under similar conditions.

STEREOSCOPIC AND RETINAL SIZE

So far, we have considered stereoscopic size-distance for targets of constant angular size. In this section we shall consider the question of whether two targets at different stereoscopic depths can be made to appear equal in size if their angular subtense is adjusted so as to take into account the difference in their perceived locations. From the experiments already considered, it is clear that the perceived size of a target cannot be predicted on the basis of retinal image size alone since we have shown repeatedly that disparity interacts with perceived size even while image size remains essentially constant. If two targets of equal subtense can be made to appear different in size through an inequality in their disparities, then it seemed reasonable to assume that two targets of unequal subtense could be made to appear identical in size. While the assumption is logical, it should be pointed out that there is no reason a priori to conclude that it could be verified empirically because modulation of perceived size from a constant retinal size might very well depend upon different underlying processes than those which operate to bring unequal retinal images to perceptual equality.

Our data on size-distance dependency during stereopsis suggest, as related elsewhere, that perceived size can be predicted by the solid angle formed at the center of the interocular axis by the target while in the plane of the stereogram. Therefore, data obtained on the stereoscopic location of a target as a function of disparity should allow us to calculate its physical dimensions when projected to the plane of the stereogram.

We report here a simple experiment undertaken to verify our calculation. The stereoscopic targets consisted of two small gray squares (22 ft-L) arranged side by side and seen against a larger and darker gray square (5 ft-L). The left small square was of constant size (10 mm on a side, $1° - 17'$ of arc), and it never carried any disparity with reference to the larger background square. The right small square was of one of two sizes (10 or 11.3 mm on a side, $1° - 17'$ or $1° - 26'$ of arc), and it carried each of two levels of disparity (0 and $+14'$ of arc). In all, there were four experimental stereograms used in the study: equal sized squares with and without disparity in the right square and unequal sized squares with and without disparity in the right square.

Each of six observers was instructed to consider the stereoscopic distance between himself and the left gray square as equal to 100 and to use this distance as a reference modulus to judge the distance to the right gray square. Further, observers were instructed to consider the vertical height of the left square as a ruler equal to 10 and to estimate the height of the right gray square relative to this modulus.

The size of the right target at 11.3 mm was the calculated value of the size of a 10 mm target with 14′ of arc of crossed disparity projected back to the reference plane.

The results of the experiment appear in Table X-I for each of our six observers. In stereogram 1, both squares were of equal angular size in the plane of the stereogram, but the right one carried a crossed disparity and therefore was seen closer. As expected, it was judged to be smaller by all observers. Its mean perceived size of 8.7 was precisely the size predicted on the basis of our solid angle calculation. Stereogram 2 served as a control in that the squares were of equal size and neither had any disparity. Again, as expected, observers judged their sizes as approximately equal (9.9 *versus* 10.0). In the third stereogram the squares were of unequal physical size, with the right one larger and seen closer (mean depth relative to the modulus was 86.4). Nevertheless, both squares appeared to be equal in size. When the disparity of the right square was removed (stereogram 4), its size was judged veridically.

In summary, the present findings indicate that two targets of the same physical size are perceived as different in size when seen in different stereoscopic depth planes (stereogram 1) and equal in size when seen in the same stereoscopic depth plane (stereogram 2). Further, two targets of different physical size are perceived as the same size when seen in different stereoscopic depth planes (stereogram 3) and unequal in size when seen in the same depth plane (stereogram 4). The finding that disparity contributes to perceived size is important because it indicates that disparity provides two types of perceptual information about visual ob-

Table X-I. Perceived size of the right square as a function of its size and disparity.

Right square	Stereograms			
	1	2	3	4
Angular size	1.28°	1.28°	1.43°	1.43°
Disparity	+0.23°	0.0°	+0.23°	0.0°
O_1	8.5	10.0	10.0	11.4
O_2	9.0	10.0	9.8	11.5
O_3	9.0	10.2	10.0	11.0
O_4	8.3	9.7	9.9	11.0
O_5	8.5	10.0	10.0	11.2
O_6	9.0	10.0	10.0	12.0
$\overline{X}$ observed	8.7	9.9	9.9	11.3
Geometrical prediction	8.7	10.0	10.0	11.3

jects. First, we must continue to consider it as the primary stimulus for stereoscopic localization; and, second, we must now consider disparity as a cue that contributes systematic information about stereoscopic size. The impact that disparity can have upon perceived size is demonstrated again and made clearer in the next and final section of this chapter where we treat stereoscopic size and distance in relation to convergence.

BINOCULAR DISPARITY AND CONVERGENCE

In all of our experiments on the influence of binocular disparity upon stereoscopic size and distance, we have presented our stereoscopic targets at an average distance of 70 cm. This distance is well within the limits in which convergence can influence size and distance judgments (*2, 13, 14, 15, 17, 20, 23*). Consequently, we wanted to determine what influence, if any, convergence would have upon size and distance estimates for dot-matrix and classical stereograms. In one experiment we determined the effects of a change in convergence angle upon the relative size and egocentric distance of objects defined by stereoscopic contours, and in another experiment we obtained stereoscopic distance judgments for classical stereograms where changes in convergence were prohibited by the brevity of the target exposure.

In the first experiment we presented dot-matrix stereograms which contained two disparate squares in each half-image, as shown in Fig. 10.11. Each disparate square carried a crossed disparity of 0, 19, or 38′

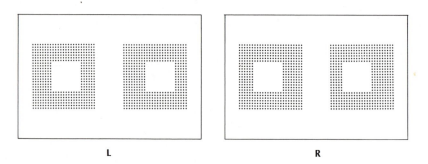

L   R

Fig. 10.11 A sample of a stereogram used to study the effect of convergence on estimates of the size and distance of the squares within the dot matrices. When in binocular register, there appear two square matrices side by side in a single depth plane with a stereoscopically contoured square interposed in front of each. The right one appears closer than the left one.

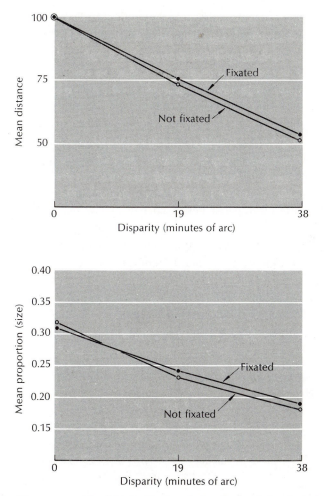

Fig. 10.12 Mean egocentric distance (top) and size (bottom) for fixated and not fixated targets as a function of disparity in minutes of arc.

of arc. The disparities were assigned so that each experimental stereo-gram contained two unequally disparate squares with each disparity level paired with every other disparity condition. The inner squares and the outer edges of the surrounding matrix subtended constant visual angles of $1°$ and $1° - 55'$, respectively. The observers employed the same magnitude estimation technique as outlined earlier in this chapter in order to estimate egocentric distances (module = 100). For size estimates, the observers estimated what proportions the height and the width of the inner square were of the height and width of the outer square matrix of dots. These proportionality judgments were later converted and plotted as decimal values.

In order to estimate the effects of a change in convergence, each observer was required to fixate upon the left inner square and then estimate the size and distance of *both* inner squares. Thereafter, he switched his fixation to the right inner square and once again estimated the size and distance of both inner squares.

A comparison of the fixated and nonfixated estimates shown in Fig. 10.12 indicates clearly that perceived size and distance varied directly with binocular disparity, and that changes in convergence had little effect upon the size-distance relationships. The fact that changing convergence from one target to another did not influence either size or distance estimates indicates that disparity was the primary carrier of information. That convergence alone has a very weak effect upon apparent size has long been known. That binocular disparity alone has a very strong effect upon apparent distance and size is now clear.

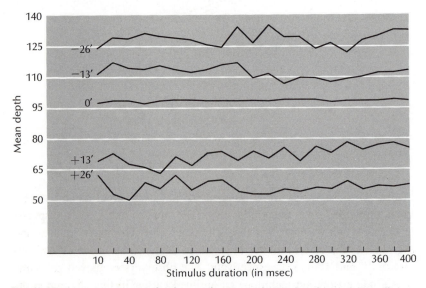

Fig. 10.13   Mean egocentric depth as a function of stimulus duration in milliseconds for each of five levels of disparity, as noted. Data from Godek (12).

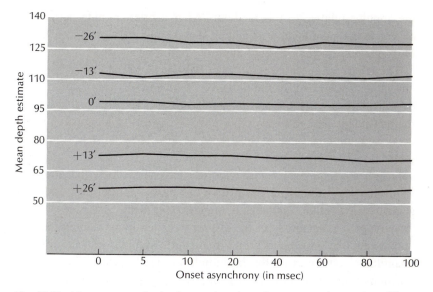

Fig. 10.14   Mean egocentric depth as a function of onset asynchrony, in milliseconds, between the right and left half-images for each of five levels of disparity, as noted. Data from Godek (12).

In the second experiment, Godek (12), working in the Vermont laboratory, conducted a study in which she eliminated convergence adjustments by presenting briefly to each eye the half-images of a disparate target. She employed stereoscopic patterns consisting of a solid black circle (56' visual angle) within a larger black annulus (3° − 21' visual angle). The annulus was displaced laterally relative to the inner circle to yield one of five disparities (+26, +13, 0, −13, and −26' of arc). The half-images were displayed in two channels of a three-channel tachistoscope. The third channel contained a small red fixation light which remained visible throughout the experiment.

Each half-image was presented to the six observers at stimulus duration times of 10 to 400 msec, in 10 msec steps, and the half-images had onset asynchronies of 0 to 100 msec. It is important to realize that for stimulus duration times below 200 msec there was not enough time for the modification of the convergence response through feedback based on sensory information.

Each observer was instructed to consider the distance to the inner solid black circle as equal to 100 units and to estimate the distance of the annulus relative to this modulus. After a brief training period, the observers had no difficulty estimating stereoscopic depth for training stereograms presented at selected durations and asynchronies.

The effects of successive and brief half-image presentations are clear and quite striking. All of the observers were able to report stereoscopic depth estimates when the half-image flashed to one eye was followed by the half-image flashed to the other eye. The effects of stimulus duration times and stimulus onset asynchronies at all levels of disparity are presented in Figs. 10.13 and 10.14, respectively. The stimulus duration data indicate that, even for the shortest exposure times, the observers were able to discriminate positive from negative disparities, and they generated magnitude estimates of stereoscopic depth that were a direct function of the magnitude of the disparity carried by the targets. Similar findings for the onset asynchrony treatment conditions indicate that the quantitative estimates of the magnitude of depth varied directly as a function of disparity in the absence of any changes in convergence.

References

1. Adams, O. S. Stereogram decentration and stereo-base as factors influencing the apparent size of stereoscopic pictures. *Amer. J. Psychol.,* 1955, *68,* 54-68.
2. Biersdorf, W. R. Convergence and apparent distance as correlates of size judgments at near distances. *J. Genet. Psychol.,* 1966, *75,* 249-264.
3. Biersdorf, W. R., and Baird, J. C. Effects of an artificial pupil and accommodation on retinal image size. *J. Opt. Soc. Amer.,* 1966, *56,* 1123-1129.
4. Blakemore, C., and Campbell, F. W. Adaptation to spatial stimuli. *J. Physiol.,* 1969, *200,* 11-13.
5. Blakemore, C., and Campbell, F. W. On the existence of neurones in the human visual system selectively sensitive to the orientation and size of retinal images. *J. Physiol.,* 1969, *203,* 237-260.
6. Blakemore, C., Garner, E. T., and Sweet, J. A. The site of size constancy. *Perception,* 1972, *1,* 111-119.
7. Bleything, W. B. Factors influencing stereoscopic localization. *Amer. J. Optom.,* 1957, *34,* 416-429.
8. Bridgman, C. S. Analysis of a recently discovered stereoscopic effect. *Amer. J. Psychol.,* 1964, *77,* 138-143.
9. Bunge, J. V., and Bechtoldt, H. P. Size-distance relationships in random letter stereograms. Paper presented at *Midwestern Psychological Association Meetings,* Chicago, 1967.

STEREOSCOPIC SIZE-DISTANCE RELATIONSHIPS 273

10. Fraser, A. C. *Selections from Berkeley*. New York: Macmillan & Co., 1884.
11. Gilinsky, A. S. Orientation-specific effects of patterns of adapting light on visual acuity. *J. Opt. Soc. Amer.*, 1968, *58*, 13-18.
12. Godek, Cynthia L. The effects of stimulus duration, time between presentation of stimuli, and magnitude of disparity upon human stereoscopic depth perception. Unpublished master's thesis, Univ. of Vermont, Burlington, Vt., 1972.
13. Gogel, W. C. Convergence as a cue to absolute distance. *J. Psychol.*, 1961, *52*, 287-301.
14. Gogel, W. C. Convergence as a determiner of perceived absolute size. *J. Psychol.*, 1962, *53*, 91-104.
15. Gogel, W. C. The effect of convergence on perceived size and distance. *J. Psychol.*, 1962, *53*, 475-489.
16. Heinemann, E. G. Photographic measurement of the retinal image. *Amer. J. Psychol.*, 1961, *74*, 440-445.
17. Heinemann, E. G., Tulving, E. and Nachmias, J. The effect of oculomotor adjustments on apparent size. *Amer. J. Psychol.*, 1959, *72*, 32-45.
18. Hering, E. *Spatial Sense and Movements of the Eye*. Translated by C. A. Radde. Baltimore: The American Academy of Optometry, 1942.
19. Hermans, T. G. The relationship of convergence and elevation changes to judgments of size. *J. Exper. Psychol.*, 1954, *48*, 204-208.
20. Holst, E. von. Aktive Leitsungen der menschlichen Gesichtswahrnehmung. *Studium Generale*, 1957, *10*, 231-243.
21. Humphrey, N. K., and Weiskrantz, L. Size constancy in monkeys with inferotemporal lesions. *Quart. J. Exper. Psychol.*, 1969, *21*, 225-238.
22. Judd, C. H. Some facts of binocular vision. *Psychol. Rev.*, 1897, *4*, 374-389.
23. Künnapas, T. Distance perception as a function of available visual cues. *J. Exper. Psychol.*, 1968, *77*, 523-530.
24. Lie, I. Convergence as a cue to perceived size and distance. *Scand. J. Psychol.*, 1965, *6*, 109-116.
25. Marg, E., and Adams, J. E. Evidence for a neurological zoom system in vision from angular changes in some receptive fields of single neurons with changes in fixation distance in the human visual cortex. *Experientia*, 1970, *26*, 270-71.
26. Pascal, J. I. Effect of accommodation on the retinal image. *Brit. J. Opthal.*, 1952, *36*, 676-678.
27. Richards, W. Spatial remapping in the primate visual system. *Kybernetik*, 1968, *4*, 146-156.
28. Roelofs, C. O., and Zeeman, W. P. Apparent size and apparent distance in binocular and monocular vision. *Ophthalmologica*, 1957, *133*, 188-204.
29. Von Kries, J. Notes. In Helmholtz, H. von *Helmholtz's Treatise on*

Physiological Optics, vol. 3, J. P. C. Southall (Ed.), New York: Optical Society of America, 1925.

30. Wheatstone, C. Contributions to the physiology of vision. Part II. On some remarkable, and hitherto unobserved, phenomena of binocular vision (continued). *The London, Edinburgh, and Dublin Phil. Mag. and J. of Sci.,* 1852, ser. 4, *3,* 504-523.

Appendix

This appendix provides a computer program, written in the BASIC language, that calculates the retinal disparity of a given point in space when the attitude of the eyes is also specified. Use is limited to points that lie in a horizontal plane that includes the centers of the eyes.

INSTRUCTIONS FOR USE

The program is designed for the naive user, one who is not skilled on computer use. However, there are several simple matters that must be made plain.

First, the program requires three parameters of the visual system; namely, the *radius of curvature* of the eye, the *interocular distance* from center of curvature to center of curvature, and the *distance between the center of curvature and the nodal point* of the eye. The values for these parameters, based on average measures cited in the text for the human, are 1.1, 6.5, and 0.6 cm, respectively, and these values are written into the program as it appears in this appendix. As we shall show, these values can be altered by a user with ease, should he wish to change them in order to calculate disparity for the visual system of a different organism.

Second, the attitude of the eyes is determined by the location of a point of fixation, specified in terms of its distance in centimeters from the midpoint of the interocular axis (center to center) and its azimuth relative to the same axis. The azimuth is defined as the angle formed with the interocular axis by a line through the fixation point and the mid-

275

point of the interocular axis, measured counterclockwise. Thus, a point straight ahead of an observer would lie at an azimuth of 90 degrees, a point to the right of straight ahead would lie between 0 and 90 degrees, and a point to the left of straight ahead would lie between 90 and 180 degrees. All azimuth angles must lie between 0 and 180 degrees and all distances must be in centimeters.

Third, the program also requires the user to specify the distance in centimeters and the azimuth of all points (up to 100) for which disparities are to be calculated. As with fixation, the same method of specification is employed.

ACTUAL USE

When a user calls for the program, it begins with a question to the user printed out on the teletype. It reads,

NEW EYE PARAMETERS {ENTER <YES> OR <NO>}

If answered NO , the program takes the parameters for the human visual system specified earlier in these instructions. If answered YES , the program asks the user to give the parameters (in centimeters) one at a time in response to each of three statements.

Thereafter, the program asks another question of the user. It reads,

AZIMUTH AND DISTANCE TO FIXATION POINT

The user types in the azimuth in degrees and the distance in centimeters, with the two numbers separated by a comma. For example, *90,100* would mean that the fixation point had an azimuth of 90 degrees and was 100 cm from the midpoint of the interocular axis.

The program then asks a final question of the user. It reads,

AZIMUTH AND DISTANCE TO OTHER POINT{S}

The user responds by typing in a pair of numbers for each point in question where azimuth is entered first followed by distance in centimeters. Up to 100 azimuth-distance pairs (100 points) can be entered at once, but only one pair (1 point) need be entered.

Output. The output of the program appears as a printed table of the form shown below for each point calculated.

	ANGLE {DEG}		DISPARITY	
	L EYE	R EYE	MIN	RAD
RE: NODAL PT	*	*	*	*
RE: CNTR EYE	*	*	*	*

The first and second columns of the table give the angle in degrees between the fixation point and the point in question for the left eye (column 1) and the right eye (column 2), as measured both at the nodal point and the center of curvature of the eye. Column 3 gives the angular disparity of the point in question in minutes of arc relative both to the nodal point and the center of curvature of the eye. Plus (+) and minus (−) signs denote crossed and uncrossed disparity, respectively. Column 4 simply expresses the disparity in radians rather than in minutes of arc.

When more than one azimuth-distance pair of numbers is entered in a single run of the program, the table is repeated for each point entered in the order of entry.

Computer Program

```
DISPARIT

100 DIM A{20}, P{200}, S{20}

110

120 PRINT "
            NEW EYE PARAMETERS {ENTER <YES> OR <NO>}";

130 LINPUT AS

140 IF A$="NO" THEN 220

150 PRINT "
            RADIUS OF CURVATURE OF EYE:"

160 INPUT R

170 PRINT "
            INTEROCULAR DISTANCE:"

180 INPUT S{1}

190 PRINT "
            SEPARATION BETWEEN CENTER OF CURVATURE AND NODAL POINT:"

200 INPUT S{6}

210 GOTO 240

220 READ R, S{1}, S{6}  'DEFAULT EYE PARAMETERS SPECIFIED HERE

230 DATA 1.1, 6.5, .6

240 LET S{1}=S{1}/2
```

```
DISPARIT {CONTINUED}

250

260 PRINT "
                AZIMUTH AND DISTANCE TO FIXATION POINT:"

270 INPUT A{1}, S{2}

280

290 PRINT "
                AZIMUTH AND DISTANCE TO OTHER POINT{S}:"

300

310 'IF MORE THAN 100 POINTS {200 ITEMS} ARE TO BE ENTERED IN

320 'RESPONSE TO THE MAT INPUT STATEMENT, P{} MUST BE REDIMENSIONED

330 'TO ACCOMODATE ALL OF THE ENTRIES.

340

350 MAT INPUT P

360 LET N=NUM

370 IF MOD{N,2}=0 THEN 410

380 PRINT "WRONG NUMBER OF ENTRIES--RETRY:"

390 GOTO 350

400

410 LET P=3.1415926535   'PI

420 DEF FNA{X}=ATN{X/SQR{1-X^2}}   'ARCSINE FUNCTION

430 DEF FNB{X}=P*X/180   'DEGREE-RADIAN CONVERSION FUNCTION

440

450 LET A{1}=FNB{A{1}}

460

470 'OUTPUT FORMAT

480 PRINT "
                ANGLE {DEG}                        DISPARITY"

490 PRINT"            L EYE         R EYE         MIN         RAD"

500 PRINT"          ========      =======      =======     ======="

510 PRINT
```

DISPARIT {CONTINUED}

520

530 FOR I=1 TO N STEP 2

540

550 LET A{3}=FNB{P{I}}

560 LET S{4}=P{I+1}

570

580 'RIGHT EYE

590 LET S{3}=SQR{S{1}^2+S{2}^2-2*S{2}*S{1}*COS{A{1}}}

600 LET A{2}=FNA{S{2}*SIN{A{1}}/S{3}}

610 IF S{2}*COS{A{1}}>S{1} THEN 630

620 GO TO 640

630 LET A{2}=P-A{2}

640 LET S{5}=SQR{S{1}^2+S{6}^2-2*S{1}*S{6}*COS{A{2}}}

650 LET A{9}=FNA{S{6}*SIN{A{2}}/S{5}}

660 LET S{9}=SQR{S{4}^2+S{5}^2-2*S{4}*S{5}*COS{A{3}-A{9}}}

670 LET A{10}=FNA{S{4}*SIN{A{3}-A{9}}/S{9}}

680 IF S{4}*COS{A{3}-A{9}}>S{5} THEN 700

690 GO TO 710

700 LET A{10}=P-A{10}

710 LET A{7}=A{2}+A{9}

720 LET A{6}=ABS{A{7}-A{10}}

730 LET C1=FNA{S{6}*SIN{A{6}}/R}+A{6}

740

750 'LEFT EYE

760 LET S{13}=SQR{S{1}^2+S{2}^2-2*S{1}*S{2}*COS{P-A{1}}}

770 LET A{12}=FNA{S{2}*SIN{P-A{1}}/S{13}}

780 IF S{2}*COS{P-A{1}}>S{1} THEN 800

790 GO TO 810

DISPARIT (CONTINUED)

```
800 LET A(12)=P-A(12)
810 LET S(15)=SQR(S(1)^2+S(6)^2-2*S(1)*S(6)*COS(A(12)))
820 LET A(19)=FNA(S(6)*SIN(A(12))/S(15))
830 LET A(17)=A(19)+A(12)
840 LET S(19)=SQR(S(15)^2+S(4)^2-2*S(15)*S(4)*COS(P-A(3)-A(19)))
850 LET A(20)=FNA(S(4)*SIN(P-A(3)-A(19))/S(19))
860 IF S(4)*COS(P-A(3)-A(19))>S(15) THEN 880
870 GO TO 890
880 LET A(20)=P-A(20)
890 LET A(16)=ABS(A(20)-A(17))
900 LET C2=FNA(S(6)*SIN(A(16))/R)+A(16)
910
920 'OUTPUT
930 IF A(1) > A(3)  THEN 970
940 LET D1=A(6)-A(16)
950 LET D2=C1-C2
960 GO TO 990
970 LET D1=A(16)-A(6)
980 LET D2=C2-C1
990 LET D3=(360*D1)/(2*P)*60
1000 LET D4=(360*D2)/(2*P)*60
1010 PRINT "RE: NODAL PT", A(16),A(6),D3,D1
1020 PRINT "RE: CNTR EYE",C2,C1,D4,D2
1030 PRINT
1040
1050 NEXT I
1060
1070 END
```

Glossary

ABBREVIATIONS

m	meter(s)
cm	centimeter(s)
sec	second(s)
msec	millisecond(s)
0°-0′-0″	degrees, minutes, seconds of arc
C	center of eye
O	optical node of eye
⊙	binocular visual direction
γ	convergence angle
Δ	change
η	disparity
F	point of fixation
f	fovea
ϕ	angle of subtense
+	crossed disparity
−	uncrossed disparity

TERMS

binocular correlation

The extent of analogous target features between the right and left half-images. Identical half-images have a perfect correlation. In the case of matrix targets, the presence of disparity in a subset of the dots does not alter perfect binocular correlation provided that for each dot in the right view there is an analogous dot in the left view with which to form a fused pair.

binocular locking

The stereoscopic combination of half-image targets according to their analogous features, whether disparate or not, and it is always accompanied by perfect binocular correlation.

281

binocular re-locking

The stereoscopic combination of half-image targets according to their nonanalogous features as a consequence of inappropriate vergence, and it is never accompanied by perfect binocular correlation.

binocular visual direction

The angle of inclination (Θ) from the mid-sagittal of an imaginary line drawn between a point in space and the middle of the interocular axis. In the text negative and positive values denote locations left and right of straight ahead, respectively.

central matrix

A geometrical construct that refers to a cyclopean map of the right and left retinas superimposed with the foveas and major axes congruent.

contour

The monocular or binocular perception of a well-defined and continuous target boundary.

cyclopean density

Refers to the number of dots in a matrix target per $1°$ solid angle which appear in a single stereoscopic depth plane.

dichoptic

Stereoscopic combinations of right and left half-images wherein one or more of the binocularly combined target element pairs differ along some stimulus dimension, such as size or luminance.

dioptic

Stereoscopic combinations of right and left half-images wherein combined target elements that form a pair are identical.

directional separation

The absolute angular difference between the binocular visual directions to each of two points in space.

edge

The boundary of a target defined by an abrupt luminance gradient.

egocentric depth

The judged depth of a target from the observer made by him through the method of magnitude estimation, usually given in depth units relative to a defined depth modulus.

geometrical horopter

The location of points in space that are imaged on geometrically corresponding loci on the retinas for a given attitude of the eyes, whether convergence is symmetrical or asymmetrical.

global density

Refers to the total number of matrix cells, whether vacant or filled, per $1°$ solid angle in dot stereograms. Global density ignores matrix density.

matrix density
> Refers to the percentage of matrix cells which contain a dot, and it ignores global density.

null horopter
> A geometrical horopter for cases of symmetrical convergence.

retinal density
> Refers to the number of imaged dots per $1°$ solid angle.

stereoscopic contour
> The binocular perception of a well-defined and continuous target boundary which occurs in the absence of an abrupt luminance gradient and for which stereopsis is necessary.

Name Index

A number in italics indicates that the name appears in the reference section at the end of a chapter.

Subject Index